THEORIES
AND
PRACTICES OF LIBRARIANSHIP

By

Rakeshkumar Shantilal Prajapati

B.Lib., M.Lib.

Librarian

Swami Vivekanand Sarvoday Bank Education College

Mehsana (Gujarat)

(India)

DPH

DISCOVERY PUBLISHING HOUSE PVT. LTD.

NEW DELHI-110 002

Published by:
Tilak Wasan

DISCOVERY PUBLISHING HOUSE PVT. LTD.
4383/4B, Ansari Road, Darya Ganj
New Delhi-110 002 (India)
Phone : +91-11-23279245, 43596064-65
Fax : +91-11-23253475
E-mail : discoverypublishinghouse@gmail.com
sales@discoverypublishinggroup.com
parul.wasan@gmail.com
web : www.discoverypublishinggroup.com

***First Edition:* 2013**

ISBN: 978-93-5056-380-9

Theories and Practices of Librarianship

Printed at:
Dynamic Printers
Delhi

Contents

Preface

A librarian is a person in-charge of a library, and is usually trained in librarianship. Traditionally, a librarian is associated with collections of books, as demonstrated by the etymology of the word librarian. The role of a librarian is continuously evolving to meet social and technological needs. However, a modern librarian may deal with information in many formats, including books, magazines, newspapers, audio recordings, video recordings, maps, manuscripts, photographs and other graphic material, bibliographic databases, web searching, and digital resources. A librarian may provide other information services, including computer provision and training, co-ordination of public programmes, basic literacy education, and assistive equipment for people with disabilities, and help with finding and using community resources.

Public service librarians work with the public, frequently at the reference desk of lending libraries. Some specialize in serving adults or children. Children's librarians provide appropriate material for children at all age levels, include pre-readers, conduct specialized programs and work with the children to help foster interest and competence in the young reader.

—Author

1

Understanding the Librarianship

WHY WE BECOME LIBRARIANS

Why do we choose librarianship? Some people know they want to become librarians from a young age. They were read to as toddlers, attended library story hours, learned to love reading and discover the hidden joys in books, felt comfortable in the children's room of their local library, loved attending children's and teen programmes as they were growing up, and maybe found a mentor in a librarian. People interested in technology may aspire to be systems librarians.

Inquisitive types may strive to be reference librarians, desiring to help people find information by using electronic databases, while others might long to contribute to the educational role of libraries as centers of lifelong learning in their communities. Future leaders in our profession may see themselves playing an instrumental role in the acquisition, collection, organization, retrieval, and dissemination of information. When *American Libraries* editor Leonard Kniffel asked a class of library school students at Dominican University what made them choose librarianship, he found that "they were attracted by the books, the place, the people, and the need to find a job worth doing."

HOW WE BECOME LIBRARIANS

How do we become librarians? Those determined early on to become librarians proceed straight through school, graduating from high school and college and going directly to graduate school. Although this is the most straightforward path to librarianship, it is not the most common way people become librarians. For most of us it is a much longer and more circuitous road-in fact, librarianship may not even be our first career choice. Some people may earn their bachelor's degrees only to find out that there are no jobs available in their field or that they are not suited to that particular field. Those with bachelor's degrees in English, history, philosophy, religion, or fine arts, for example, often require advanced degrees to secure a job in their field, which are limited primarily to college or university teaching, research, or scholarly publishing positions. If you aren't interested in a lifetime of teaching or scholarly research and publishing, you might start looking for another career. Librarianship attracts people with education, interests, and backgrounds in all subject areas.

No specific undergraduate programme of study is required for acceptance into library school, so people from many disciplines enter LIS graduate programmes. Librarian positions in most public, academic, and special libraries, as well as in some school libraries, require a master's degree in library science (MLS) or library and information science (MLIS). The U.S. government requires that the librarians it employs have an MLS or the equivalent in education and experience, while other employers often require librarians to be graduates of the more than 50 schools accredited by the *American Library Association* (ALA).

The ALA website states that the educational requirements for a librarian position can span a large range:

* Four-year undergraduate degree in any field
* Master of library science (MLS) degree
* MLS degree from an ALA-accredited school
* ALA-accredited MLS degree plus a teaching certificate (often the case in school libraries) or an ALA-accredited MLS plus a second degree, for example, a law degree

School media specialists (also known as school librarians or teacher-librarians) can pursue either an ALA-accredited master's degree or a master's degree in education with a specialty in school library media from an educational unit accredited by the National Council for Accreditation of Teacher Education (NCATE).

LIBRARY SCHOOL EDUCATION

Melvil Dewey founded the first library school in 1887 at the Columbia School of Library Economy in New York. Dewey pioneered the education of librarians, believing that the best way to prepare people for library work was through classroom instruction combined with practical work in a library. He helped to set standards for the profession of librarianship in terms of education, ethics, and the role of the librarian in society. Columbia admitted women to its first class, which was a point of contention with the trustees. This disagreement eventually resulted in the school's closing two years later and its move to the state library in Albany in 1889. The curriculum in early library schools emphasized technical subjects such as cataloging and bibliography.

Graduate-level education for librarians wasn't introduced until 1926, when the Graduate Library School at the University of Chicago opened. The Carnegie Corporation provided funding for the school to create an advanced, research-oriented library school; its first graduates accepted positions as academic librarians, library school teachers, and deans. The need for this level of education was slow to be accepted by librarians; however, several important works and conferences on library education between 1936 and 1948 led to the consensus that professional librarians needed a graduate degree.

Library education thrived in the 1950s and 1960s, when federal funding supported libraries, library schools, and students of librarianship to a greater degree than ever before. Libraries improved, the demand for librarians increased, and library school recruiters were busy enrolling new students. The 1970s were not so favourable for the profession, and in recent decades a number of library schools have closed. Over the last 60 years, library science education has continuously adapted to the changing needs for library and information services.

The increasing importance of library automation, electronic information systems, and online access to information has caused some changes in library school curricula, but ALA's Standards for Accreditation of Master's Programmes in Library and Information Studies does not include a core curriculum. The standards mention that curricula "encompass information and knowledge creation, communication, identification, selection, acquisition, organization and description, storage and retrieval, preservation, analysis, interpretation, evaluation, synthesis, dissemination, and management."

However, since these 14 elements aren't defined, and the standards don't mention which ones require greater emphasis, there are wide differences among ALAaccredited schools in how these areas are covered and what MLS librarians need to know. Due to this lack of a common core curriculum in LIS education, graduates from ALA-accredited LIS programmes aren't mastering comparable skills. Some schools cover in a week what others take a semester to teach. This inability to define a core curriculum contributes to the difficulty in maintaining the status of librarianship as a profession.

Other professions, such as medicine, nursing, dentistry, law, architecture, and real estate, have clearly defined standards, comparable certification exams from state to state, and minimum requirements for continuing education. You can earn undergraduate and graduate degrees in library science, associate's degrees, and certifications as a library assistant or library technician. Some states certify library media specialists, public librarians, and library directors. Continuing education, online education, and distance education opportunities have become more important than ever as a way to keep up with constant change, learn new skills, and acquire degrees and certificates. Today, you can earn LIS degrees and certifications wherever you may live.

KINDS OF LIBRARIANS

Librarians are generally categorized according to the type of library in which they work:

* *Public librarians* work in public libraries.

* *School librarians, library media specialists,* and *teacher librarians* work in school libraries or media centres.
* *Academic librarians* work in college, university, or postsecondary school libraries.
* *Special librarians* work in specialized information centers such as corporate libraries, government agencies, military libraries, law libraries, art libraries, museum libraries, or medical libraries.

In larger organizations, librarians may specialize in technical services, administrative services, electronic services, or user services. In small libraries, librarians typically perform duties encompassing all aspects of librarianship. Some librarians choose to work with specific groups such as children, young adults, students, adults, or special populations.

WHAT IS AN ACCIDENTAL LIBRARIAN

ALA itself recognizes that the educational requirements for librarian positions do vary, including a four-year undergraduate degree in any field. In states where an MLS is not required to practice public librarianship, librarians-even library directors-without MLS degrees are common. Many smaller libraries, especially those in rural areas, have a difficult time filling librarian and library director positions. They often hire people with other degrees or equivalent experience. In many rural areas throughout the U.S., there is no MLS librarian to be found for miles.

Even if there were, most small towns cannot afford (or are not willing to pay) an MLS librarian's salary. Many small communities cannot afford librarians with college degrees, much less those with graduate degrees in library science. Librarians without MLS degrees are essentially accidental librarians-increasingly being hired as frontline librarians in libraries of all kinds and sizes, performing duties that were formerly carried out exclusively by professional librarians, while MLS librarians can be found working behind the scenes in management and administrative positions, including technical services, marketing, systems administration, and personnel.

It is not uncommon to see advertisements for librarian jobs in large city systems that require a four-year degree in any field plus library experience, while an ALA-accredited MLS degree is listed only as being "preferred." A recently posted Assistant Librarian position in my area required only a high school diploma or GED, plus two years of postsecondary education. Successful accidental librarians share their stories of how they found success and what they do in their jobs. I hope they will motivate, inspire, and encourage you to learn more about librarianship as you move ahead on your chosen path.

The Facts About Accidental Librarians

Accidental librarians may be more numerous–and important–than you think:

* For decades, great research libraries have hired scholars over degreed librarians for director positions.
* Many deans of library school programmes do not hold MLS degrees.
* No special qualifications are prescribed by law for Librarians of Congress, who have come from the varied professions of newspaperman, novelist, poet, physician, and diplomat. In 1899, at the urging of the ALA, President McKinley appointed the first experienced librarian, Herbert Putnam, to the position of Librarian of Congress. L. Quincy Mumford, Librarian of Congress from 1954 through 1974, was the first Librarian of Congress to have graduated from library school.
* The Council on Library and Information Resources (CLIR) offers postdoctoral fellowships in research libraries to humanities scholars to develop meaningful linkages between disciplinary scholarship, libraries, archives, and evolving digital tools. Study in the area of LIS is not a requirement for this fellowship.
* The Virginia code does not require the state librarian to have an MLS. Sandra Treadway served as Deputy State Librarian at the Library of Virginia for more

than a decade and became the Virginia State Librarian before she had a library degree. Treadway "learned about library operations the old-fashioned way—climbing the ladder to the top one rung at a time." She never intended to do library work.

Many accidental librarians are both accomplished and prominent. *Public Libraries in the United States,* only 67.9 per cent of FTE (full-time equivalent) public librarians in the U.S. hold ALA-accredited MLS degrees. Table 1.1 lists the states in which less than half of the total FTE public librarians have ALA-accredited MLS degrees.

Table 1.1. States in which Less than Half of Public Librarians have ALA Accredited MLS Degrees.

State	Total FTE Librarians (%)
Montana	20.9
Wyoming	21.5
North Dakota	22.6
Kentucky	23.8
Iowa	25.6
Mississippi	26.3
Vermont	26.9
Nebraska	27.2
West Virginia	27.2
South Dakota	28.9
Oklahoma	33.6
Idaho	33.7
Kansas	36.8
New Hampshire	37.2
Alabama	38.4
Arkansas	40.3
Louisiana	41.2
New Mexico	43.2
Maine	45.6
Tennessee	49.4

Table 1.2 lists the states where more than half of the total FTE public librarians hold ALA-accredited MLS degrees.

Table 1.2. States in which More than Half of Public Librarians have ALA Accredited MLS Degrees.

State	Total FTE Librarians (%)
Delaware	50.7
Maryland	52.0
Utah	53.5
Wisconsin	53.6
Missouri	55.0
Alaska	58.1
Illinois	62.8
Massachusetts	64.9
Indiana	65.0
Minnesota	65.5
Pennsylvania	67.7
Michigan	68.0
Colorado	70.0
Nevada	71.8
Texas	71.8
Ohio	73.3
Oregon	75.3
Connecticut	76.3
Arizona	78.3
South Carolina	78.9
Florida	83.4
Virginia	83.9
New York	84.0
Rhode Island	85.5
District of Columbia	88.5
California	93.2
Washington	94.3
Georgia	95.1
North Carolina	95.4
New Jersey	99.6
Hawaii	99.7

The situation varies considerably between Montana, where 20.9 per cent of FTE public librarians hold an

ALAaccredited MLS, and Hawaii, where 99.7 per cent hold such a degree. Inmost states, school librarians (also known as teacher-librarians or school media specialists) are not required to have MLS degrees. School librarians are usually required to have an undergraduate degree in education, with a school library media specialist certification. This certification requires coursework in library science or passing a qualifying test. School librarians are certified at the state level, and each state has its own requirements.

Often an organization or corporation will add a librarian's duties to the job of a secretary or administrative assistant when materials purchased for shared use by employees have accumulated to the point that they are no longer accessible. In such a case, management realises the need for someone to organize and manage the collection, track usage, and retrieve information. They may not recognize that this is a "librarian" position, or that the job requires any special skill or knowledge. Other special librarians, such as church or synagogue librarians, often begin as volunteers. Many prison librarians are not required to hold MLS degrees; some hold the title of Library Aide or Library Technician, but are actually running their libraries single-handedly.

Because academic librarians work in an environment that values the degree, postsecondary, college, or university libraries are less likely to hire librarians without MLS degrees, making it less common to find accidental librarians in academic situations. Mary McKinley Ingraham, University Librarian at Acadia University in Nova Scotia, driving force of the Maritime Library Institute and editor of its *Bulletin,* said in a 1939 editorial,

"There is no doubt that specialized training is a necessity for most of us who would work in libraries, but is there any absolute norm by which we may determine the method or content of that training?

Despite the unquestioned value of the many schools of library service, we have to admit that the greatest librarians in the world, from Zenodatus at Alexandria to Putnam at Washington, were not graduates of library schools." She was careful to stress that librarianship requires education and training, calling it a "learned profession," but suggested that this training can take place in many contexts and by diverse means.

WHAT MAKES A LIBRARIAN

By now you can see that there really are no universal criteria in the U.S. for determining what makes a librarian. It's no wonder that librarians have such varying levels of education, experience, and knowledge about library and information science. Librarians come from all subject backgrounds and educational levels, and have varying degrees of library experience. Although some states and schools have established standards, with very few exceptions these are voluntary or optional. Some state standards can easily be met with very little education, experience, or training, and it may be possible to be certified as a librarian or library director in your state with no library education or experience.

If you don't qualify as a librarian in one state, you can go to another state and easily become certified as a library director there. Some people assume that passing their state certification test is equivalent to an MLS, but even if you have an MLS there is no common basic foundation of knowledge you are required to master in graduate school. Confused? The lacxk of national standards in the U.S. for qualifying librarians creates a chaotic professional atmosphere.

Disagreements about who is and isn't a librarian abound. We engage in ongoing discussions about the state of LIS education and our profession, "illegal librarians," and what makes a "real" librarian. In this atmosphere, insisting that someone has to have an MLS to be a librarian is unrealistic: There are plenty of practicing librarians who do not have the degree. Unfortunately, when nondegreed librarians reject learning from MLS librarians because they feel threatened by them, and when MLS librarians reject nondegreed librarians because of the belief that they are not "real" librarians, they overlook some of their greatest opportunities to learn from each other, advance our profession, and improve our libraries.

Misunderstandings on both sides of this issue abound, causing our profession to be fragmented. We cannot afford a "librarian vs. librarian" mentality. We are facing some of the most challenging and exciting changes in our field, and this is the time to join together and move forward. Degreed and nondegreed librarians alike are responsible for creating and upholding the standards of our profession, and for valuing librarianship and each other.

WHAT DO LIBRARIANS DO

The primary functions of a librarian are to:

* Collect information
* Acquire information
* Organize information
* Retrieve information
* Disseminate information based on the needs of the populations we serve.

These five functions create a foundation for the practice of librarianship, and understanding them as such helps librarians stay focused on our main purpose. As our profession rapidly changes and evolves it is essential for us to be grounded in a set of core functions that we can easily apply to new developments in the information field.

Collect Information

Librarians develop collections to meet the information needs of their communities. They must constantly assess their community's changing information needs and collect, as well as deselect, materials and resources based on those needs.

Acquire Information

Librarians evaluate, select, and purchase or lease materials and information resources to meet the information needs of the populations they serve.

Organize Information

Librarians organize information by:

* Classifying it according to subject, and

* Cataloging it by describing it in a way that makes the information easily accessible.

Librarians also make library resources, services, and programmes available electronically in a way that users can easily access and utilize.

Retrieve Information

Librarians find information to meet the needs of library users. This involves analysing users' needs to determine what it is they want and at what level, and searching for and extracting information in multiple formats from multiple sources. Librarians also assist people in finding the information they need.

Disseminate Information

Librarians play an important role in facilitating the transfer of knowledge and ideas from the sources of the knowledge and ideas to the people who need and want the information. Librarians do this by synthesizing and delivering information to people who request it in a form that is useful to them.

WHAT ELSE DO LIBRARIANS DO

In the process of acquiring, collecting, organizing, retrieving, and disseminating information, librarians also:

* Assist and instruct
* Provide services and programmes
* Utilize technology
* Preserve and conserve library materials

In the process of doing our work, librarians are also responsible for upholding the basic principles of intellectual freedom, or the right of every individual to both seek and receive information from all points of view without restriction. ALA's Library Bill of Rights affirms that all libraries are forums for information and ideas and articulates basic principles to guide their services. Librarians support the Freedom to Read and the Freedom to View under the Constitution of the United States, and we are responsible for advocating for these rights.

Additionally, we must be aware of legislation that affects libraries or that may threaten these basic rights. We need to take responsibility for acting in support of the freedom of information on behalf of libraries and the citizens of our country. We are expected to protect the creators of works being shared in our libraries by seeing to it that the Copyright Act is observed.

ASSIST AND INSTRUCT

Librarians play an instructional role, which includes teaching users how to access information, synthesize it, and use it. They also teach users how to effectively use library tools, technology, and resources. The desired result is for users to be able to search for information, analyse it, synthesize it, and use it on their own in the future. Librarians also develop content and design materials for instructional purposes.

PROVIDE SERVICES AND PROGRAMMES

Librarians plan, budget, and manage programmes such as story hours, literacy skills classes, book groups, programmes for all ages, and educational classes based on the needs of the community. Other services librarians provide include reference service and readers' advisory service.

UTILIZE TECHNOLOGY

Because technology has become such a large part of information storage and delivery, librarians evaluate information technologies; develop, design, and manage digital access and content; use technology appropriately and effectively; administer and manage computer systems; and train users on using technology to retrieve information and for other purposes.

PRESERVE AND CONSERVE

Librarians are responsible for maximizing the life of library materials by preserving and conserving them.

WHAT SKILLS DO LIBRARIANS NEED

In recent years, the LIS field and the practice of librarianship have undergone tremendous changes due to the growth of information technology and the resulting changes in the methods of acquiring, collecting, organizing, retrieving, and disseminating information. There has been a fundamental shift in libraries from ownership to access, and a corresponding shift in the skills librarians need.

Today, librarians not only need to understand the basics of managing and disseminating information, they also need to:

* See the big picture
* Make things happen
* Remove barriers
* Create vision and mission
* Work independently and on teams
* Exercise initiative and independent judgment
* Think creatively and innovatively
* Create partnerships and alliances
* Evaluate, select, and apply new technologies
* Troubleshoot technology
* Communicate clearly and effectively verbally and in writing
* Seek additional funding to meet unmet community needs
* Write grant proposals
* Develop new systems and adapt old ones to new situations
* Work with diverse populations
* Teach

WHAT ARE THE CHARACTERISTICS OF LIBRARIANS

Librarians are:

* Change agents
* Proactive
* Creative
* Inquisitive
* Initiators
* On the leading edge
* Customer service oriented
* Collaborators

* Risk-takers
* Active communicators
* Flexible
* Advocates
* Continuous lifelong learners
* Leaders
* Networkers
* Visionaries
* Team players
* Analytical thinkers
* Strategic planners.

Don't be shocked if you are beginning to realise that there is much more to librarianship, what librarians do, what they need to know, and the skills and qualities they need to possess than you previously thought. You aren't alone. Perhaps you haven't had a positive librarian role model or mentor, you didn't work in a library before becoming a librarian, or you were never in a position where you learned what is really involved in librarianship. You came into this profession accidentally, or as a second career, without the benefit of education or professional experience, easily meeting your state's qualifications to practice librarianship.

You thought, "The state certified me, so I must know all there is to know about being a librarian." Although this is not uncommon, it is a mistake to think that passing a certification test or meeting your state's qualifications to be a library director is the same as earning a graduate degree in library and information science. It's not quite that simple. When you accepted your job as a librarian for your municipality, school, organization, or corporation, you became professionally obligated to perform your job competently and to continue to learn about librarianship.

Most of you have taken this responsibility seriously and have worked hard to live up to the standards of our profession. A few of you, though, may find it easy and safe to keep doing what you've always done, resisting change and new ideas proposed by staff members. Over the years you may have surrounded yourselves with supportive friends, volunteers, and library users who praise you for the good job you are doing—but do they know what librarians do? You might attend your state library association conference every year and an occasional local workshop to fulfill continuing education requirements, but do you challenge yourself, apply new concepts, or plan to change?

Do you wonder why you should put in all that hard work to become a better librarian when things are fine just the way they are? If this sounds at all like you, it is time to take notice. You have an obligation to an entire profession and to the people you serve to take the next step. Librarianship is a dynamic, exciting, and challenging profession with room for many great librarians. By joining together to establish a common understanding of our profession and our role as librarians, as suggested, all help ensure the survival of librarianship and libraries.

2

Leadership Theories and Management Functions

REVIEW OF LEADERSHIP THEORY

A review of the leadership literature reveals an evolving series of 'schools of thought' from "Great Man" and "Trait" theories to "Transformational" leadership.

Whilst early theories tend to focus upon the characteristics and behaviours of successful leaders, later theories begin to consider the role of followers and the contextual nature of leadership:

* *Great Man Theories*: Based on the belief that leaders are exceptional people, born with innate qualities, destined to lead. The use of the term 'man' was intentional since until the latter part of the twentieth century leadership was thought of as a concept which is primarily male, military and Western. This led to the next school of Trait Theories.
* *Trait Theories:* The lists of traits or qualities associated with leadership exist in abundance and continue to be produced. They draw on virtually all the adjec-tives in the dictionary which describe some positive or virtuous human attribute, from ambition to zest for life.
* *Behaviourist Theories*: These concentrate on what leaders actually do rather than on their qualities. Different patterns of behaviour are observed and categorised as 'styles of leadership'. This area has probably attracted most attention from practising managers.

* *Situational Leadership:* This approach sees leadership as specific to the situation in which it is being exercised. For example, whilst some situations may require an autocratic style, others may need a more participative approach. It also proposes that there may be differences in required leadership styles at different levels in the same organization.
* *Contingency Theory:* This is a refinement of the situational viewpoint and focuses on identifying the situational variables which best predict the most appropriate or effective leadership style to fit the particular circumstances.
* *Transactional Theory*: This approach emphasises the importance of the relationship between leader and followers, focusing on the mutual benefits derived from a form of 'contract' through which the leader delivers such things as rewards or recognition in return for the commitment or loyalty of the followers
* *Transformational Theory*: The central concept here is change and the role of leadership in envisioning and implementing the transformation of organisational performance.

Each of these theories takes a rather individualistic perspective of the leader, although a school of thought gaining increasing recognition is that of "dispersed" leadership. This approach, with its foundations in sociology, psychology and politics rather than management science, views leadership as a process that is diffuse throughout an organisation rather than lying solely with the formally designated 'leader'.

The emphasis thus shifts from developing 'leaders' to developing 'leaderful' organisations with a collective responsibility for leadership. In the current section as suggested, focus primarily on the more traditional, individualistic views of the leader as we feel these have greatest relevance to the development of management and leadership standards. As suggested, finish, however, with an introduction to "dispersed leadership".

THE TRAIT APPROACH TO LEADERSHIP

The Trait Approach arose from the "Great Man" theory as a way of identifying the key characteristics of successful leaders. It was believed that through this approach critical leadership traits could be isolated and that people with such traits could then be recruited, selected, and installed into leadership positions. This approach was common in the military and is still used as a set of criteria to select candidates for commissions.

The problem with the trait approach lies in the fact that almost as many traits as studies undertaken were identified. After several years of such research, it became apparent that no consistent traits could be identified. Although some traits were found in a considerable number of studies, the results were generally inconclusive.

Some leaders might have possessed certain traits but the absence of them did not necessarily mean that the person was not a leader. Although there was little consistency in the results of the various trait studies, however, some traits did appear more frequently than others, including: technical skill, friendliness, task motivation, application to task, group task supportiveness, social skill, emotional control, administrative skill, general charisma, and intelligence. Of these, the most widely explored has tended to be "charisma". Table 2.1 lists the main leadership traits and skills identified by Stogdill in 1974.

THE BEHAVIOURAL SCHOOL

The results of the trait studies were inconclusive. Traits, amongst other things, were hard to measure. How, for example, do we measure traits such as honesty, integrity, loyalty, or diligence? Another approach in the study of leadership had to be found. After the publication of the late Douglas McGregor's classic book The Human Side of Enterprise in 1960, attention shifted to 'behavioural theories'. McGregor was a teacher, researcher, and consultant whose work was considered to be "on the cutting edge" of managing people. He influenced all the behavioural theories, which emphasize focusing on human relationships, along with output and performance.

Table 2.1. Leadership Skills and Traits

Traits	Skills
– Adaptable to situations	– Clever (intelligent)
– Alert to social environment	– Conceptually skilled
– Ambitious and achievement-orientated	– Creative
– Assertive	– Diplomatic and tactful
– Cooperative	– Fluent in speaking
– Decisive	– Knowledgeable about group task
– Dependable	– Organised (administrative ability)
– Dominant (desire to influence others)	– Persuasive
– Energetic (high activity level)	– Socially skilled
– Persistent	
– Self-confident	
– Tolerant of stress	
– Willing to assume responsibility	

McGregor's Theory X and Theory Y Managers

Although not strictly speaking a theory of leadership, the leadership strategy of effectively-used participative management proposed in Douglas McGregor's book has had a tremendous impact on managers. The most publicized concept is McGregor's thesis that leadership strategies are influenced by a leader's assumptions about human nature. As a result of his experience as a consultant, McGregor summarised two contrasting sets of assumptions made by managers in industry.

Theory X and Y Managers:

* Theory X managers believe that:
  - The average human being has an inherent dislike of work and will avoid it if possible.

   - Because of this human characteristic, most people must be coerced, controlled, directed, or threatened with punishment to get them to put forth adequate effort to achieve organizational objectives.
   - The average human being prefers to be directed, wishes to avoid responsibility, has relatively little ambition, and wants security above all else.
* Theory Y managers believe that:
   - The expenditure of physical and mental effort in work is as natural as play or rest, and the average human being, under proper conditions, learns not only to accept but to seek responsibility.
   - People will exercise self-direction and self-control to achieve objectives to which they are committed.
   - The capacity to exercise a relatively high level of imagination, ingenuity, and creativity in the solution of organizational problems is widely, not narrowly, distributed in the population, and the intellectual potentialities of the average human being are only partially utilized under the conditions of modern industrial life.

It can therefore be seen that a leader holding Theory X assumptions would prefer an autocratic style, whereas one holding Theory Y assumptions would prefer a more participative style.

BLAKE AND MOUTON'S MANAGERIAL GRID

The Managerial Grid developed by Robert Blake and Jane Mouton focuses on task and employee orientations of managers, as well as combinations of concerns between the two extremes. A grid with concern for production on the horizontal axis and concern for people on the vertical axis and plots five basic leadership styles. The first number refers to a leader's production or task orientation; the second, to people or employee orientation.

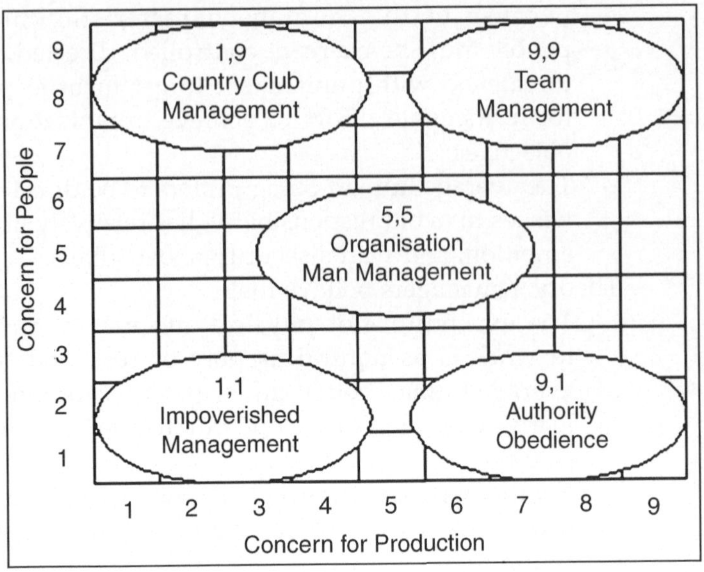

Fig 2.1. "Team Management"-a High Concern for Both Employees and Production-is the Most Effective Type of Leadership Behaviour.

The Contingency or Situational School

Whilst behavioural theories may help managers develop particular leadership behaviours they give little guidance as to what constitutes effective leadership in different situations. Indeed, most researchers today conclude that no one leadership style is right for every manager under all circumstances. Instead, contingency-situational theories were developed to indicate that the style to be used is contingent upon such factors as the situation, the people, the task, the organisation, and other environmental variables.

Fiedler's Contingency Model

Fiedler's contingency theory postulates that there is no single best way for managers to lead. Situations will create different leadership style requirements for a manager. The solution to a managerial situation is contingent on the factors that impinge on the situation. For example, in a highly routine environment where repetitive tasks are the norm, a relatively directive leadership style may result in the best performance, however, in a dynamic environment a more flexible, participative style may be required.

Fiedler looked at three situations that could define the condition of a managerial task:

* *Leader Member Relations*: How well do the manager and the employees get along?
* *Task Structure:* Is the job highly structured, fairly unstructured, or somewhere in between?
* *Position Power*: How much authority does the manager possess?

Managers were rated as to whether they were relationship oriented or task oriented. Task oriented managers tend to do better in situations that have good leader-member relationships, structured tasks, and either weak or strong position power. They do well when the task is unstructured but position power is strong. Also, they did well at the other end of the spectrum when the leader member relations were moderate to poor and the task was unstructured.

Relationship oriented managers do better in all other situations. Thus, a given situation might call for a manager with a different style or a manager who could take on a different style for a different situation. These environmental variables are combined in a weighted sum that is termed "favourable" at one end and "unfavourable" at the other. Task oriented style is preferable at the clearly defined extremes of "favourable" and "unfavourable" environments, but relationship orientation excels in the middle ground.

Managers could attempt to reshape the environment variables to match their style. Another aspect of the contingency model theory is that the leader-member relations, task structure, and position power dictate a leader's situational control. Leader-member relations are the amount of loyalty, dependability, and support that the leader receives from employees. It is a measure of how the manager perceives he or she and the group of employees is getting along together. In a favourable relationship the manager has a high task structure and is able to reward and or punish employees without any problems.

In an unfavourable relationship the task is usually unstructured and the leader possesses limited authority. The spelling out in detail of what is required of subordinates affects task structure. Positioning power measures the amount of power or authority the manager perceives the organization has given him or her for the purpose of directing, rewarding, and punishing subordinates. Positioning power of managers depends on the taking away or increasing the decision-making power of employees.

The task-motivated style leader experiences pride and satisfaction in the task accomplishment for the organization, while the relationship-motivated style seeks to build interpersonal relations and extend extra help for the team development in the organization. There is no good or bad leadership style. Each person has his or her own preferences for leadership. Task-motivated leaders are at their best when the group performs successfully such as achieving a new sales record or out-performing the major competitor. Relationship-oriented leaders are at their best when greater customer satisfaction is gained and a positive company image is established.

The Hersey-Blanchard Model of Leadership

The Hersey-Blanchard Leadership Model also takes a situational perspective of leadership. This model posits that the developmental levels of a leader's subordinates play the greatest role in determining which leadership styles are most appropriate.

Their theory is based on the amount of direction and socio-emotional support a leader must provide given the situation and the "level of maturity" of the followers:

* Task behaviour is the extent to which the leader engages in spelling out the duties and responsibilities to an individual or group. This behaviour includes telling people what to do, how to do it, when to do it, where to do it, and who's to do it. In task behaviour the leader engages in oneway communication.
* Relationship behaviour is the extent to which the leader engages in two-way or multi-way communi-

cations. This includes listening, facilitating, and supportive behaviours. In relationship behaviour the leader engages in two-way communication by providing socio-emotional support.

* Maturity is the willingness and ability of a person to take responsibility for directing his or her own behaviour. People tend to have varying degrees of maturity, depending on the specific task, function, or objective that a leader is attempting to accomplish through their efforts.

In summary therefore leader behaviours fall along two continua:

* Directive Behaviour
  - One-Way Communication
  - Followers' Roles Clearly Communicated
  - Close Supervision of Performance
* Supportive Behaviour
  - Two-Way Communication
  - Listening, providing support and encouragement
  - Facilitate interaction Involve follower in decision-making

For Blanchard the key situational variable, when determining the appropriate leadership style, is the readiness or developmental level of the subordinate.

As a result, four leadership styles result:

* *Directing:* The leader provides clear instructions and specific direction. This style is best matched with a low follower readiness level.
* *Coaching*: The leader encourages two-way communication and helps build confidence and motivation on the part of the employee, although the leader still has responsibility and controls decision making. Selling style is best matched with a moderate follower readiness level.
* *Supporting:* With this style, the leader and followers share decision making and no longer need or expect the relationship to be directive. Participating style is best matched with a moderate follower readiness level.

* *Delegating:* This style is appropriate for leaders whose followers are ready to accomplish a particular task and are both competent and motivated to take full responsibility. Delegating style is best matched with a high follower readiness level.

To determine the appropriate leadership style to use in a given situation, the leader must first determine the maturity level of the followers in relation to the specific task that the leader is attempting to accomplish through the effort of the followers. As the level of followers' maturity increases, the leader should begin to reduce his or her task behaviour and increase relationship behaviour until the followers reach a moderate level of maturity. As the followers begin to move into an above average level of maturity, the leader should decrease not only task behaviour but also relationship behaviour. Once the maturity level is identified, the appropriate leadership style can be determined.

Tannenbaum and Schmidt's Leadership Continuum

One criticism of early work on leadership styles is that they looked at styles too much in black and white terms. The autocratic and democratic styles or task-oriented and relationship-oriented styles which they described are extremes, whereas in practice the behaviour of many, perhaps most, leaders in business will be somewhere between the two. Contingency theorists Tannenbaum and Schmidt suggested the idea that leadership behaviour varies along a continuum and that as one moves away from the autocratic extreme the amount of subordinate participation and involvement in decision taking increases. They also suggested that the kind of leadership represented by the democratic extreme of the continuum will be rarely encountered in formal organisations.

Four main leadership styles can be located at points along such a continuum:

* *Autocratic:* The leader takes the decisions and announces them, expecting subordinates to carry them out without question.
* *Persuasive*: At this point on the scale the leader also takes all the decisions for the group without discussion

or consultation but believes that people will be better motivated if they are persuaded that the decisions are good ones. He or she does a lot of explaining and 'selling' in order to overcome any possible resistance to what he or she wants to do. The leader also puts a lot of energy into creating enthusiasm for the goals he or she has set for the group.

* *Consultative:* In this style the leader confers with the group members before taking decisions and, in fact, considers their advice and their feelings when framing decisions. He or she may, of course, not always accept the subordinates' advice but they are likely to feel that they can have some influence. Under this leadership style the decision and the full responsibility for it remain with the leader but the degree of involvement by subordinates in decision taking is very much greater than telling or selling styles.
* *Democratic*: Using this style the leader would characteristically lay the problem before his or her subordinates and invite discussion. The leader's role is that of conference leader, or chair, rather than that of decision taker. He or she will allow the decision to emerge out of the process of group discussion, instead of imposing it on the group as its boss.

What distinguishes this approach from previous discussions of leadership style is that there will be some situations in which each of the above styles is likely to be more appropriate than the others:

* *Telling:* In an emergency, a telling style may be most appropriate and would normally be considered justified by the group.
* *Selling:* The selling style would tend to fit situations in which the group leader, and he or she alone, possesses all the information on which the decision must be based and which at the same time calls for a very high level of commitment and enthusiasm on the part of group members if the task is to be carried through successfully.

* *Consulting:* The consulting style is likely to be most appropriate when there is time in which to reach a considered decision and when the information on which the decision needs to be based lies among the members of the group.
* *Joining:* The joining style is appropriate under similar conditions, with the important exception that this is likely to be appropriate only in those instances where the nature of the responsibility associated with the decision is such that group members are willing to share it with their leader, or alternatively the leader is willing to accept responsibility for decisions which he or she has not made personally.

Adair's Action-Centred Leadership Model

John Adair has a long pedigree in the world of leadership. The Adair model is that the action-centred leader gets the job done through the work team and relationships with fellow managers and staff.

According to Adair's explanation an action-centred leader must:

* Direct the job to be done
* Support and review the individual people doing it
* Co-ordinate and foster the work team as a whole

His famous three circle diagram fig. 2.2 is a simplification of the variability of human interaction, but is a useful tool for thinking about what constitutes an effective leader/manager in relation to the job he/she has to do. The effective leader/manager carries out the functions and exhibits the behaviours depicted by the three circles. Situational and contingent elements call for different responses by the leader. Hence imagine that the various circles may be bigger or smaller as the situation varies *i.e.* the leader will give more or less emphasis to the functionally-oriented behaviours according to what the actual situation involves.

The challenge for the leader is to manage all sectors of the diagram:

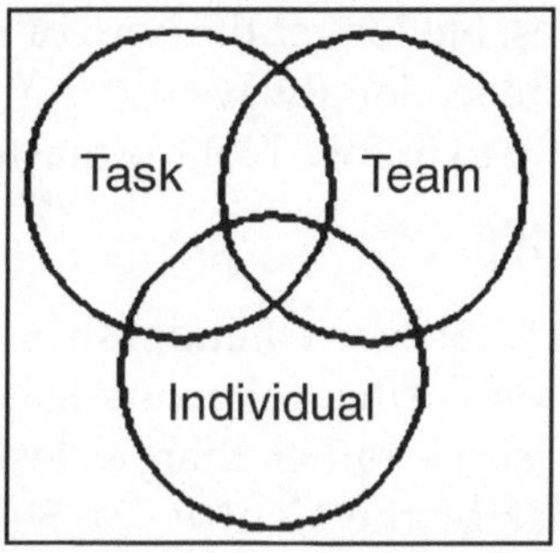

Fig 2.2. Action-Centred Leadership Model.

* Task:
  - Define the task
  - Make the plan
  - Allocate work and resources
  - Control quality and rate of work
  - Check performance against plan
  - Adjust the plan
* Team:
  - Maintain discipline
  - Build team spirit
  - Encourage, motivate, give a sense of purpose
  - Appoint sub-leaders
  - Ensure communication within group
  - Develop the group
* Individual:
  - Attend to personal problems
  - Praise individuals
  - Give status
  - Recognise and use individual abilities
  - Develop the individual

LEADERS AND FOLLOWERS

The models discussed so far have dwelt on the leader as some frontal figure who stands out from the rest as being somehow different and "leading" the rest of the people. The discussion now moves to recognition of the importance of the leaders' relationship with his/her followers and an interdependency of roles. No longer the hero or solo leader but the team leader. Not the leader always out in front but the leader who has the capacity to follow. Not the master, but the servant.

Servant Leadership

The notion of "Servant Leadership" emphasises the leaders' duty to serve his/her followers-leadership thus arises out of a desire to serve rather than a desire to lead Robert Greenleaf, founder of the Centre for Servant Leadership describes it as follows:

* "The servant-leader is servant first. . . It begins with the natural feeling that one wants to serve, to serve first. Then conscious choice brings one to aspire to lead. He or she is sharply different from the person who is leader first, perhaps because of the need to assuage an unusual power drive or to acquire material possessions. For such it will be a later choice to serve–after leadership is established. The leader-first and the servant-first are two extreme types. Between them there are shadings and blends that are part of the infinite variety of human nature.
* The difference manifest itself in the care taken by the servant-first to make sure that other people's highest priority needs are being served. The best test, and difficult to administer, is: do those served grow as persons; do they, while being served, become healthier, wiser, freer, more autonomous, more likely themselves to become servants? And, what is the effect on the least privileged in society; will they benefit, or, at least, will they not be further deprived?"

Characteristics of Servant Leaders are as follows:

* "Servant-Leadership is a practical philosophy which supports people who choose to serve first, and then lead as a way of expanding service to individuals and institutions. Servantleaders may or may not hold formal leadership positions. Servant-leadership encourages collaboration, trust, foresight, listening, and the ethical use of power and empowerment."

The emphasis on serving a higher purpose has made this model popular within the Church and other religious institutions.

The Following Part of Leading

Katzenbach and Smith, authors of 'The Wisdom of Teams' talk of the "following part of leading", saying that the critical behaviours of leaders are:

* Key Behaviours of Leaders:
  - *Asking Questions Instead of Giving Answers*: By asking such questions such as "What do you think we should do?" or "How do you suggest we proceed?" you take a step behind another person. Whether you stay behind, of course, depends on your intention to actually follow the suggestion or answer of that other person.
  - *Providing Opportunities for others to Lead you:* This goes beyond the traditional notion of looking for growth opportunities for other people. Unless the opportunity in question bears a real risk for your personal performance outcome, you are not actually positioning yourself as a follower.
  - *Doing Real Work in Support of others Instead of only the Reverse*: Rolling up your sleeves and contributing "sweat equity" to the efforts and outcomes of other people earns you their appreciation as someone upon whom they can depend, regardless of the relative hierarchical or functional position each of you holds.
  - *Becoming a Matchmaker Instead of a "Central Switch"*: In addition to following other people yourself, you must learn to help them follow each other. This requires you to get beyond considering yourself the "central switch" through which all decisions flow. Instead, you need to look for every possible chance to help people find their best collaborators. "Have you asked Sally or Rasheed what they think?" is often the

only input required to facilitate the effort at hand, although you then must submit your effort and support to whatever the people in question suggest.

- *Seeking Common Understanding Instead of Consensus*: The pejorative meaning associated with consensus management has nothing to do with either effective leading or effective following. Leaders who know when and how to follow build deep common understanding, not superficial consensus, around the purpose, goals, and approach at hand. They submit themselves and others to the discipline of ensuring that all sides to any disagreement are fully understood by everyone, recognizing that mutual understanding is far more powerful than any particular decision to choose path A over path B. All people will follow strong, commonly understood purposes and goals more easily than the "put-up jobs" associated with consensus.

They go on to say that the indicators of when a leader must follow are:

* When a leader must follow Leaders:
  - Individual performance: As a leader, you must follow another individual, regardless of hierarchy, if:
    a. That individual, through experience, skill, and judgement, knows best.
    b. That individual's growth demands that you invest more in his or her skill and self-confidence than in your own.
    c. Only that individual, not you, has the capacity to "get it done"
  - Team performance: As a leader, you must follow the team if:
    a. The team's purpose and performance goals demand it
    b. The team, not you, must develop skills and self-confidence

c. The team's agreed-upon working approach requires you, like all the others, to do real work

- *Organizational Performance*: As a leader, you must follow others, regardless of hierarchy, if:
  a. The organization's purpose and performance goals demand it
  b. The need for expanding the leadership capacity of others in the organization requires it
  c. "Living" the vision and values enjoins you to do so

Team Leadership

In the late 1970's Meredith Belbin conducted a study of teams focusing on the factors separating successful and unsuccessful teams via a college business game at Henley a feature of which was shared leadership. Through the game Belbin found that the composition of the team was important and that individual differences in style, role and contribution far from underlining personal weaknesses, were a source of potential team strength. Balanced teams comprised of such individuals who engaged in complementary role behaviour performed better than unbalanced teams.

Nine distinctive roles were identified in the study, with most people being found to embrace a mix of two or three roles whilst also avoiding others with which they were uncomfortable. Where there was an individual with clear, useful and appreciated attributes they would fit into a team on the basis of the strengths they brought. These people would also have weaknesses that belonged to the same cluster of characteristics as the strength itself. These potential deficiencies were considered the price that has to be paid for a particular strength, a price that is worth paying, and were referred to as 'allowable weaknesses.

Belbin found no 'ideal' team member, individual who could perform all of the roles. From this work, Belbin drew the distinction between the "Solo" and the "Team" leader. He suggests that "leaders are not notable for admitting their weaknesses, whether allowable or not. They act as though they have no weaknesses". To many people the image of the leader-a person heading up a team of followers, ever ready to take on any role and assuming any responsibility-is very familiar to us for it is the one based upon our past experiences and beliefs.

Belbin classified such leaders as 'Solo leaders' and in the workplace this type of behaviour may have great advantages, for internal barriers can be overcome and decisions, especially those of an urgent nature, can be made and put into effect with little or no delay. The increasing complexity and the discontinuous nature of modern work however, poses greater problems where Solo leadership is less appropriate and 'Team leadership' more suited. The key difference between the 'Solo leader' and 'Team leadership' revolves around the behaviour and participation of the two.

Solo and Team Leader:

* Solo Leader:
  - *Plays Unlimited Role:* The Solo Leader interferes in everything
  - *Strives for Conformity*: The Solo Leader tries to mould people to particular standards
  - *Collects Acolytes:* The Solo Leader collects admirers and sycophants
  - *Directs Subordinates*: Subordinates take their leads and cues from the Solo Leader
  - *Projects Objectives*: The Solo Leader makes it plain what everyone is expected to do 1. Chooses to limit role to preferred team roles–delegates roles to others
* Team Leader:
  - *Chooses to Limit Role to Preferred Team Roles*: Delegates roles to others
  - *Builds on Diversity*: The Team Leader values differences between people
  - *Seeks talent:* The Team Leader is not threatened by people with special abilities

- *Develops colleagues*: The Team Leader encourages the growth of personal strengths
- *Creates mission*: The Team Leader projects the vision which others can act on as they see fit

Using Team Role theory the word 'shape' indicates to us 'shaper', whilst the word 'vision' implies 'plant'. Looking at leadership using Handy's definition is interesting for vision is certainly important to leadership, but does it have to be unique to an individual? Where it is unique to an individual with a drive to enact it such as a 'Shaper', strong Solo leadership is likely to prevail. Vision alternatively may be 'borrowed' by a 'Shaper' who treats it as a product of the self and similarly will adopt a Solo leadership style.

Many organisations have rewarded Solo leadership behaviour by promoting individuals to management and leadership positions, for such individuals have met past organisational needs In today's organisation the alternative approach, the Team Leader, is more appropriate. Whilst Team leadership may not be as natural as Solo leadership, Belbin suggests it can be learned through understanding the nature of leadership and the qualities required.

In the rapidly changing and uncertain work environment of today no one person has all the answers to leadership. A Team leadership style based upon the development of the strengths and the allowable weaknesses of all of the roles will permit a more holistic, or participative, style of leadership where teamwork, problem solving, decision making and innovation can flourish with heightened teamwork and work performance.

Transactional and Transformational Leadership

James MacGregor Burns writing in his book 'Leadership' was the first to put forward the concept of "transforming leadership". To Burns transforming leadership.

"Is a relationship of mutual stimulation and elevation that converts followers inyo leaders and may convert leaders into moral agents".

Burns went on to also further define it by suggesting that:

* "[Transforming leadership] occurs when one or more

persons engage with others in such a way that leaders and followers raise one another to higher levels of motivation and morality..."

Burns draws upon the humanistic psychology movement in his writing upon 'transforming leadership' by proposing that the transforming leader shapes, alters, and elevates the motives, values and goals of followers achieving significant change in the process. He proposed that there is a special power entailed in transforming leadership with leaders

"Armed with principles [that] may ultimately transform both leaders and followers into persons who jointly adhere to modal values and end-values".

Burns sees the power of transforming leadership as more noble and different from charismatic leadership, which he terms 'heroic' leadership, and executive or business leadership. Despite this it is surprising that most of the application of Burns' work has been in these two types of leadership. Bernard Bass developed Burns' concept of transforming leadership in 'Leadership and Performance Beyond Expectations' into 'transformational leadership' where the leader transforms followers–the direction of influence to Bass is thus one-way, unlike Burns' who sees it as potentially a two-way process. Bass, however, deals with the transformational style of executive leadership that incorporates social change, a facet missing from Burns' work.

For Bass 'transformational leaders' may:

* Expand a follower's portfolio of needs
* Transform a follower's self-interest
* Increase the confidence of followers
* Elevate followers' expectations
* Heighten the value of the leader's intended outcomes for the follower
* Encourage behavioural change
* Motivate others to higher levels of personal achievement.

Tichy and Devanna in their book 'Transformational Leadership' built further on the work of Burns and Bass in organisational and work contexts.

They described the hybrid nature of transformational as *"...Not due to charisma. It is a behavioural process capable of being learned"*.

Bass writing with a research colleague Avolio suggested that

"Transformational leadership is closer to the prototype of leadership that people have in mind when they describe their ideal leader, and it is more likely to provide a role model with which subordinates want to identify".

Transactional leadership has been the traditional model of leadership with its roots from an organisational or business perspective in the 'bottom line'. Stephen Covey writing in 'Principle-Centred Leadership' suggests that transformational leadership "focuses on the 'top line'" and offers contrast between the two.

Comparison of Transactional and Transformational Leadership:

* Transactional Leadership:
  - Builds on man's need to get a job done and make a living
  - Is preoccupied with power and position, politics and perks
  - Is mired in daily affairs
  - Is short-term and hard data orientated
  - Focuses on tactical issues
  - Relies on human relations to lubricate human interactions
  - Follows and fulfils role expectations by striving to work effectively within current systems
  - Supports structures and systems that reinforce the bottom line, maximise efficiency, and guarantee short-term profits
* Transformational Leadership
  - Builds on a man's need for meaning
  - Is preoccupied with purposes and values, morals, and ethics
  - Transcends daily affairs

- Is orientated towards long-term goals without compromising human values and principles
- Focuses more on missions and strategies
- Releases human potential–identifying and developing new talent
- Designs and redesigns jobs to make them meaningful and challenging
- Aligns internal structures and systems to reinforce overarching values and goals

Both kinds of leadership are necessary. Transactional leadership has remained the organisational model for many people and organisations who have not moved into or encouraged the transformational role needed to meet the challenges of our changing times.

* "The goal of transformational leadership is to 'transform' people and organisations in a literal sense– to change them in mind and heart; enlarge vision, insight, and understanding; clarify purposes; make behaviour congruent with beliefs, principles, or values; and bring about changes that are permanent, self-perpetuating, and momentum building"

Transformational leaders display behaviours associated with five transformational styles.

Table 2.2. Transformational Leadership Styles and Behaviours

Transformational Style	Leader Behaviour
1) Idealized Behaviours: living one's ideals	* Talk about their most important values and beliefs * Specify the importance of having a strong sense of purpose * Consider the moral and ethical consequences of decisions * Champion exciting new possibilities * Talk about the importance of trusting each other

Table Contd...

2) Inspirational Motivation: inspiring others **Transformational Style**	* Talk optimistically about the future **Leader Behaviour**
	* Talk enthusiastically about what needs to be accomplished * Articulate a compelling vision of the future * Express confidence that goals will be achieved
	* Provide an exciting image of what is essential to consider * Take a stand on controversial issues
3) Intellectual Stimulation: stimulating others	* Re-examine critical assumptions to question whether they are appropriate * Seek differing perspectives when solving problems * Get others to look at problems from many different angles * Suggest new ways of looking at how to complete assignments * Encourage non-traditional thinking to deal with traditional problems * Encourage rethinking those ideas which have never been questioned before
4) Individualized Consideration: coaching and development	* Spend time teaching and coaching * Treat others as individuals rather than just as members of the group * Consider individuals as having different needs, abilities, and aspirations from others

Table Contd...

	* Help others to develop their strengths
Transformational Style	**Leader Behaviour**
	* Listen attentively to others' concerns * Promote self development
5) Idealized Attributes: Respect, trust, and faith	* Instill pride in others for being associated with them * Go beyond their self-interests
	for the good of the group * Act in ways that build others' respect * Display a sense of power and competence * Make personal sacrifices for others' benefit * Reassure others that obstacles will be overcome

Transformational leadership is a process in which the leaders take actions to try to increase their associates' awareness of what is right and important, to raise their associates' motivational maturity and to move their associates to go beyond the associates' own self-interests for the good of the group, the organization, or society. Such leaders provide their associates with a sense of purpose that goes beyond a simple exchange of rewards for effort provided.

The transformational leaders are proactive in many different and unique ways. These leaders attempt to optimize development, not just performance. Development encompasses the maturation of ability, motivation, attitudes, and values. Such leaders want to elevate the maturity level of the needs of their associates. They convince their associates to strive for a higher level of achievement as well as higher levels of moral and ethical standards. Through the development of their associates, they optimize the development of their organization as well. High performing associates build high performing organizations.

Hooper and Potter extend the notion of transformational leadership to identify seven key competences of "transcendent leaders": those able to engage the emotional support of their followers and thus effectively transcend change:

* Setting direction
* Setting an example
* Communication
* Alignment
* Bringing out the best in people
* The leader as a change agent
* Providing decision in a crisis and on the ambiguous

DISPERSED LEADERSHIP

The importance of social relations in the leadership contract, the need for a leader to be accepted by their followers and a realisation that no one individual is the ideal leader in all circumstances have given rise to a new school of leadership thought. Referred to as 'informal', 'emergent' or 'dispersed' leadership, this approach argues a less formalised model of leadership where the leaders' role is dissociated from the organisational hierarchy. It is proposed that individuals at all levels in the organisation and in all roles can exert leadership influence over their colleagues and thus influence the overall leadership of the organisation.

Heifetz distinguishes between the exercise of "leadership" and the exercise of "authority"–thus dissociating leadership from formal organisational power roles whilst Raelin talks of developing "leaderful" organisations through concurrent, collective and compassionate leadership. The key to this is a distinction between the notions of "leader" and "leadership". "Leadership" is regarded as a process of sense-making and direction-giving within a group and the "leader" can only be identified on the basis of his/her relationship with others in the social group who are behaving as followers.

In this manner, it is quite possible to conceive of the leader as emergent rather than predefined and that their role can only be understood through examining the relationships within the group. The origins of such an approach have their foundations more in the fields of sociology and politics than the more traditional management literature and draw on concepts such as organisational culture and climate to highlight the contextual nature of leadership. It is a more collective concept, and would argue for a move from an analysis and development of individual leader qualities to an identification of what constitutes an effective leadership process within an organisation. A move in focus from the individuals to the relationships themselves.

LEADERSHIP MODELS AND COMPETENCY FRAMEWORKS

This section of the report will look at some different leadership models and frameworks used in practice across the public and private sector organisations. The chosen models were selected as the organisations were known to researchers at the Centre for Leadership Studies and/or details of the framework were publicly available. They are not intended to represent a comprehensive, or even representative, sample of available frameworks but rather a preliminary examination of readily available materials.

The inclusion of a particular framework does not necessarily indicate that it is in any way assumed "better" or more "typical" than those that were not included and, indeed, there may well be many excellent models which have not been discussed. To many participating organisations the material reviewed represents an element of their "competitive advantage" and is thus confidential. We have therefore chosen in this report, not to include the full framework but simply to refer to the key elements. Where further information is available on the Internet we have included the web address. For ease of presentation, they have been divided into private-sector, public-sector and generic frameworks.

PRIVATE SECTOR FRAMEWORKS

AstraZeneca Leadership Capabilities

The AstraZeneca Leadership Capabilities were defined

shortly after merger in 1999 and have been used in performance management, development planning and management planning across the global company. They are a central part of leadership development programmes and a 360 degree feedback tool has been developed to support their application. The leadership behaviours provide a link between business priorities and the AZ values of: respect for the individual and for diversity; openness, honest, trust and support for each other; integrity and high ethical standards; and leadership by example at all levels.

There are seven key capabilities, each with associated indicators/behaviours:

* Provides clarity about strategic direction.
* Ensures commitment.
* Focuses on delivery.
* Builds relationships.
* Develops people.
* Demonstrates personal conviction.
* Builds self-awareness.

BAE Performance Centred Leadership

Performance Centred Leadership competencies provide a set of related behaviours used to improve business performance. They have been developed from 360 degree feedback information, benchmarked against the competencies of high performing organisations, changed to reflect input from the Senior leader focus groups and statistically evaluated by London University. The competencies and related behaviours are used to evaluate performance in Peer Recognition and Employee opinion survey, identifying development opportunities through 360 degree feedback and are used as part of the appointment process.

There are five core competences, each with a set of related behaviours:

* Achieving High Performance.
* Focusing on the Customer.
* Developing Others.
* Continuously Improving.
* Working Together.

The framework forms a basis for leadership development in BAE which is fully integrated with all other strategic processes in the organisation through the Performance Centred Leadership Development Framework.

Federal Express Leadership Qualities

FedEx has a system for rating aspiring leaders according to nine attributes:

* Charisma.
* Individual consideration.
* Intellectual stimulation.
* Courage.
* Dependability.
* Flexibility.
* Integrity.
* Judgement.
* Respect for others.

Lufthansa Leadership Compass

The Lufthansa Leadership Compass sets out a framework for effective leadership that is used by the Lufthansa School of Business in its leadership development education.

It includes the following six key categories, which set out a range of skills and behaviours including: vision, decisiveness, concern for people, self-reflection and professional know-how:

* Entrepreneurial leadership
* Breakthrough problem solving
* Winning others
* Leading people
* Attitude and drive
* International business competencies.

Development Centres based on this framework are used to help "high potential" employees define their current position and determine the next steps for their professional career. This involves a self-assessment exercise, development centre and a post DC process whereby the participant develops an individual development plan with the support and coaching of their superior. It is intended that this process should occur about one year before moving into grade post.

Philips Leadership Competencies

Six Leadership Competencies define the behaviour that is required to achieve business success in Phillips. They provide a balanced approach, stating the importance of task aspects while recognising that results are obtained through people.

These competencies are as follows:

* Shows determination to achieve excellent results
* Focuses on the market
* Finds better ways
* Demands top performance
* Inspires commitment
* Develops self and others

Shell Leadership Framework

The Leadership Framework used by Shell includes nine key elements:

* Builds Shared Vision
* Champions Customer Focus
* Maximises Business Opportunities
* Demonstrates Professional Mastery
* Displays Personal Effectiveness
* Demonstrates Courage
* Motivates, Coaches and Develops
* Values Differences
* Delivers Results

Vodafone Global Leadership Competencies

The Vodafone leadership competencies underlying their Global Leadership Programme are divided into five categories:

* Values communication
* International team development
* Strategic vision

* Building organisational capability
* Commercial drive

PUBLIC SECTOR FRAMEWORKS

Senior Civil Service Competency Framework

This framework sets out key attributes that have been identified by Civil Service Corporate Management as required for the *Senior Civil Service* (SCS). There are six main sets of competences, each with a series of related behaviours.

The competencies are as follows:

* Giving purpose and direction
* Making a personal impact
* Thinking strategically
* Getting the best from people
* Learning and improving
* Focusing on delivery

DfES-Management and Leadership Attributes

This framework sets out what is expected of managers and leaders in the Department for Education and Skills as the organisation moves forward to deliver the Department's Strategic Framework. It is based on the SCS Competency Framework and was developed following a period of internal consultation in the DfES.

It distinguishes between "effective" and "ineffective" behaviours in relation to three clusters of attributes each of which comprises a set of behaviours, skills and knowledge:

* *Interpersonal Attributes*: Making a personal impact, Giving purpose and direction
* *Delivery Attributes*: Focussing on delivery, Thinking strategically
* *Improvement Attributes:* Getting the best from people, Learning and improving

The framework takes a situational/contingency view of leadership in that it states that:

* Competent DfES managers and leaders at all levels will demonstrate varying combinations of these attributes

in different circumstances and at different times. The effective behaviours and skills within each attribute are examples of what competent managers and leaders do when they are modelling good management and leadership–they may not do all of them all of the time!"

Northern Ireland Senior Civil Service Core Criteria

This is the Northern Ireland equivalent of the SCS Competency Framework, covering 8 key competencies including leadership:

* *Leadership:* Envisioning, Team building, Standards and integrity
* *Conceptual and Strategic Thinking and Planning:* Conceptual thinking, Strategic thinking, Planning
* *Focus on Outcomes:* Customer orientation, Outcomes focus, Meeting and improving performance standards
* *Managing and Developing Staff:* Managing staff effectively, Promoting and facilitating development
* Managing relationships and partners
* *Communication:* Oral/written, Influencing, Presentation
* *Managing Resources Innovatively:* Cost awareness, Improvement orientation
* *Personal Effectiveness:* Change orientation, Develop orientation, Self confidence and resilience, Commitment, Intellect in action

Scottish Executive Framework

This framework, devised for the Scottish parliament, identifies seven sets of criteria and, for each, what everyone should do and what managers and leaders should also do. Indicators are also given as to when development needs may be identified.

The specific leadership dimensions of the framework are as follows:

* Achieving
* Self management
* Analysis and investigation
* Outward focus

* Communication
* Managing others
* Working with others

Ministry of Defence

The MoD uses a number of competency frameworks related to leadership for annual appraisal, including a revised SCS Competency Framework and *Officers Joint Appraisal Report* (OJAR).

MD Senior Civil Service Competency Framework

This is based on the SCS Competency Framework and redefines it:

* *Leading and Working Together:* Working together, Providing the lead, Enabling others to give of their best
* *Being Personally Effective:* Striving to achieve results, Promoting change and continuous improvement, Communicating and influencing, Solving problems and taking decisions, Taking a wider perspective
* *Delivering Results:* Focussing on customers and service delivery, Developing and delivering effective policies and programmes, Managing work and resources to achieve results, Exploiting information and knowledge

Officers Joint Appraisal Report

The OJAR, introduced in March 2001, covers 10 performance attributes explored during annual appraisals for officers across the forces.

These are as follows:

* Leadership
* Professional effectiveness
* Effective intelligence
* Judgement
* Management
* Initiative
* Reliability
* Powers of communication
* Subordinate development
* Courage and values.

EO for Local Government–Compendium of Competencies

The *Employers' Organisation* for local government's (EO) role is to help councils achieve the high standards of people management needed to ensure the continuous improvement of services. Their website includes a compendium of leadership competencies developed by and/or used by local authorities across the U.K.

These have been classified into 20 different categories:

* *Change:* includes Challenge, Leadership for Change, Managing Change/Strategic Thinking.
* *Communication*: Includes Communicating, Communication and Customer Care, Listening and Organising
* *Corporate Focus:* Includes Collective Responsibility, Corporate Focus, Developing a Learning Organisation, Evaluating and Improving Organisational Performance, Organisational Awareness, Organi-sational Effectiveness
* *Customer Focus:* Includes Commitment to Quality Customer Service, Customer Focused Service Delivery, Sharpening Customer and Service Focus
* *Decision Making*: Includes Analysing and Solving Problems, Decision Making, Identifying and Solving Problems, Judgement.
* *Equality and Diversity*: Includes Achieving Equal Opportunities, Demonstrating Leadership in Implementing Equalities, Managing Equitably, Valuing Diversity
* *Focus on Results:* Includes Achievement Focused, Focusing on Results, Managing for Results
* *Impact and Influence*: Includes Acting Assertively, Impact and Influence, Interpersonal Skills, Networking and Influencing, Partnership Working, Persuasiveness
* *Information Management:* Includes Gathering and Using Information, Getting Unbiased Information, Giving Clear Information, Information and Communication Management, Searching for Information
* *Integrity*: includes Behaving Ethically, Integrity
* *Leading People:* Includes Appraising People and

Performance, Developing Others, Disciplining and Counselling, Enabling, Leadership, Managing People, Managing, Developing and Understanding Others, Personal and Staff Development, Training, Coaching and Delegating, Valuing People

* *Partnerships:* Includes Community Leadership, Co-operating with Others, Leading Integrated Working, Networking and Influencing, Working in Partnership
* *Personal Management and Drive*: Includes Determination, Managing Self, Motivation and Drive, Personal Effectiveness, Personal Management, Planning and Scheduling Work, Setting Goals and Standards, Time Management and Prioritising
* *Political Awareness:* Includes Democratic Support, Political and Organisational Awareness, Working Competently within the Political Environment
* *Project and Process Management*: Includes Managing Projects, Organisational and Project Management
* *Resource Management:* Includes Managing Resources
* Safety
* *Service Improvement*: Includes Continuous Improvement to Service Delivery, Delivering Excellence, Leading the Challenge on Continuous Service Improvement, Managing the Executive Programme and Performance, Service Co-ordination and Management, Sharpening Customer and Service Focus
* *Strategic Focus:* Includes: Acting Strategically, Developing Strategy, Managing Change/Strategic Thinking, Strategic Behaviour, Vision
* *Team Building:* Includes Building Teams, Working in and Developing Teams

NHS Leadership Qualities Framework

The NHS Leadership Qualities Framework, developed by the NHS Leadership Centre, identifies 15 key qualities across three broad clusters: Personal qualities, Setting direction and Delivering the service.

* *Personal Qualities:* Self belief, Self awareness, Self

management, Drive for improvement, Personal integrity

* *Setting Direction:* Seizing the future, Intellectual flexibility, Broad scanning, Political astuteness, Drive for results
* *Delivering the Service:* Leading change through people, Holding to account, Empowering others, Effective and strategic influencing, Collaborative working

As with the DfES model, there is an emphasis on the situational nature of leadership and an attempt to indicate the circumstances under which different leadership qualities will take precedence.

National College for School Leadership — Hay McBer Model

In 1999 the NCSL commissioned Hay McBer to research leadership in schools. This research led to the development of a model of school leadership which formed the basis of further discussion. The NCSL now seems to be moving away from this approach towards an integrated leadership development framework.

The 17 school leadership qualities in the Hay McBer Model are as follows:

* Analytical Thinking
* Challenge and Support
* Confidence
* Developing Potential
* Drive for Improvement
* Holding People Accountable
* Impact and Influence
* Information Seeking
* Initiative
* Integrity
* Personal Convictions
* Respect for Others
* Strategic Thinking
* Teamworking
* Transformational Leadership

* Understanding the Environment
* Understanding Others.

Senior Executive Service

This framework sets out leadership competencies for the *Senior Executive Service* (SES) in the US.

It identifies 26 competencies across five categories:

* *Leading Change:* Continual Learning, Creativity and Innovation, Resilience, Service Motivation, Strategic Thinking, Vision.
* *Leading People:* Conflict Management, Leveraging Diversity, Integrity/Honesty, Team Building
* *Results Driven*: Accountability, Customer Service, Decisiveness, Entrepreneurship, Problem Solving, Technical Credibility
* *Business Acumen:* Financial Management, Human Resources Management, Technology Management
* *Building Coalitions/Communication:* Influencing/ Negotiating, Interpersonal Skills, Oral Communi-cation, Partnering, Political Savvy, Written Comm-unication

GENERIC FRAMEWORKS

CEML Framework of Management and Leadership Abilities

The Council for Excellence in Management and Leadership conducted an extensive piece of research using primary and secondary data sources to identify a key set of management and leadership abilities. The resultant framework identified 83 distinct management and leadership abilities which were grouped into 8 meta-groups and three generic categories.

The categories and meta-groups are as follows:

* *Thinking Abilities:* Think Strategically
* *People Abilities:* Manage self, Manage and lead people, Lead direction and culture, Manage relationships
* *Task Abilities:* Manage information, Manage resources, Manage activities and quality

METO Management Standards

These are the previous management standards developed by METO, the Management Education Training Organisation.

The seven key roles are as follows:

* Manage Activities
* Manage Resources
* Manage People
* Manage Information
* Manage Energy
* Manage Quality
* Manage projects

Investors in People Leadership and Management Model

The IIP Leadership and Management Model sets out a framework for the assessment of leadership and management capabilities in relation to the new "leadership and management" dimension of the Investors in People Award. There are four main principles each with associated indicators.

EFQM Business Excellence Model

The European Foundation for Quality Management Award is an internationally recognised quality award based around business processes.

The leadership dimension covers the following four areas:

* Leaders develop the mission, vision and values and are role models of a culture of Excellence;
* Leaders are personally involved in ensuring the organisation's management system is developed, implemented and continuously improved;
* Leaders are involved with customers, partners and representatives of society;
* Leaders motivate, support and recognise the organisation's people.

Institute of Chartered Management–Chartered Management Skills

Chartered Manager candidates need to demonstrate

learning, development and impact in the workplace against two of these six categories:

* Leading People
* Meeting Customer Needs
* Managing Change
* Managing Information and Knowledge
* Managing Activities and Resources
* Managing yourself

IMF Management Competencies

As a first step in fostering effective managerial practices, the International Monetary Fund has defined a set of effective managerial behaviours, encapsulated in management competencies. Management competencies comprise a set of critical knowledge, skills, and behaviours that lead to effective management practices. These management competencies are tools you, as a manager, can use to perform your supervisory functions. Effective performance of each competency is described by a series of behavioural benchmarks.

The 15 different management competencies, grouped in five broad categories:

* *Intellectual Leadership Factor:* Sound Judgment/ Analytical Skills, Strategic Vision
* *Work Management Factor:* Planning and Organizing, Drive for Results, Adaptability
* *Communication Factor:* Oral Presentation Skills, Creating Open Communication, Written Communi-cation Skills
* *Interpersonal Factor*: Building Relationships, Negotiating and Influencing, Country/Client Relations
* *People Management Factor:* Motivating Performance, Delegating, Fostering Teamwork, Appraising and Developing Staff

IMF Management competencies are used in a number of ways:

* They are the starting point for developing managerial performance expectations. Competencies can help senior managers articulate the skills needed to be an effective manager—as distinct from those needed to be an effective economist or technical contributor.

* Competencies are the basis for assessing potential managers in the Management Development Center.
* Competencies are the basis for identifying training and development areas.
* They form a common basis on which to assess managers within and across departments.

Hamlin's Generic Model of Managerial and Leadership Effectiveness

This model is based upon a meta analysis of leadership and management behaviours in four U.K. public-sector organisations. It distinguishes between positive and negative indications of management and leadership.

* Positive indicators:
  - Effective organisation and planning/proactive management
  - Participative and supportive leadership/Proactive team leadership
  - Empowerment and delegation
  - Genuine concern for people/Looks after the interests and development needs of staff
  - Open and personal management approach/ Inclusive decision making
  - Communicates and consults widely/Keeps people informed
* Negative indicators:
  - Shows lack of consideration or concern for staff/ ineffective autocratic or dictatorial style of mana-gement
  - Uncaring, self serving management/undermining, depriving and intimidating behaviour
  - Tolerance of poor performance and low stan-dards/ignoring and avoidance
  - Abdicating roles and responsibilities
  - Resistant to new ideas and change/negative approach

The results have been compared to the Zenger Miller Grass-Roots Leadership Model and used to argue for a universalistic model of leadership/management.

The Zenger Miller Grass-Roots Leadership Model

This model was developed from empirical research in which collected 1,871 "critical incidents" from 450 US and Canadian organisations.

The model has been refined from the original Zenger Miller CLIMB strategies model:

* *Create a Compelling Future:* Create and describe a vision, Manager changes required to realise a vision
* *Let the Customer Drive the Organization*: Respond to identified customer needs
* *Involve Every Mind*: Support individual effort, Support team effort, Share information, Make decisions that solve problems, Manage work horizontally, Build personal credibility
* *Manage Work Horizontally:* Manage cross-functional processes, Display technical skills, Manage projects, Manage time and resources
* *Build Personal Credibility*: Take initiative beyond job requirements, Take responsibility for your own actions and the actions of your group, Handle emotions in yourself and others, Display professional ethics, Show compassion, Make credible presentations

A SELECTION OF LEADERSHIP DEVELOPMENT INITIATIVES

The models and competency frameworks detailed, in most cases, used as a basis for the development of leadership and management development provision within organisations as well as appraisal and performance review. It is beyond the scope of this report to offer a detailed review of the associated programmes and the range of leadership and management development initiatives available, however, we would like to introduce a number of approaches that we feel are particularly interesting in the manner in which they seek to develop the behaviours, skills and attitudes of leaders.

NHS CHIEF EXECUTIVES PROGRAMMES

The NHS manage a wide range of programmes through

their Leadership Centre, including a suite of programmes for Chief Executives. These comprise a number of initiatives based upon the NHS Leadership Qualities Framework, including: National and International Learning Experiences:

* Development Assignments
* Transformational Thinking
* Study Tour to Canada
* Duality Leadership Programme
* Action Learning Sets

Modular Programmes:

* Experienced Chief Executives Development Programme
* Drive for Results

Of interest here, is the range of learning opportunities being offered, from action learning sets, study tours and exchanges to modular programmes. The participants are free to choose their preferred modes of learning yet the thinking behind the programme implies that each will contribute towards developing qualities from the Leadership Qualities Framework.

NCSL LEADERSHIP DEVELOPMENT FRAMEWORK

The National College for School Leadership is one of the leading organisations in relation to their awareness of the importance of distributed leadership. Recent years have seen an increasing move from the competency-based approach of the Hay McBer Model to the development of a Leadership Development Framework. The outcomes of a Think Tank report lead to 10 propositions about school leadership.

School leadership must:

* Be purposeful, inclusive and values driven
* Embrace the distinctive and inclusive context of the school
* Promote an active view of learning
* Be instructionally focused
* Be a function that is distributed throughout the school community
* Build capacity by developing the school as a learning community
* Be futures oriented and strategically driven

* Be developed through experiential and innovative methodologies
* Be served by a support and policy context that is coherent and implementation driven
* Be supported by a National College that leads the discourse around leadership for learning

These propositions have been actualised through a series of programmes aimed at five different stages in a school leader's career:

* Emergent leadership, when a teacher is beginning to take on management and leadership responsibilities and perhaps forms an aspiration to become a headteacher
* Established leadership, comprising assistant and deputy heads who are experienced leaders but who do not intend to pursue headship
* Entry to headship, including a teacher's preparation for and induction into the senior post in a school
* Advanced leadership, the stage at which school leaders mature in their role, look to widen their experience, to refresh themselves and to update their skills
* Consultant leadership, when an able and experienced leader is ready to put something back into the profession by taking on training, mentoring, inspection or other responsibilities

The focus on, and research into, leadership at different organisational levels and career stages is refreshing when contrasted to the majority of competency/quality frameworks which tend to be based on research with senior managers only. The model therefore, reflects a contingency approach, but without being prescriptive, and seeks to develop a "leadership culture" rather than just a finite number of "leaders".

ACEVO-LEADERSHIP JOURNEY

The "leadership journey" currently being delivered to members of the *Association of Chief Executives of Voluntary Organisations* (ACEVO) uses a somewhat emergent group learning process to develop and explore leadership capabilities, whereby a group of 12 or so Chief Executives from different voluntary-sector organisations embark on a one-year learning experience together. The programme, run by a consultancy organisation is based around a series of two-day residential modules and associated action learning sets and individual and group challenges.

Whilst the basic structure of the programme is outlined in advance, the emphasis is very much on getting the group to agree on future topics, activities and speakers and thus input and develop the programme as it proceeds. A further central element of the programme is the "make a difference challenge" which is an active development challenge for participants to complete within their organisation and share with other members of the group. The programme is, therefore, very experiential and depends to a large extent on peer-group interaction, support and development.

LEAD2LEAD

The Lead2Lead programme, managed by Lancaster University, uses the process of leadership exchange and reflection to help improve leadership awareness. It involves a process of careful paring of participants, often from different organisations, sectors, and even countries. Once matched, participants are given training in observation and reflection techniques, followed by a three-day exchange to each others work place, and a facilitated debriefing session. The process of observing and being observed can generate significant insights and awareness that could not be delivered through more formalised training. It gives first-hand experience, stories, and personal insights that can be very important to leadership. Furthermore, the "time-out" and reflection elements give the leader space to think and consider their leadership practises.

INTERNATIONAL MASTERS IN PRACTISING MANAGEMENT (IMPM)

The International Masters Programme in Practicing Management is designed to be the "Next Generation" Masters

Programme, combining management development with management education. It is a degree programme that focuses directly on the development of managers in their own contexts-their jobs and their organizations. The IMPM is therefore deeper than conventional programmes of management development and more applied than traditional degree programmes. It was launched in March of 1996 to acclaim from participants and their companies alike, as well as from the international business press.

The IMPM seeks to break the mold of the functional "silos" so common in management education-marketing, finance, organization behaviour, and so on. Instead, the Programme is structured around managerial "mindsets", one for each module. It opens in Lancaster with Managing in general and the *reflective* mindset in particular. Then it moves to McGill, where attention turns to Managing Organizations and the *analytic* mindset. Bangalore follows with Managing Context, the *worldly* mindset. In Japan, it takes up Managing Relationships, the *collaborative* mindset. The Programme closes at INSEAD with Managing Change, the *action* mindset.

More detail is given about each of these mindsets by Mintzberg and Gosling:

* *The Reflective Mindset Refers to "Managing Self"*: Developing the ability to reflect and make meaning–a form of emotional intelligence.
* *The Analytic Mindset Refers to "Managing Organisations"*: Developing the ability to analyse and synthesise not only the hard data, but also the soft–"to appreciate scores and crowds while never losing sight of the ball".
* *The Worldly Mindset Refers to "Managing Contexts"*: To appreciate cultural and local differences and similarities and respond accordingly.
* *The Collaborative Mindset Refers to "Managing Relationships"*: Developing partnerships and networks; working with people–managing "relationships" not "people".
* *The Action Mindset Refers to "Managing Movement"*:

Managing change without losing track of continuity.

It is argued that the good manager/leader must master and integrate each of these mindsets and so offers a more cognitive and reflective approach to management development than more traditional behaviour and skills-based programmes.

THE LEADERSHIP GAME

The Leadership Game is a dynamic action-learning event for senior to middle managers designed to maximise learning through experiential techniques supported by expert analysis, feedback and coaching.

It is a two-day programme that creates a temporary learning zone to explore issues such as:

* Leadership and decision-making under pressure
* Leaders within hierarchies, virtual teams and self-managed teams
* Team effectiveness under different leadership styles/structures
* How teams work together across functional boundaries
* Understanding the big picture: strategic vision and organisational dynamics.

Day 1 – "The leadership Game" uses a mixture of plenary, work team and cross-team groups and a real-life work related challenge. The process is observed by expert consultants who give team and individual analysis and feedback as required. Day 2 – "Learning Assessment and Implementation" unleashes the learning from Day 1 to address the personal and organisa-tional challenges that arise from the Leadership Game. The programme is run in conjunction with the Tavistock Consultancy Service and represents a current manifestation of the "Human Relations" school started by Kurt Lewin and applied through the National Training Labs of the 1950s. This approach encourages a contextualisation of emotional intelligence and a coming to terms with authority. It offers an alternative to the trait theories of leadership and provides a forum for exploring the emotional aspects of leadership in context and through activities.

TOWARDS AN ALTERNATIVE FRAMEWORK OF LEADERSHIP

REVIEW OF COMPETENCIES

From the review of leadership theory, current models and competency frameworks in use throughout the public and private sectors it would appear that a somewhat limited version of "transformational" leadership is being promoted. Most frameworks go beyond simple definitions of behaviours, to also consider some of the cognitive, affective and interpersonal qualities of leaders, however, although the role of followers may be recognised it is usually in a rather simplistic, unidirectional manner.

Leadership, therefore, is conceived as a set of values, qualities and behaviours exhibited by the leader that encourage the participation, development, and commitment of followers. It is remarkable how few of the frameworks refer to the leader's ability to "listen" and none refer to the word to "follow". The "leader" is thus promoted as the sole source of "leadership". He/she is seen to act as an energiser, catalyst and visionary equipped with a set of tools that can be applied across a diverse range of situations and contexts. Whilst contingency and situational leadership factors may be considered, they are not generally viewed as barriers to an individuals' ability to lead under different circumstances.

Fewer than half of the frameworks cited refers directly to the leaders' ability to respond and adapt their style to different circumstances. In addition to the "soft" skills, the leader is also expected to display excellent information processing, project management, customer service and delivery skills, along with proven business and political acumen. They build partnerships, walk the talk, show incredible drive and enthusiasm, and get things done. Furthermore, the leader demonstrates innovation, creativity and thinks "outside the box". They are entrepreneurs who identify opportunities-they like to be challenged and they're prepared to take risks. Of interest, too, is the emphasis on the importance of values such as honesty, integrity, empathy, trust, ethics and valuing diversity.

The leader is expected to show a true concern for people that is drawn from a deep level of self-awareness and personal reflection. This almost evangelistic notion of the leader as a multi-talented individual with diverse skills, personal qualities and a large social conscience, however, posses a number of difficulties. Firstly it represents almost a return to the trait theory of leadership, just with a wider range of attributes. Secondly when you attempt to combine attributes from across a range of frameworks the result is an unwieldy, almost over-powering list of qualities such as that identified in the CEML research. And thirdly there is little evidence in practice that the "transformational" leader is any more effective than his/her alternatives.

Personal qualities of the leader are undoubtedly important but are unlikely to be sufficient in themselves for the emergence and exercise of leadership. Furthermore, the manner in which these qualities translate into behaviour and group interaction is likely to be culturally specific and thus depend on a whole host of factors, such as the nature of the leader, followers, task, organisational structure, national and corporate cultures, etc.

EXPERIENCE OF USING COMPETENCY FRAMEWORKS

The very fact that organisations will go to great effort and expense to develop their own leadership framework is perhaps evidence in itself that there is no "one size fits all" even though there does seem to be a remarkably great degree of similarity between them. Perhaps, in this case, it is not so much the framework in itself that is important, but the process by which it is developed. The identification of what is required of leaders and the manner in which this integrates with other activities is an important voyage of discovery for the organisation and one for which it is vital that key players take ownership.

To achieve this takes time, reflection and discussion-simply printing off or copying a pre-defined set of standards wouldn't achieve the same results. In the organisations with whom we've spoken the leadership competency framework is an integral element of the leadership development process–

whereby it is used to define the content and mechanism of delivery and to help individuals measure and explore their own level of development. It frequently forms the basis of the 360-degree feedback process, by which they can monitor their progress and identify personal learning and development needs, and also underlies assessment and appraisals.

AstraZeneca expressed the importance of keeping the framework to a manageable number of dimensions so that it remains easier to operationalise. Experience of larger frameworks confirms that longer lists may result in a box-ticking mentality which does little, if anything, to enhance leadership and management capability.

A further challenge also remains: what is the realistic life-span of a framework? Once formalised and implemented it is becomes easy to stop challenging and developing the framework-the search for leadership competencies within an organisation could thus become self-fulfilling and stagnate. Like any continuous improvement process, the development and identification of leadership talent needs to remain dynamic and current. It needs to move with the times and encourage creativity and diversification.

EVIDENCE-BASED LEADERSHIP DEVELOPMENT

For many of the frameworks little, if no information, was available on how they were developed and it seems likely that no detailed research was conducted. Alan Hooper reported that following his research with companies to develop the "transcendent leadership" competencies he found the majority of corporate leadership frameworks to be loosely based on notions of the company culture, guidance of the CEO and "what seems to be acceptable around here".

Even for those frameworks where research has been performed, there are some concerning methodological omissions. For example, the NHS Leadership Framework was developed following interviews with 150 Chief Executives yet is being used to direct leadership development at all levels within the organisation. Such a lack of empirical grounding is concerning for a number of reasons. Firstly, there is a danger that the qualities identified have little bearing on the effectiveness of leadership in the organisation.

Secondly, there is a danger of forming a clique, whereby people are selected into leadership positions because of their similarity to existing leaders, thus neglecting those individuals who don't fit this mould and forming leadership "blind spots". And thirdly, a lack of concern over research at this stage is frequently translated into a lack of concern for the evaluation of leadership development activities. Research is increasingly stressing the necessity of building evaluation structures into leadership and management development.

Huge spending is made on this type of activity yet to most organisations this remains a leap of faith. It may be a difficult task to evaluate beyond immediate post-course reactions but the ability to identify whether such activities are leading to behavioural, attitudinal and organisational changes is a major source of competitive advantage. It not only enables the improvement of existing provision and identification of future provision but also an appreciation of the wider-scale impact of the intervention.

Multi-stakeholder evaluation, for example, explores the aspirations and experiences of diverse stakeholder group and may well reveal that activities beneficial for one may have a negative effect on others. James and Burgoyne argue that "evaluation, like breathing, is not optional" whether done formally or informally it will always influence subsequent decisions about investments and budgets. It would be best, therefore, that this is based on some proof rather than vague aspirations–few businesses would survive if they based business decisions on such weak logic.

EMERGENT AND COLLECTIVE LEADERSHIP DEVELOPMENT

The findings of our review are very similar to those of another recent review of leadership and leadership development literature for the Learning and Skills Research Centre. The authors developed a useful model for the consideration of both leadership and leadership development along two dimensions.

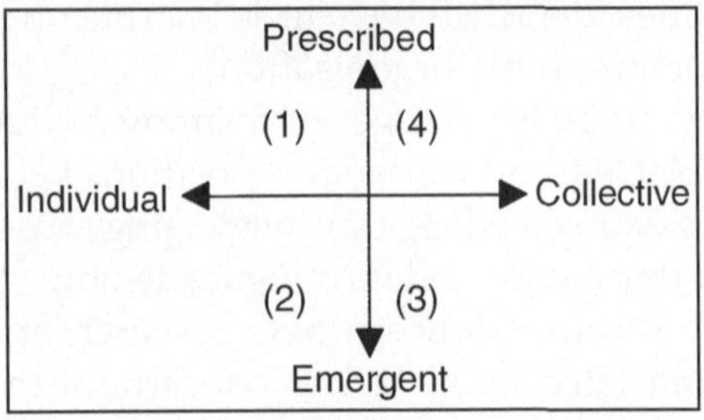

The model proposes that leadership development initiatives differ in the degree to which they focus on individual or collective processes and prescriptive or emergent models and approaches. It is proposed that the vast majority of leadership initiatives lie within cell of the grid, with about 15% in cell and the remaining 5% on the collective side. The authors also argue that there is an almost exclusive emphasis on the leadership inputs and outputs with little attention being paid to the processes in between and they challenge us to consider a more "relational" notion of leadership.

In the Lead2Lead and Leadership Game approaches, for example, far greater attention is paid to the processes than the specific inputs or outputs. To this extent, the process is conceived as one which is likely to generate leadership insights, understanding and awareness but the exact inputs will be different in every case and the outputs will emerge from the process rather than being predefined. Indeed, there is also an extent to which emergent and collective methodologies are used within programmes closely associated with a competencies/qualities framework. For example, the study tours and exchanges on the NHS Chief Executives programme assume that relevant knowledge and understanding will somehow arise from these experiences.

Furthermore, in a review of the Experienced Chief Executives Development Programme, the programme designers report how they used Activity Theory as a basis for programme conception. The programme was "designed to help participants step back from day-today pressures, reflect on the activities in which they were engaged and their inherent dilemmas, and explore new options".

The National College for School Leadership is likewise looking for means to develop a more collective form of leadership within schools. It is moving away from the relatively individualistic approach of the Hay McBer framework to a more fluid Leadership Development Framework that specifies a strategy for developing school leaders at all levels.

AN ALTERNATIVE TO LEADERSHIP AND MANAGEMENT FRAMEWORKS

In our research and discussion related to the current review, we have begun to hear voices of dissent. The Scottish Leadership Foundation, for example, is currently working with public-sector organisations in Scotland to move them away from competency and standards frameworks. The National College for School Leadership seems to be reconsidering its position; and the Institute for Leadership and Management is launching a process to develop its own leadership standards in reaction to the current project under way by the Management Standards Centre.

It seems much has already been done to define what "qualities", "competencies", "standards" should be sought from our leaders but, as the current debate would imply, this has done little to improve the quality of our leaders and leadership other than, perhaps, for specific organisations. Take, for example, the work of CEML on identifying management and leadership abilities. They produced a list of 83 attributes based on a meta analysis of previous research, however, this has not been adopted as the norm as the current exercise contests. What is to ensure that the new National Occupational Standards in Management and Leadership will be any more successful?

Perhaps, therefore, it is time to conceive of alternative ways to view management and leadership standards:

* Should we be recommending ethically and socially acceptable forms of behaviour?–almost a "Leadership Charter" that leaders can sign up to?

* Should we be promoting "mindsets" that leaders need to master rather than the behaviours they exhibit?
* Should we be questioning leadership styles, approaches, behaviours and methods to reveal their weaknesses rather than searching for some Holy Grail of leadership?
* Should we focus instead on leadership development to explore what does and doesn't help improve organisational performance rather than providing a post-hoc description of leadership qualities?

In many ways a leadership competencies or standards framework is like a psychometric profile–useful for illuminating current practice in comparison to a norm but dangerous and potentially damaging if misused. To work as a psychometric assessor you must be qualified in the tools' application and interpretation–perhaps the same should be true of leadership and management frameworks to prevent their abuse.

3

Understanding yourself and your Leadership Potential

Consultants cannot work completely separate from their client's organizations. The moment that a consultant begins to communicate with members of the client's organization, that consultant begins to make a difference in the organization–that consultant is an "instrument of change." You cannot be a successful change consultant if you do not understand yourself as the "tool" and how that tool is used. Guidelines in this part will help you to understand how you can be a successful instrument for change in your client's organization. The guidelines are useful in all phases of the collaborative consulting cycle.

The guidelines are applicable whether you are an external or internal consultant. We often perceive what we believe and our perception is reality. Our beliefs are based on our perceptions and assumptions about ourselves and the world around us. The accuracy with which you understand your clients, their problems and their organizations, depends a great deal on how well you understand yourself. You must recognize your own biases about organizations, including how organizations should be led and managed. You need to recognize the "lens" through which you filter your perceptions about organizations.

You also need to recognize how you prefer to collect and organize information, along with how you solve problems and make decisions about that information. Those features of yourself comprise your "mental model," or your mental framework that drives your perceptions, assumptions, beliefs and, ultimately, what actions you take in the world.

SUCCESS COMES FROM YOUR EXPERTISE AND FROM WHO YOU ARE

There are other advantages to having a clear understanding of yourself during consulting projects. The quality of the working relationship between you and your client often determines the quality of the project itself. Successful organizational change projects require the strong, ongoing ownership, commitment and participation of your clients. To get that from your clients, you must engage in a highly collaborative relationship with your clients.

However, first your clients need to feel respected and trusted by you. They need to believe that your values and style are compatible with theirs. You can influence your client's impressions by understanding how you "come across" to people in different situations. That kind of self-awareness is a great asset for you, particularly when working to understand and adapt to different cultures. The guidelines throughout this overall section will help you to maintain a strong awareness of yourself and how clients might perceive you during your projects.

USE GUIDELINES IN THIS SECTION TO UNDERSTAND CLIENTS

Experts in organizational change assert that it is critical for consultants to understand the culture of their client's organization. They assert that successful organizational change often means successful change in the culture, as well. One of the approaches that you might use to understand the nature of your clients, and others with whom you work in your client's organization, is to tactfully ask them about their biases on organizations, their "lens" through which they view organizations, the style they prefer when working with others, and their preferred approach to problem solving.

UNDERSTAND YOUR BIASES – WE ALL HAVE THEM

Your biases play a major role in how you perceive your client. Your perceptions are your reality, whether they are the reality for someone else or not. Differences in perception between you and your client can make the difference between a successful project and a complete disaster. So know your own biases!

For example:

* Do you believe that leaders should "take charge" and lead from the front of the organization? If so, you might encounter frustration and resistance when working with clients who believe that leaders should lead from the middle.
* Do you believe that, if an organization struggles for a year or so, it should just be shut down? If so, you might find it difficult to accept a small organization working hard to sell a certain product, but just cannot get enough resources.
* Do you believe that clients should just "shut up and listen to you?" If so, you will probably find that clients will either seem glad that you are there or they will kick you out of their offices.
* Do you believe that all businesses should maximize profits as soon as possible? If so, you will be frustrated when they place priorities on mission and passion, rather than on the "bottom line."
* Do you believe that meetings should start and end on time? If so, you will certainly be frustrated with people from cultures that place far less emphasis on time.
* Do you believe that most problems would be solved if people just did what they were supposed to do? If so, you probably should not be a consultant.

DO YOU TALK ABOUT "PROBLEMS" OR "OPPORTUNITIES"

This might seem like a trivial consideration. However, it can make a huge difference in how you and your clients perceive and participate in projects. Perhaps no philosophy or movement has made this point better than that of *Appreciative Enquiry* (AI). AI makes the point that, very often, we create problems and issues by considering and calling them as such.

Practitioners of AI might focus project activities especially on the organization's opportunities and strengths. For example, they might help clients to clarify a positive vision for the future and then use those opportunities and strengths to reach that vision. The overall philosophy and associated attitudes that you choose to use in your consulting activities is up to you. Realise that that choice might also influence the quality of the relationships between you and your clients, depending on the philosophies and attitudes of your client.

UNDERSTAND YOUR PREFERRED CONSULTING STYLE

You should understand your own style, including your overall goals in consultation and your basic assumptions about the consulting process. You must recognize your own philosophy of consulting, which ultimately determines your priorities and personal biases. If you are a leader acting as an internal change agent-an internal consultant–you should understand your leadership style.

UNDERSTAND YOUR NATURAL RESPONSES TO FEEDBACK AND CONFLICT

HOW DO YOU RESPOND TO FEEDBACK

One of the best ways to influence your client during a project is to model the behaviour that you want from your client. Usually, you want your client to be open to receiving feedback, whether the feedback is about their organization and its problems or even about the role that your client plays in the problems. Thus, to model that kind of behaviour, you want to be open to feedback yourself. Often, that is easier said than done. In this context, feedback is information about your actions or performance and is information that you act on. This is in contrast to information about others or either too vague or indirect to be useful to you.

Feedback from clients might make you feel uncomfortable. However, you can manage your actions in response to their feedback. Even if you feel threatened, frustrated or angry about the feedback, you can remind yourself that the feedback is not necessarily directed at you personally. Often, the feedback has more to do with your client's fear about the project than about you as a person.

You can also remind yourself that feedback from clients is a valuable gift to you. For example, it is not uncommon that consultants get so highly involved in their client's organizations and problems that they lose the professional objectivity required to be effective as consultants. Feedback from clients can be valuable forms of learning for consultants in these situations. Based on their learning, they realise they are too close to the problems in their client's organization and so they regain their perspective and effectiveness with their clients.

HOW DO YOU RESPOND TO CONFLICT

Experienced consultants realise that conflict is a natural outcome from interactions among different people and from changes in an organization. Conflict can have a variety of causes, for example, differences in perceptions among people, feelings of fear or disrespect, power conflicts, poor communication techniques or just plain fatigue during organizational change. Conflict is not inherently bad. Problems come from how the conflict is addressed. Effective conflict management includes focusing on the issue at the heart of the conflict, rather than on the personalities of the people involved. It includes using effective means of communication, such as effective listening, supportive questioning and noticing non-verbal communications.

You want your clients to advantageously recognize and manage their conflicts, rather than denying that those conflicts exist or engaging in ongoing destructive arguments with others. You can model successful conflict management by effectively responding to conflict within yourself. It is not uncommon for clients and consultants to have strong emotions about change at various times during a project. It will be important for you to carefully respond to those emotions from your clients, recognizing the emotions and allowing your clients the freedom to express them. How you respond to conflict yourself is often how you to respond to the strong emotions of others.

WHAT IS YOUR EMOTIONAL INTELLIGENCE

There are different definitions for *emotional intelligence* (EI), but it is probably fair to generalize that it is the ability to recognize our emotions and then manage our responses to those emotions in a manner that enhances our health and relationships with others. There are some basic guidelines that might be useful in enhancing your own EI.

Consider the following basic guidelines:

* Notice how you are feeling and be able to name the emotion, for example, mad, glad, sad or bad. Be careful not to get confused between your thoughts and feelings. Notice the difference between and then use "I feel ..." and "I think ..." statements.
* Notice how you judge those emotions, for example, you might believe that "it is scary and bad to feel angry."
* Notice what situations typically evoke those emotions in you.
* Notice the difference between your emotions and your outward responses to those emotions–what others would see you do and say. Ask yourself how you choose to feel about something and whether your behaviour is aligned with that choice.
* Realise that it is OK to have strong emotional reactions. It is what you do with those emotions that can be a problem for you and others.
* Notice how long you retain those emotions. What changes them?

* Notice what makes you happy and plan for those situations on a regular basis.
* Notice how you make conclusions about other peoples' feelings. What are they doing or saying?

UNDERSTAND YOUR NATURAL APPROACHES TO PROBLEM-SOLVING AND DECISION-MAKING

Different people have quite different preferences and approaches for solving problems and making decisions. Those differences can often cause conflict between people unless they each understand their own particular preferences. The following preferences represent probably the most common preferences. It is important for you to note that any preference is not necessarily better than others. Certain preferences might work better in certain situations. The important point for you to realise is the diverse ways that people - including you - address problems and decisions. Always consider that diversity in your consulting projects.

RATIONAL VERSUS ORGANIC APPROACH TO PROBLEM SOLVING

Rational

A person with this preference often prefers using a comprehensive and logical approach similar to the following procedure.

For example, the rational approach is often used when addressing large, complex matters in strategic planning:

* Define the problem.
* Examine all potential causes for the problem.
* Identify all alternatives to resolve the problem.
* Carefully select an alternative.
* Develop an orderly implementation plan to implement that best alternative.
* Carefully monitor implementation of the plan.
* Verify if the problem has been resolved or not.

A major advantage of this approach is that it gives a strong sense of order in an otherwise chaotic situation and provides a common frame of reference from which people can communicate in the situation. A major disadvantage of this approach is that it can take a long time to finish. Some people might argue, too, that the world is much too chaotic for the rational approach to be useful.

Organic

Many believe that it can be quite illusory to believe that an organizational consultant is there to identify and solve problems for the client. Some people assert that the dynamics of organizations and people are not nearly so mechanistic as to be improved by solving one problem after another. Often, the quality of an organization or life comes from how one handles being "on the road" itself, rather than the "arriving at the destination." The quality comes from the ongoing process of trying, rather than from having fixed a lot of problems. For many people it is an approach to organizational consulting.

The following quote is often used when explaining the organic (or holistic) approach to problem solving:

* "All the greatest and most important problems in life are fundamentally insoluble...They can never be solved, but only outgrown. This "outgrowing" proves on further investigation to require a new level of consciousness. Some higher or wider interest appeared on the horizon and through this broad-ening of outlook, the insoluble lost its urgency. It was not solved logically in its own terms, but faded when confronted with a new and stronger life urge."

A major advantage of the organic approach is that it is highly adaptable to understanding and explaining the chaotic changes that occur in projects and everyday life. It also suits the nature of people who shun linear and mechanistic approaches to projects. The major disadvantage is that the approach often provides no clear frame of reference around which people can communicate, feel comfortable and measure progress towards solutions to problems.

INTUITIVE VERSUS SENSING APPROACHES TO GATHERING INFORMATION

There are a variety of assessment instruments that are often referenced when helping people understand their own unique styles when solving problems and making decisions, for example, the Myers-Briggs Type Indicator® instrument. One of the dimensions of the Myers-Briggs is "Intuitive versus Sensing," which considers how a person gathers information.

Intuitive

A highly intuitive person often gathers information instinctively. They thrive on ideas and possibilities. They might seem oblivious to what is going on around them, yet they often effectively solve problems and make decisions based on surprisingly valid information. Many times, they might not even know how they did it. Some experts on leadership and management assert that highly experienced people often have developed intuition that enables them to make quick, effective decisions. A major advantage of this approach is that it can save a great deal of time. A major challenge can be how to explain their choices to others.

Sensing

These people thrive on facts and information. They are detail-oriented and accuracy is important to them. They are aware of their physical surroundings, of who is saying what. They solve problems and make decisions by considering the "data" around them. One of the major advantages of a sensing person is that their actions are often based on valid information. Thus, they are able to explain their reasoning and their actions to others. A major challenge is the time and care required for them to solve problems and make decisions.

THINKING VERSUS FEELING APPROACHES TO PROCESS INFORMATION

Another major dimension of the Myers-Briggs Indicator® instrument is "Thinking versus Feelings," which considers how a person makes decisions about information.

Thinking

A thinking person often uses a highly objective, sometimes rational approach to organizing, analysing and making decisions about information. At their extreme, they might shun consideration of emotions. The thinking person probably prefers the rational approach to problem solving. The advantage of this approach is that it often generates valid problem solving and decision-making. A major challenge can be that it might require an extensive amount of time to come to action.

Feeling

The feeling approach is used most often by individuals who are quite sensitive to their values in processing information. When people focus on their values, emotions often come into play. A major advantage of this approach is that it can help to ensure that people are happy and fulfilled in the situation–that their values have been considered during the process and are reflected in the outcome. A major challenge is that there are a variety of short-term factors that can influence a person's emotions other than the current major problem or decision, for example, their not having had enough sleep or having eaten right.

UNDERSTAND YOUR PREFERRED "LENS" THROUGH WHICH YOU VIEW ORGANIZATIONS

One of the most frequent reasons that organizational consultants argue about the best methods for organizational change is because consultants often have different perspectives, or lens, through which they view organizations. The impact of these differences is often underestimated. For example, you can have two different consultants interact with an organization and they might later provide different descriptions of the same organization. Therefore, it is critical that consultants understand their own perspective and be sensitive to the organizational perspectives of others.

Table 3.1. Various "Lens" Through which we View Organizations

Lens	Examples of What is Noticed or Talked About from That Lens
Structural	Goals, objectives, roles, responsibilities, performance, policies and procedures, efficiency, hierarchy and coordination and control
Human Resource	Participation, feelings, fulfillment, communication, needs of people, relationships, motivation, enrichment and commitment
Political	Power, conflict, competition, authority, experts, coalitions, allocation of resources, bargaining and decision making
Symbolic	Rituals, culture, values, stories, different perspectives, language, expressions, myths, commitment and metaphors

Note that these are horizontal lens regarding what different people notice across the activities in organizations. There are also many vertical lens through which we view intrapersonal dynamics, for example, the many perspectives put forth in the increasing amount of books on personal development. It is important for you to realise that no lens, or perspective, is better than the others. Experienced consultants have learned that the more perspectives that they can get from their clients about an issue in their organization, often the more accurate and useful are the plans to address that issue. Thus, the more lens through which you can view organizations, the more useful you will be to yourself and your clients.

UNDERSTAND YOUR PREFERRED FOCUS ON ORGANIZATIONS

People naturally focus on different areas of the same organization during the same project. That difference can cause conflict and confusion, especially during the initial phases of the project. Therefore, it is important for you to recognize your own preferred scope during projects and, if possible, recognize the scope preferred by your clients. The following are probably some of the most common areas of focus viewed by people during projects.

FOCUS ON "20/80" (PRAGMATIC APPROACH)

This perspective tends to generate activities focused on quick, up-front, practical action plans that take 20% of your client's time and energy, but might address 80% of the problems in your client's organization. The disadvantage of the 20/80 approach is that ongoing, renewed action plans are sometimes necessary to generate long-term results.

FOCUS ON FUNCTIONS (SILO APPROACH)

This perspective focuses primarily on the scope of the "presenting" priority–the priority that is first noticed and reported to you by your client. It might be a major problem in the organization that your client wants to solve, or it could be an exciting goal that your client wants you to help them to achieve. Note that the presenting priority often is a symptom of deeper, more entrenched problems. For example, many leaders complain about lack of money, yet their real problem is ineffective strategic and business planning. A major advantage of this silo approach can be that it often gives quick comfort to your client who wants a "quick fix" and strongly believes where the problem lies in the organization. A major disadvantage is that, because organizations are complex and often rapidly changing, problems often require a larger focus than the particular function first reported as having the problem

FOCUS ON HOLISTIC, SYSTEMS APPROACH

This perspective places strong focus on the overall system and especially on the relationships among subsystems within the system. This is an example of whole systems thinking. A major advantage of this approach is that it is more likely to effectively address complex challenges in organizations. A major challenge is in mastering systems thinking and use of systems tools.

HOW TO INVENTORY YOUR SKILLS AS AN ORGANIZATIONAL DEVELOPMENT CONSULTANT

There can be a wide range of services and associated skills that are applicable to organizational change projects. Without a clear understanding of one's strong interests and skills as a consultant, you are more likely to lose motivation and succumb to burnout. Also, you are much more likely to hurt your client's organization and your own professional career. In addition, you will not know when and how to adapt your approach to consulting in various situations. You will not know when to ask for help or even when to leave a project, if necessary. One of the most important assets of any consultant is their reputation, their credibility.

Credibility often comes from doing what you say you are going to do and doing it well, so credibility often comes from knowing what skills you are good at. Therefore, it is critical for you to have a clear sense about what services you are excited about and interested in, and what services you dislike and often want little or nothing to do with. That sense can come from conducting an inventory of your skills and expertise.

They can be organized into a variety of categories, but the following three might be most clear and meaningful to you:

* *Technical:* Includes mastery of content-specific information and practices, for example, with phases of consulting or with specific functions and processes in organizations.
* *Interpersonal*: Includes mastery of skills to understand and manage oneself and others and to maintain high-quality relationships with others.
* *Process*: Includes mastery of skills to work with others to effectively and efficiently develop and implement project plans.

Consider the following guidelines when attempting to identify what consulting services you want to provide and what skills you have to provide those services.

GENERAL GUIDELINES FOR A SELF-INVENTORY

* *Use the 20/80 Rule*: Attempt to identify the 20% of interests and skills that generate 80% of the most fulfilling services that you could provide as a consultant.
* *Reference a List of Competencies, if Possible, Rregarding your General Interest:* Many professions have established a list of competencies associated with high-performers in that field.
* *Consider Major Types of Consultants*: Many times, it is easier for us to relate broad roles rather specific service areas, such as Boards, marketing or finance.
* *Get feedback from others*: Our opinions of what we like and dislike can often change, depending on our moods, or even if we have not been sleeping well lately. Thus, we often get a much more accurate and valid impression of our preferences if we ask family, friends or peers to give us their opinions about us.
* *Reference Past Experiences More than Fantasies and Daydreams*: Consider past experiences when identifying your preferences. Our history is often a more reliable indicator of our preferences than, for example, our fantasies or daydreams about the future.
* *Start with your Feelings First*: What services are you passionate about? What gives you "goose bumps," or thrills? In contrast, what services do you dislike?
* *Next, Consider your Interests*: What have you been reading or talking a lot about lately regarding services to organizations? What conversations do you notice the most?
* *Then, Consider Trends in the Particular Service:* For example, you might prefer to provide services in the areas of face-to-face marketing. However, a great deal

of marketing is now being done over the Internet. That might change your preference.

* *Assess your Skills in your Preferred Area of Service:* A powerful approach to assessing your skills is to work with a mentor in that area. For example, you might find an organization in which you could volunteer and work with a more experienced consultant to get an impression of your skill level.

COMPETENCIES FOR OD CONSULTANTS

One powerful approach for organizational change consultants to inventory their relevant skills is to review a list of recommended competencies. The focus of the field of Organization Development is on the values, theories and models, and tools and techniques to successfully accomplish organizational change. Therefore, it might be useful for you to examine a list of competencies for high-performing OD consultants.

KNOWLEDGE AREAS FOR ORGANIZATIONAL DEVELOPMENT CONSULTANTS

In addition to the competencies suggested for consultants in the field of Organization Development, there are certain major functions about which you should have knowledge. The degree of knowledge required depends on the nature of the particular services that you offer as a consultant.

All organizational consultants should have at least basic, general knowledge about some of the major functions, including:

* *Board of Directors:* Board members should be aware of, and sometimes approve and oversee, consulting projects that affect a significant portion of a corporation. You should understand at least the roles and respon-sibilities of a governing Board, including how they compare to the roles and responsibilities of employees.
* *Strategic Planning:* Project plans for organization-wide

projects are often most effective if integrated into an overall strategic planning process. You should have a fairly good working knowledge of the typical strategic planning process, including its major phases and activities.

* *Marketing*: Marketing is managing the relationship between the business and its customers to ensure that both parties want to work with each other and receive equitable value from the relationship. Marketing includes research, identifying target markets, products and packaging, pricing, unique value propositions, and advertising and promotions.
* *Product development:* Consulting projects often are meant, ultimately, to improve products and services. You should have at least a basic understanding of the process to design, develop and provide a product or service.
* *Staffing (Human Resources)*: It is likely that employees will be highly involved in your projects. You should have at least a basic understanding of how staffing roles are typically analysed, how employees are trained and organized, and how employees are supervised.
* *Financial Management:* Projects will likely incur substantial cost to your client's organization and various types of financial transactions. You should be aware that financial management typically includes budgeting, projecting, recording transactions, generating financial statements and analysing those statements on a regular basis.
* *Evaluation*: Evaluation of your projects might be more efficient in they are integrated with evaluation activities that are already underway. Businesses might conduct evaluations of employees, products, the Chief Executive Officer and the Board.

You might require some degree of knowledge in other major functions in business or organizations, such as market research, advertising and promotions or facilities management.

HOW TO ARTICULATE YOUR PROFESSIONAL MISSION AND VALUES

Your professional mission and values serve as your "compass" in life and work. This is true whether you are an external or internal consultant. They guide how you make decisions and solve problems, especially during complex and challenging activities. For many of us, our mission and values are implicit–we have not taken the time to clarify them explicitly or to write them down. Without explicitly proclaiming the mission and values from which we want to operate as professional consultants, we are prone to getting ourselves into situations–and operating in those situations – in a manner that does not match our nature and needs. Your professional mission and values can be communicated to clients to help them to understand and trust you, which is critical in collaborative consulting. Therefore, it is important for professional consultants to consider articulating their own mission and value, ideally in mission statements and values statements.

DEVELOPING YOUR PROFESSIONAL MISSION STATEMENT

Your professional mission statement describes at least the overall purpose of your consulting activities. There are various perspectives on mission statements. Some people believe the statements should describe an overall purpose. Some people believe the mission should also include a description of a vision, or future state. Some people believe the mission should also include a description of overall values. Mission statements can be just a few sentences long. There are also various perspectives on how to develop a mission statement. The suggestions are associated with one of the ways to develop your own professional mission statement to describe the purpose of your consulting activities. The process of producing your own professional mission statement is as important as the mission statement itself. Therefore, it is important for you to carefully think about your own mission before you reference any mission statements produced by others.

When you write your professional mission statement, it should:

* Succinctly describe the purpose of your consulting activities.
* Succinctly describe the overall type(s) of clients you serve in your work.
* Mention the particular results that you work to help your clients achieve.
* Convey a strong public image.
* Mention any particular strengths and expertise that you have.
* Be clearly understandable by you and your clients.

DEVELOPING YOUR PROFESSIONAL VALUES STATEMENT

Your professional values statement describes the most important priorities in the nature of how you want to operate as a consultant. Some people might prefer to do a principles statement. Principles are descriptions of values in action and often begin with the phrase, "I will..." or "I believe ..." Similar to the mission statement, the process of producing the values statement is as important as the values statement itself.

The following guidelines will be helpful to you as you develop your own professional values statement:

* *When Identifying Values, Think about Behaviours Produced by those Values:* Many of us struggle to directly identify desired values. We can get bogged down in words that seem too general, idealized–even romanticized–to be useful. Often, it helps first to identify desired behaviours and then the values that produce those behaviours.
* *Consider Any Relevant Laws and Regulations that Pertain to your Consulting:* Identify behaviours or values that will help you operate in a manner so as to avoid breaking these laws and to follow the necessary regulations.
* *Consider Suggested Overall Goals and Assumptions for Effective Consultants:* Block suggests certain overall goals and working assumptions for any consultant.

* *Consider Suggested Principles for Effective Consulting:* Consider behaviours and values that are in accordance with the most important principles for consulting for you.
* *Consider your Own Lens, Biases, Style, Response to Feedback and Conflict:* You might identify behaviours and values that will help you to counter any potential misperceptions or obstacles that you might develop because of your own particular nature and needs.
* *Consider Any Current, Major Issues in your Work:* Identify the behaviours needed to resolve these issues. Identify which values would generate those preferred behaviours. There may be values included that some people would not deem as moral or ethical values, for example, team-building and promptness, but for many, these practical values may add more relevance and utility to a values statement.
* *Consider Any Ethical Values that might be Prized by your Clients:* For example, consider expectations of their customers, suppliers, investors and members of the local community. Before you identify these "public relations" values, be careful that you do not select values that you really cannot adhere to in your work.
* *From the Above Steps, Select the Top Five to Ten Values*: You cannot be all things to all people, including to yourself. Even if you do include all the values on your statement, it is still important for you to carefully think about which values are most important to you.
* *Associate with Each Value, Two Example Behaviours which Reflect Each Value*: Examples of behaviours for each value make the values much more explicit and understood to you and to others.
* *Update the Statement at Least Once a Year:* The most important aspect of the statement is developing it, not the statement itself. Continued dialogue and reflection around your values cultivates awareness

and sensitivity to act in accordance to your values. Therefore, revisit your statement at least once–preferably two or three times–a year.

DEVELOPING LEADERSHIP SKILLS

No one is a born leader—everyone can develop leadership skills and everyone can benefit from using them.

FIRST, TAKE TIME TO HONESTLY ANALYSE YOURSELF

Learn to understand yourself.

It's the first step to understanding others. Consider these important questions:

* What kind of leader am I? One who helps solve problems? A leader who helps people get along? How do others see me as a leader?
* What are my goals, purposes, and expectations in working with this particular group?

IDENTIFY AREAS FOR IMPROVEMENT

Ask yourself these questions:

* Do I try to be aware of how others think and feel?
* Do I try to help others perform to the best of their abilities?
* Am I willing to accept responsibility?
* Am I willing to try new ideas and new ways of doing things?
* Am I able to communicate with others effectively?
* Am I a good problem solver?
* Do I accept and appreciate other perspectives and opinions?
* Am I aware of current issues and concerns on campus or in my community?

THEN - AFTER ANALYSING YOUR STRENGTHS AND WEAKNESSES - TAKE ACTION

Devise a strategy for upgrading your skills. Here are a few strategies to consider.

Communicate Effectively

Effective communication is dialogue. Barriers are created by speaking down to people, asking closed questions that elicit yes or no answers, using excessive authority, and promoting a culture that depends on unanimity. If your focus is winning the argument or if you react defensively to criticism, you'll create fear of openness and hinder the organization's growth.

Try these steps to effective communication:

* *Listen Actively*-ask open questions. Be genuinely interested in what other's say.
* *Thank People* for their openness - stress how much you value it - even if you don't like specifically what is being said.
* *Point to Areas of Agreement* before jumping on areas of disagreement-this reduces defensiveness; members wont fear being "attacked."
* *Set Aside your Authority* to create an atmosphere of partnership to reduce fear in group members.
* *Promote a Culture of Constructive Dissent*-though not to the point of paralysis.
* *Portray Disagreement as Simply a Difference of Opinion.* Get rid of the "I'm right, you're wrong" attitude.

Encourage Enthusiasm and a Sense of Belonging. Show

* *Friendliness:* Others will be more willing to share ideas if you're interested in them as people too.
* *Understanding:* Everyone makes mistakes. Try to be constructive, tolerant and tactful when offering criticism.
* *Fairness:* Equal treatment and equal opportunity lead to an equally good effort from all group members.
* *Integrity:* Members will take tasks more seriously if you show that you're more interested in group goals than your own personal gain.

Keep Everyone Working Towards Agreed upon Goals

* *Remind everyone* of the group's purposes from time

to time. It's easy to become too narrowly focused and lose sight of the larger goals.

* *Provide encouragement* and motivation, by showing your appreciation for good ideas and extra effort.
* *Harmonize differences* and disagreements between group members by stressing compromise and cooperation.
* *Involve everyone* in discussions and decisions, even if asking for opinions and ideas means a longer discussion.

Get to Know the People around you

Everyone has different abilities, wants, needs, and purpose in life.

To get along with others and get results, you need to get to know them:

* *Interact with Group Members as Often as Possible:* The only way to get to know someone is through direct personal contact.
* *Become Familiar with Every Member of your Group:* Take note of each person's unique qualities and characteristics.

Treat others as Individuals

Put your knowledge and understanding of each group member to work:

* *Be Aware of Expectations:* Everyone expects something different: recognition, a chance to learn, a chance to work with other people, etc.
* *Be Creative:* A repetitious routine can cause boredom. A successful leader thinks of new and better approaches to old ways of doing things.
* *Provide Rewards:* Recognition by the group is a source of personal satisfaction and positive reinforcement for a job well done.
* *Delegate Responsibilities:* If everyone shares the work, everyone can share pride in the group's accomplish-

ments. Let each member know what's expected of him/her, available resources, deadlines, etc.

Accept Responsibility for Getting Things Done

* *Take the Initiative:* Why stand around and wait for someone else to get things started? Set an example.
* *Offer Help and Information:* Your unique knowledge and skills may be just what's needed.
* *Seek Help and Information:* Ask for advice if you need it. This will encourage group involvement and help accomplish group goals.
* *Make Things Happen:* By being decisive, energetic, and enthusiastic, you can and will help get things done!
* *Know when and how to Say "No":* If your time and resources are already committed, turn down extra tasks, but do it nicely.

Problem Solve in a Step-by-step Way

Whether you are faced with a decision to make or a conflict to resolve, following a logical approach will help:

* State the problem as simply and clearly as possible.
* Gather all relevant information and available resources.
* Brainstorm as many ideas or solutions as you can think of.
* Evaluate each idea or solution and choose the best one.
* Design a plan for using your idea or solution. Include a timetable, assigned roles, and resources to be used.
* Follow up on your plan by asking if your idea worked and why or why not.

4

Listening Skills

COMMUNICATION AND LISTENING SKILLS

Communication is any means by which an individual relates experiences, ideas, knowledge, and feelings to another. Communication can be expressed through both speech and gestures. It is important that mentors know how to effectively communicate with mentees. This section is devoted to information and activities designed to develop active listening and communication skills effective for working with an adolescent population.

When establishing a mentoring relationship, it is important to create a comfortable communication environ-ment. This can be done by using the theory of reciprocity. Following this theory enables mentors to control the flow and direction of a conversation by the rate at which information is revealed. For example, if the mentor reveals something about him-or herself, the mentee would likely respond by revealing the same sort of information. This pattern tends to repeat. If at some point the mentee does not respond in kind, the pattern of the conversation should be redirected to make the mentee feel more comfortable. This type of interaction pattern fosters the development of trust in the mentoring relationship.

GUIDELINES FOR COMMUNICATION

To encourage the development of trust in the mentoring relationship:

* Make communication positive, clear, and specific.
* Recognize that each individual sees things from a different point of view.

* Be open and honest about your feelings and accept others. feelings.
* Ask questions for clarification on an issue.
* Learn to listen. Allow time for the student to talk without interruptions.

These suggestions should be used as guidelines. There may be situations that require mentors to act differently.

ACTIVE LISTENING SKILLS

Active listening is an essential mentoring skill. One of the most common mistakes mentors can make is confusing .hearing. and .listening.. Hearing is merely noting that someone is speaking. Listening, however, is making sense of what is heard and requires the individual to constantly pay attention, interpret, and remember what is heard. Hearing is passive; listening is active. The passive listener is much like a tape recorder. If the speaker is providing a clear message, the listener will probably get most of what is said. For mentors, this is not enough. They must be active listeners. *Active listening requires the listener to hear the words and identify the feelings associated with the words.* Mentors should be able to understand the speaker from his or her point of view.

There are four essential requirements for active listening:

* Intensity
* Empathy
* Acceptance
* Willingness to take responsibility for completeness

An active listener concentrates on what the speaker is saying. The human brain is capable of handling a speaking rate six times that of the average speaker. Thus, the listener must focus on the speaker. Tuning out distractions will increase listening ability.

SUGGESTIONS FOR IMPROVING ACTIVE LISTENING SKILLS

* *Make Eye Contact:* Lack of eye contact may be interpreted as disinterest or disapproval. Making eye contact with the speaker focuses attention, reduces

the chance of distraction, and is encouraging to the speaker.

* *Exhibit Affirmative Nods and Appropriate Facial Expressions:* The effective listener shows signs of being interested in what is said through nonverbal signs. Together with good eye contact, non-verbal expressions convey active listening.
* *Avoid Distracting Actions or Gestures*: Do not look at other people, play with pens or pencils, shuffle papers, or the like. These activities make the speaker feel like the listener is not interested in what is being said.
* *Ask Questions*: Questioning helps ensure clarification of what the speaker is saying, facilitates understanding, and lets the speaker know that the listener is engaged.
* *Paraphrase:* Paraphrasing means restating what the individual has said in different words. This technique allows the listener to verify that the message was received correctly.
* *Avoid Interrupting the Speaker*: Allow the speaker to complete his or her thought before responding, and do not anticipate what he/she will say.
* *Do Not Talk Too Much:* Talking is easier than listening intently to someone else. An active listener recognizes that it is impossible to talk and listen acutely at the same time.

POSITIVE FEEDBACK

Mentors should focus on providing positive feedback. Negative feedback inhibits the mentee from talking freely and usually meets more resistance. Positive feedback, however, is typically met with acceptance.

Suggestions for providing positive feedback:

* *Focus on Specific Behaviours:* Avoid vague, general statements like.You did a good job. or.That was a really bad decision. Instead, provide information that tells *why* you feel what you expressed. For instance.You played a great game today. I liked the way you played defence.

* *Keep Feedback Goal Oriented*: Make sure statements are relevant to what the speaker is saying.
* *Keep Feedback Well Timed:* Providing immediate feedback is much more effective than comments given at a later time.
* *Ensure Understanding:* Just as it is important for listeners to understand the speaker, it is also important for listeners to be understood by the speaker. Asking the mentee to rephrase what has been said helps to ensure confirmation.

Effective communication requires practice. By following the advice in this unit and finding opportunities to practice the skills with other mentors or with friends and family, mentors, over time, should feel more comfortable with effective communication styles. Additionally, mentors can contact the mentee.s parents. It is a good idea for a mentor to include the mentee in the letter writing so that the mentee knows exactly what is happening.

Here are guidelines for writing a letter to parents:

* Introduce yourself as a mentor.
* Tell the parents about yourself.field of study, interests, where you are from, and how you became involved in the programme.
* Express your desire to form a positive relationship with their child and your willingness to work in partnership on any particular issues they feel could be beneficial to their child. Express your sincere interest in the growth and well-being of their child.
* Include the day and time of the week that you and your mentee will be meeting.
* Tell parents how much you are looking forward to getting to know their child and express excitement about growing closer to them in the coming year!
* You may include an address for them to write back, if you choose. Use a neutral address such as a P.O. Box, school, or corporate address. Be aware that this may put you in an awkward situation.

LESSON PLAN

OBJECTIVES

To help mentors understand communication guidelines and listening skills while building rapport with their mentees.

LESSON

The instructor will discuss:

* Guidelines for communication
* Active listening skills
* Suggestions for improving active listening
* Positive feedback

MATERIALS

* 5 Guidelines of Communication
* Essential Requirements of Active Listening
* Ways to Improve Active Listening Skills
* Suggestions for Providing Positive Feedback

5 Guidelines of Communication

* Make your communication positive, clear, and specific.
* Recognize that each individual sees things from a different point of view.
* Be open and honest about your feelings and accept others feelings.
* Ask questions for clarification on an issue.
* Learn to listen actively and allow time for the mentee to talk without interruption.

Essentials of Active Listening

* Intensity
* Empathy
* Acceptance
* Recognizing responsibility for completeness

Ways to Improve Active Listening Skills

* Make Eye Contact
* Use Affirmative Nods and Appropriate Facial Expressions

* Avoid Distracting Actions or Gestures
* Ask Questions
* Paraphrase
* Avoid Interrupting the Speaker
* Do Not Talk Too Much

Providing Positive Feedback

* Focus on Specific Behaviours
* Keep Feedback Goal Oriented
* Keep Feedback Well Timed
* Ensure Understanding

LISTENING SKILLS

Listening skills have broad applications. Many of you may find that you use them quite naturally. Good listening is about 50 per cent of counseling, and it is also a useful tool with family, with friends, and at work. This book does not teach you how to become a therapist. Listening is only part of helping, hut it is a crucial part. A means of support, good listening helps people explore what they are thinking and feeling. Developing your skills may therefore help another person solve or clarify a problem.

A word of caution about what good listening is not. It is not doing all the talking. It is not giving advice. It is not manipulating. It is not taking the responsibility for the other person's problem and its solution. The material in this chapter is based on the work of Alan Ivey. We hope it will demystify the skills of active listening. These skills can be defined, taught, and learned. You do not have to be superhuman to grasp them. In fact, you may find you have acquired one or more of the skills quite naturally, while you need to learn a few others. What is most important is a sincere desire to understand other people accurately and to he more aware of these skills—skills that do facilitate interpersonal interactions.

MINIMAL ATTENDING SKILLS

Minimal attending skills are the foundation that supports all the other skills. Sometimes called "the art of listening with your mouth closed," this set of skills helps you be a more effective and empathetic listener. Although we are not consciously aware of it much of the time, our body language is a critical part of how we relate and what we communicate. Of particular interest in this regard are eye contact and body posture.

Good *eye contact* is important but complex. Different cultures and subcultures, even different individuals, have different standards for good eye contact. Be sensitive to another person's comfort; good eye contact says, "I am with you" but is not invasive. With practice, you will come to know when you are engaging in appropriate eye contact. Just as eye contact varies from person to person or culture to culture, so does *personal space.* Being the right distance from another person is part of appropriate posture. In addition, leaning forward with an open, relaxed stance and without extraneous, distracting movement is part of an ideal posture.

Once again, it is important to remember to be yourself and to use a posture that is comfortable for you. Another element of basic attending is *verbal following.* Verbal following differs from ordinary conversation, in which each person may be pursuing his or her own line of thought. With verbal following, you let the other person determine the course of conversation while you simply nod, respond, or ask questions. Keep interruptions to a minimum and avoid "topic jumping" or changing the subject. Although it may be difficult at first, also avoid giving advice or judging the other person's motives, thoughts, and behaviour. Avoid sharing your personal experiences or "comparing notes."

Summary—Minimal Attending:

* Eye Contact
  - Look at the person most of the time.
  - *Communicate Caring*: "I am with you, I'm listening."
* Body Posture
  - Be comfortable, he relaxed, lean forward slightly.
  - Be aware of personal distance.
  - Avoid distracting gestures or fidgeting.

* Facial Expressions
  - Don't be a brick wall!
  - Display appropriate empathy.
* Following the Person's Lead
  - Don't interrupt, don't change the subject.
  - Listen, don't talk.
  - Don't share experiences 'Oh, I've been there..."

OPEN QUESTIONS

This section concentrates on what we call "the open invitation to talk." In it, we speak of "open" and "closed" questions. Open questions are questions that encourage a person to talk without feeling defensive. Closed questions are the kind asked by a census taker, a doctor, a lawyer, or a parent: in most cases, both parties in the conversation understand that very specific information is requested in very short answers.

Examples of closed questions are:

* "Did you do that last Monday?"
* "Is it true that there are three people living here?"
* "How long have you been here?"

Nothing is wrong with using a closed question if you need to—and if the client is amenable. However, such questions do tend to cut down communication; and if used unadvisedly, they can lead to frustration for the client. Especially frustrating are questions that begin with "Have you tried" or "Do you think" or "What do you think," because such questions are really sneaky ways of giving advice or airing your opinion. Open questions, on the other hand, are phrased for the purpose of exploration. An open question allows the other person to direct the flow of conversation, to bring up more data, and to deal with it in more depth.

Open questions serve several functions: they can begin the interview, they may encourage the person to elaborate on a point or explore a point further; they may elicit specific examples to clarify what is being said; and they may allow the person to focus on his or her feelings. Open questions often do something further. They lead the conversation into a more personal, here-andnow, internal mode in which the client assumes responsibility for feelings and behaviour. This contrasts with the anecdotal, external style of conversation, in which the client blames others for what is happening. As you encourage people to speak more personally, there is a greater chance they will find solutions to problems.

Example: Internal Mode:

* Counselor: How are you today?
* Client: I'm feeling kind of down, like everything is going wrong. I'm not much fun to be with.

Example: External Mode:

* Counselor: How are you today?
* Client: I'd be okay if it weren't for the people at my house. They get on my nerves and make me feel like climbing the walls.

For open questions, "How," "What," and "Could you say more about" are appropriate beginnings, Examples of open questions are: "What would you have done then?" and "How did it happen that you were there at that time?" One especially good kind of question is, "What would you like to have happen?" or "If you could have things just the way you wanted, what would they be like?" This type of question gives people permission to fantasize, and answering the question often triggers a new insight, a new alternative. Be careful of using "why."

Beginning a question with "why" often puts the other person on the defensive. It seems to call for an explanation or justification. Using *"why"* is good if one is asking how something works but it is not very effective in other cases. Many times, a 'why" question can be rephrased so that it asks essentially the same thing hut does not elicit the defensive response. For instance, try saying to yourself, "Why did you do that?" and then ask, "How did it happen that you did that?" and see which sounds better to you. Or compare, "Why are you here now?" with "What brings you here now?"

As a peer counselor, you need to be sensitive to the "temperature" of your interview. If the person seems anxious or conversation is dying, open questions can stimulate the interchange. If you are feeling flooded with information from your client, use closed questions to cool down and slow the flow. But be careful: some seemingly closed questions can unleash a flood, for example, "Are you thinking about a divorce now?" On the other hand, some questions that sound like open questions are really "coolers," as in "Exactly what kinds of sexual behaviours do you engage in with your spouse?" Minimal encouragements also move the conversation along. They may be either verbal or nonverbal.

The important part is that they be brief and natural to you. Again, by experimenting, you should be able to find your own best style. Many times an encouragement or the simple restatement of something already said has a powerful effect, so do not be afraid to limit yourself to the use of minimal encouragements if you want to keep the conversation going. Although we do not often think of it in this way, *silence* is a useful minimal encouragement. Practice using silence instead of asking a question and see what occurs! Being patient and not asking questions to fill silence allows the client to think, talk, and explore.

Summary—Open Questions:

* An Open Question Is one that:
  - Can't be answered by one or two words
  - Usually starts with "how" or "what"
  - Encourages the other person to talk
* A Closed Question Is one that:
  - Can be answered by "yes" or "no" or by one word
  - Starts with "is," "do," "have you," etc.
  - Discourages the person from talking and slows the flow of conversation
* You can use open questions for:
  - Beginning a conversation
    a. "What would you like to talk about?"
    b. "What's going on with you?"
  - Clarifying and elaborating "How is this a problem for you?"
    a. "What do you mean by ______?"
    b. "What is it about the situation that bothers you?"

- Working with feelings
  a. "How do you feel about that?" (Make sure you get an answer about feelings, not thoughts.)
  b. "What is [that feeling] like for you?"
  c. "How do you feel right now?" (This helps people bring feelings into the here and now.)
  d. "What would you like to say to him/her?" (This helps people get in touch with their feeling about other people.)
- Solving problems
  a. "What options do you have?"
  b. "What have you thought of doing?"
  c. "How do you feel about each of these options?"
  d. "What's the best thing that could happen?"
  e. "What's the worst thing that could happen?"
  f. "What do you think will actually happen?"

* Don't:
  - Ask questions to satisfy your own curiosity
  - Ask "Why.?"
  - Ask long, complicated questions with lots of dependent clauses and other grammatical junk.
  - Give advice in a question (*e.g.*, "Have you tried talking to him?").
* Do:
  - Keep questions clear and simple.
  - Keep questions in the here and now and with the person. (Don't counsel someone who's not in the room.)

PARAPHRASING

A *paraphrase* reflects the essence of the verbal content; it expresses briefly the facts of the situation but pares away details. For instance, newscasters often repeat in their own words what people said during interviews. Each of you has observed the use of the paraphrase and has probably used paraphrasing, perhaps without noticing it. When you take notes in a class, you probably paraphrase the instructor's lecture. When you send a telegram, you condense the message into as few words as possible—again, a form of paraphrase. This skill is a bit sophisticated, taking more concentration and more practice than the open questions described earlier.

The paraphrase has three main functions:

* Verification of perception
* Clarification
* Demonstration of accurate empathy

First, a paraphrase acts as a perception check, to verify that you have understood what the other person has said. This is especially helpful if you are confused, or if you feel you may he identifying too closely with the person's situation. If you have heard correctly, the client may respond to your paraphrase by saying "Yes", "That's it", or "Right." Second, a paraphrase may clarify what the person has said, especially if you pick up trends, set up dichotomies, or list priorities. As an active listener with some objectivity, you may see these trends and priorities more clearly than the speaker. Third, a good paraphrase can demonstrate that you have what Carl Rogers called accurate empathy.

Accurate empathy is a nonjudgmental reflection of another person's world view; it is "walking a mile in another's shoes." It is important that a paraphrase be brief. It should almost always be shorter than what was originally said. Standard openings for a paraphrase are: "In other words," or "So I hear you saying__________" You will discover other openings with which you feel comfortable.

Make the paraphrase tentative, so that if it is not right, the person feels free to correct you. It is crucial that you know when you have not heard correctly. You might end with: "Is that right?" or something similar. Watch out for endings such as "isn't it?" or "aren't you?" since these have the effects of a closed question. What is especially tricky about paraphrasing is that if you parrot back exactly what you heard, you are not being terribly helpful and may even he irritating. (Sometimes, though, the client's wording is so apt that you may want to use some of the same words.)

On the other hand, if you add too many of your own perceptions, you may be putting words into the other person's mouth. The former is called a *restatement;* the latter is an interpretation. Although both restatements and interpretations have their appropriate places, they are both quite advanced tools, and neither should take the place of the paraphrase. With a little practice, you will be able to tell the difference between restating, paraphrasing, and interpreting.

Paraphrasing

A paraphrase is a brief, tentative statement that reflects the essence of what the person has just said.

A good paraphrase:

* Captures the essence of what the person said; leaves out the details
* Conveys the same meaning but usually uses different words
* Is briefer than what the person said
* Is clear and concise
* Is tentative

Reasons for using paraphrase include:

* *To Check Perceptions:* When you paraphrase what you think people have said, they can react to your paraphrase and tell you whether it is accurate or inaccurate.
* *To Clarify:* Hearing an accurate paraphrase helps clients clarify what they are thinking and feeling. Often a paraphrase will bring up new thoughts and feelings.
* *To Give Accurate Empathy:* An accurate paraphrase demonstrates that you ate listening and that you understand. In effect, a good paraphrase says, "I am with you."

Do:

* Keep it brief and keep it tentative!
* Use openings such as:
  - "Let me see if I've got it right..."
  - "Sounds like..."
  - "I think I hear you saying..."
  - "So, in other words..."
* End by asking, "Is that right?"

The Continuum

Restatement (OK)	Paraphrase (Best)	Interpretation (Avoid, for Now)

WORKING WITH FEELINGS

Working with feelings is difficult for two reasons. First, people are taught not to discuss feelings openly; feelings are too private, or too embarrassing, or too powerful to deal with directly. Second, partly as a result of such training, what people say may not match-or may not be *congruent* with-what they are communicating nonverbally. Nonverbal communication is more directly a reflection of feelings. Nevertheless, a timely reflection of feelings can be quite useful, since it gives people "permission" to own their feelings-it validates the emotional as well as the Cognitive expression.

Talking about feelings is a limited experience, so our vocabulary may he equally limited. When working with someone's feelings, avoid pejorative or evaluative terms, such as: "That's ridiculous", or "Why would you feel that?" Stick to more specific, simple, expressive words. This is a sensitive area, and you will want to refrain from interpreting what you sense or putting the client on the defensive. There is a vast difference between saying, "You feel" and "You feel that".

The former is a genuine reflection of feeling, while the latter moves into more cognitive areas. Say to yourself, "I feel happy" and then, "I feel that today is going to be a happy day." Notice the difference? It is of paramount importance to notice both verbal and nonverbal expressions when working with feelings. (Sometimes you may even get two dissimilar verbal or two incongruous nonverbal messages.) Although you may not always want to comment on discrepancies you notice, it is helpful to use this information as a cue for your own behaviour. Be sensitive, again as to when it would be appropriate to point out congruence or lack of it—and when it would be judgmental or threatening.

The four basic steps in working with feelings involve helping the person to:

* Identify feelings

* Define and clarify feelings
* Acknowledge feelings and take responsibility for them
* Deal with feelings

Identify Feelings

There are three ways to discover what someone is feeling. You want to be able to use all three and to learn when each is most appropriate.

Ask Feelings Questions

The main feelings question is "How do you feel?" Sometimes it is more effective to substitute "What emotions do you feel in relation to that?" Help your clients stick to the here and now. Talking about feelings in the past tends to turn into storytelling. Even when people's current problems involve past events, they have here-and-now feelings about what happened. It is essential that you get feelings for answers rather than thoughts. Statements that begin with "I feel that" *or* "I feel like" usually express a thought. Statements that begin with "I feel" usually express feelings.

If someone gives you a non-feeling answer, paraphrase it and then ask the feeling question again:

* Counselor: How do you feel about that?
* Client; Well, I feel like I should be angry at her.
* Counselor: So you think you *should* be mad at her, but how do you actually *feel*? What emotion or emotions are you experiencing?
* Client: I'm pissed off at her and frustrated that I haven't told her.

Paraphrase Spoken Feelings

It's not always necessary to pry feeling out of people. Some people express their feelings quite openly. When someone does express feelings, it's a good idea to paraphrase them.

This tends to clarify for people what they are expressing:

* Client: I get so angry when my sister comes to visit for the holidays and all she does is complain.
* Counselor: So you're feeling angry, is that right?

Reflect Feelings

Reflecting feelings is one of the most effective methods for bringing up feelings, but it is also one of the trickiest and most easily abused. The term *reflecting feelings* is slightly misleading, because what you actually reflect are a person's nonverbal expressions of feelings. For example, a woman comes in for counseling and you notice that her face and body seem very tense.

You could react in two ways:

* "You seem to be angry."
* "You seem to be very tense."

The first response reflects a feeling but is an interpretation. The woman might be nervous or scared and not angry at all. The second response is much better. It reflects the actual nonverbal message the woman is expressing, and it does not make a judgement or interpretation; it is not a conclusion in any sense. One of the most effective techniques is to reflect the person's nonverbal messages and then ask, "What are you feeling?" This opens the conversation rather than closing it. Remember that reflection of feelings deals with emotions, while paraphrase deals with content and data. Sometimes the two may seem very similar, particularly if you are talking about an emotional situation. Discuss the differences with your trainers until you are sure you understand them. When you are role playing as the client, use a situation about which you have lots of feelings.

Define and Clarify Feelings

Once you've elicited a feeling, such as "I'm upset," it is important to find out what that means to the person. This process of definition is particularly important when the feeling expressed is a *global* one, such as "I'm depressed" or "I'm lost" or "I feel good." In other words, don't assume that you know what it's like for other people. Define and clarify what their feelings, words, or expressions actually mean in *their* world.

Good questions for defining and clarifying feelings include:

* "What does [being mad] mean to you?"
* "What is being [nervous] like for you?
* "How does that feel physically?"
* "What other ways would you use to describe what you're feeling?"

What often happens as you help people define and clarify feelings is that other feelings come up.

These also can then be defined and explored:

* Client: I feel depressed.
* Counselor: How do you experience that depression?
* Client: It's like a numbness, a not wanting to do anything.
* Counselor: So you feel numb?
* Client: Yes, I feel like there are all these feelings inside me and yet I can't really feel them. [Counselor stays silent.] You know, it just feels so numb.
* Counselor: Could you describe the numbness?
* Client: It feels like there's a void within me. It's empty... no, it's not, it's full of feelings... But they're dangerous. They need to be kept under control.
* Counselor: What are those dangerous feelings?

Acknowledge the Feelings

To deal effectively with their feelings, people must first acknowledge and take responsibility for those feelings. Many people tend to place their feelings outside themselves, saying things such as "It makes me feel ____," or "He made me feel _____." Although feelings may be associated with external events, they are not "out there"; they are within the person.

Compare these statements:

* "You made me angry when you slept with Cleopatra." *vs.*
* "I felt angry when you slept with Cleopatra."

The first statement suggests causation; the second, correlation. Statements that begin "It makes me feel," "She makes me feel," or "One would feel" signal that the person is not owning or taking responsibility for his or her feelings.

All of this is well and good, but what can you do if the person is not taking responsibility?

* Client: You know, when you're working at a job you don't like, you just can't find any energy for other things. You feel bummed out and you feel disgusted, you know?
* Counselor: So you feel bummed out and disgusted, is that right?
* Client: Yeah, you just can't seem to break out of it you know?
* Counselor: When you say, "You can't seem to break out of it," do you mean "I can't seem to breakout of it"?
* Client: Yes, I just can't get rid of these feelings.
* Counselor: What make you want to get rid of those feelings?

What this counselor does is first to paraphrase the statement in a way that puts the responsibility on the client. Like many people, this client doesn't recognize the distinction and continues to say "you" instead of "I." The counselor then asks a closed question that encourages the person to acknowledge the feelings personally. This step is a tricky part of working with feelings. It is important not to challenge clients too directly, but sometimes people simply refuse to acknowledge their own feelings. When this happens, it may be necessary to take a different approach (such as a problem-solving or a "What if . . . ?" fantasy approach). It is not useful to force your point of view on people. It is often more constructive to move past or around an issue.

Deal with the Feelings

Once you have elicited the feelings, defined and clarified them, and have gotten the person to acknowledge them, then what? The first part of dealing with feelings is to place the feelings in context ("What thoughts and events are these feeling correlated with?").

Good questions are:

* "What brings up this feeling of _____ for you?"

* "What's the situation when you experience these feelings?"

People usually don't experience just one feeling at a time. The question "What other feelings are associated with _____ for you?" often brings up many related feelings. It can also be useful to relate thoughts to feelings. A question such as, "What do you say to yourself when you are feeling _____?" is helpful. An important part of dealing with feelings is to get people to express feelings that they had previously found difficult to articulate.

Examples of effective questions are:

* "How would you like to express this feeling?"
* "What would you like to say to that person?"

It may help to have clients pretend to be speaking directly to the person to whom they are expressing the feeling. So rather than "I'd say that I'm angry and that I never want him to do it again," have clients stay in the present and say, "I'm angry and I don't want you to do that again."

If people have difficulty or are uncomfortable with this, questions such as these may help:

* "What's the best (worst) thing that could happen?"
* "What would you like to see happen?"
* "How have you dealt with this before?"
* "What could you do to feel better?"

If clients depict a situation that seems hopeless and they see no possibility for improvement, then they may he really stuck. In such cases, acknowledging this reality and their feelings about it may be more helpful than encouraging a possibly premature course of action. Finally, the best preparation for working with feelings is to deal honestly with your own. This can he approached by role-play practice or co-counseling sessions specifically devoted to exploring your personal style of dealing with feelings.

Summary - Working with Feelings

Working with feeling is an *essential* part of counseling. It is difficult to explore alternative solutions to problems until the feelings surrounding the problem are clarified, vented, and dealt with.

* Identify the feelings
  - Ask feelings questions "How do you feel about that?" "How do you feel?"
  - "What feelings does that bring up in you?"
  - Paraphrase spoken feelings "So you are feeling ____, is that right?" "Sounds like you are really_____." "You must feel pretty _____."
* Define and clarify feelings
  - Elicit feelings that accompany the one that is primarily expressed
  - Discover the individual's personal experience of a given feeling (what does the person mean when he or she says, "I feel X"?)
* Acknowledge the feelings
  - Assist clients in taking responsibility for their feelings
  - Reinforce them for stating feelings in a direct, personal way (*e.g.*, "I feel X" rather than "I feel that one should feel X in this situation, don't you?")
* Deal with feelings
  - Relate thoughts to feelings
  - Further express feelings
  - Help people express hidden feelings through best/worst fantasizing and other open questions

SUMMARIZING

A counselor's summary is like a combination of one or more paraphrases and often includes a reflection of feeling. In addition, it tends to cover a relatively long period of time—several statements of the client, perhaps from even more than one session. A summary attempts to capture the essence of what the person has said, to tie together content and feeling, to put things in perspective, and to identify important trends, conflicts, or possible decisions. Even so, it is a good idea to keep the summary brief. Being concise reduces confusion. With summarization, more than with any other skill, there is the possibility of distortion or interpretation, so he especially sensitive.

Constantly check with the person to verify that you are not adding to or subtracting from what he or she has said. Be tentative in your remarks. As you sum up what you have observed as the two of you have talked, emphasize the positive aspects of the situation: what has been accomplished, what could he done, what the possibilities for the future are. Dwelling on the negative aspects rarely leads to constructive action, so while you may not he able to ignore them, do not limit yourself to enumerating them.

A good summary has several functions:

* It acts as a perception check (and is especially helpful if you find you *strongly* identify with—or cannot *at all* identify with—the problem).
* It directs the course of future interaction, decisions, and planning. Again, you should therefore be positive.
* It clarifies the situation, reflects trends, points out conflicts, and lists priorities.

When should you use a summary? A summary is useful when shifting modes (for instance, after you have explored feelings and are about to go into solving problems). Likewise, a summary is useful after main events in a counseling session—for example, after you've found out what the person considers to be the problem, it is useful to summarize and then go on, using an open question.

A summary is also good at the end of a counseling session. It ties things together for the person, giving a clear image of the session. After a good summary, there may be a pause or a sense of "what now?" This indicates that you are ready to move into new territory, and an open question is appropriate at that point. Learn to be sensitive to this forward movement; such sensitivity is one of your goals as an active listener.

Summary–Summarizing

A summary is a cumulative paraphrase. It captures the essence of what the person said. Like a paraphrase, it is brief and tentative.

Summarizing serves many of the same purposes as paraphrasing:

* It serves as a perception check.
* It demonstrates accurate empathy.
* It clarifies for you and the client.

A summary is not a sequential recounting of what the person said. A good summary organizes what has been said into a logical, usable form. It mentions both thoughts and feelings and ties them together. A summary helps people see where they've gone and where they are going.

INTEGRATING SKILLS

Integration is putting all your skills together and using each when appropriate.

This is where the art and the finesse of counseling has its fullest expression:

* Open Questions turn on the flow of conversation. They encourage people to talk. They can also direct the conversation.
* Paraphrasing tends to interrupt the *flow.* Because a paraphrase reflects what a person has just said, it focuses the conversation. Paraphrases fit together well with open questions; first, you paraphrase; then you ask an open question.
* Exploring Feelings is useful after the initial problem has been presented. Sometimes, exploring feelings will be a very effective method of counseling Some people and some types of problems respond less to feelings-oriented counseling, and in these situations you will want to take a different approach. Remember, use what works for the client.

LISTENING SKILLS IN THE WORKPLACE

Listening is perhaps the most critical element in language and language learning, for it is the key to speaking, and beyond that, reading and writing. Particularly in the workplace, listening is used at least three times as much as speaking, and four to five times as much as reading and writing. At all levels-from entry level to managerial-listening is perceived as crucial for communication. Yet listening remains one of the least understood processes in language learning. As suggested, try to summarize what is known about the listening process including the factors affecting listening. We also suggest general guidelines for teaching and assessing listening, and give examples of activities for practicing and developing listening skills for the workplace.

THE LISTENING PROCESS

Listening is a demanding process involving:

- The listener;
- The speaker;
- The content of the message; and
- Any accompanying visual support.

Imagine a workplace message being transmitted between listener and speaker using tools (a hammer, towels, a fax machine, etc.) or a video, as opposed to a message left on a telephone without visual support by an unidentified speaker. ("Put the xxx in the xxx tomorrow.") The message may be the same in both situations, but it is perceived in very different ways. Let's examine each component of the process.

The Listener

If the listener is familiar with or is interested in the topic, comprehension will increase. If not, a listener may struggle and then tune out the message. Also, a listener who is an active participant in a conversation, even though he has little background knowledge to facilitate understanding, is more likely to learn from the encounter. That means that the workplace facilitator/teacher has to explicitly teach active listening skills such as repetition, definition of points not understood, and clarification and negotiation, to enable the listener to make sense of the incoming information. These are as much listening as speaking skills.

The Speaker

When we speak, we usually do not speak in full sentences. Colloquial language and reduced forms also make comprehension more difficult. A speaker's rate of delivery may be too fast, too slow, or may have many hesitations for a listener to follow. All of these may affect concentration. Awareness of a speaker's corrections and use of rephrasing (er..., I mean... that is...) can enable the listener to recognize speech habits as clues to deciphering meaning. While teachers cannot predict how each speaker will use language, they can teach students to listen for patterns in speech and to use strategies which help them comprehend, *e.g.*, asking a speaker to slow down, or to repeat.

The Content

Content that is familiar is easier to comprehend than content that is unfamiliar. In the workplace, this becomes a bigger advantage when employees are listening and talking about their work. Hotel housekeepers, factory workers, or office clerks usually talk about topics that are familiar. The contents may be unfamiliar only when explaining a new machine or process. When background knowledge is essential to understanding content, more listening strategies may be necessary.

Visual Support

Visual support, *e.g.*, the actual tool, a video, pictures, diagrams, gestures, facial expressions, and body language, increases comprehension. However, how to use these strategies may need to be explicitly taught so the learner is able to interpret them correctly.

ACTIVE LISTENING

While the listener, the speaker, the content, and visuals are all part of the listening process, what happens in the brain to comprehend the message is key. Most of what we know comes from research into native language development. Although once labeled a "passive" process, listening is very much an "active" process of selecting and interpreting information from auditory and visual clues. Research does tell us that there are a number of events that constitute "listening".

The listener:

* Determines a reason for listening;
* Takes the raw speech and deposits an image of it in short-term memory; attempts to organize the information by identifying the type of speech event (inform, request, persuade);
* Sometimes predicts information expected to be included in the message;
* Recalls background information to interpret the message;
* Assigns a meaning to the message;
* Checks that the message has been understood;
* Transfers the original message into long-term memory; and
* Deletes the original information from short-term memory.

Although we do not know in what order or how this occurs-indeed the listener is seldom even aware of performing these steps-it is a guide for the teacher of the steps that take place when a message is perceived.

TEACHING AND ASSESSING LISTENING

To teach listening skills in the workplace, activating background knowledge and vocabulary is primary. Prelistening activities set the stage and review what the learner already knows about a subject. For example, a new type of floor polisher is being introduced in the workplace. Activities that review what the learner already knows about using the old floor polisher stimulate thinking about the new one. This might entail reviewing vocabulary such as switch on or off, brushes, or backwards and forwards, discussing steps in the polishing process, or generating a list of questions from the learner.

During the pre-listening activities, the learner recalls from long-term memory what he knows about floor polishers. The learner is then ready to do the listening task itself. The task should involve the listener in getting information that is new and immediately doing something with it, *e.g.*, "The polisher switch is on the bottom. Turn it on." The listener then turns on the switch. Post-listening activities help the learner to assess success or failure in carrying out the listening task, to build upon his background knowledge, and to integrate listening with other language skills.

To continue with our floor polisher example, have the listener reiterate sequencing tasks (first, second, next) or practice "if/then" questions or statements (if the switch is broken, then . . .). In another example, a hotel worksite where schedule changes are announced frequently at team meetings, learners may need practice recognizing details such as names, times, and dates within a longer stream of speech. In this case, a posted weekly calendar or an audiotape might be useful as post-listening activities.

GUIDELINES FOR TEACHING LISTENING

Lessons focused on listening will be enhanced by incorporating the following guiding principles. Materials should be authentic. You would not use a pillow to demonstrate tensile strength in a factory, nor would you use a hammer to demonstrate softness in a motel room. As authenticity should be evident in task, so should it be in language. The language should reflect real discourse, including hesitations, rephrasing, and a variety of accents.

Listeners at work all need to be aware that interaction between co-workers and managers may be different than interactions among co-workers, in terms of formality, vocabulary and topics. Language needs to be comprehensible, but it does not need to be constantly modified or simplified to make it easier for the listener. A guest in a hotel or customer in a restaurant is not an ESL teacher; ultimately, the worker must communicate successfully with the client, not the instructor. Level of difficulty can be controlled by the selection of the task.

At the beginning level, in a unit on listening for directions, learners might hear "May I borrow your hammer?" (or detergent, or tray). Then they choose the correct item. At an intermediate level, the learner might hear a series of instructions ("Go to the broom closet, get the new floor polisher, take it to the hall in front of classroom 301, polish the floor there, then go to the cafeteria..."). The learner then draws a map of the worksite and directions.

An advanced level learner might listen to an audiotape of an actual workplace meeting and write a summary of instructions that the supervisor gave the team. This use of authentic material as a teaching tool not only represents the familiarity of the working environment, but increases transferability to listening outside of the workplace context in the community. As well as workplace training videos, audiotapes of actual workplace exchanges, TV and radio broadcasts about the industry. Using authentic materials is a good way to develop listening strategies.

Predicting, asking for clarification, using non-verbal cues are examples of strategies that increase chances for successful listening. For example, using a training video segment—with the sound off-of the new floor polisher or a workplace team meeting would give listeners a chance to predict what was happening by answering questions about the setting, action, and interaction. Viewing the segment again with the sound on allows employees to confirm or modify their hypothesis. It also gives them a chance to check for accuracy in hearing sounds, intonation, words, and grammatical structures. These strategies for listening go far beyond the workplace. Most of all, listening should be relevant.

To keep motivation high, listeners must have a purpose for listening. (In eavesdropping, how often do we listen intently for details when the conversation is of interest to us, and how often do we tune out when it is not?) If learners at the workplace need to be able to understand new policies and procedures at staff meetings, then classroom practice can help to develop the abilities to identify main ideas and supporting details, to identify cause and effect, to indicate comprehension or lack of, and certainly to ask for clarification.

CLASSROOM LISTENING ACTIVITIES

So, what kind of listening activities are appropriate for the workplace class?

The following seven different tasks can be used to teach, as well as test for success:

* *Doing:* The listener responds physically to the stimulus, such as "open the door" or "stand up" or "write your name". (This is often called Total Physical Response.) There are many variants: sometimes the learner repeats what is said, then does it; sometimes he or she responds to directions of three or four steps.
* *Choosing:* The listener selects from alternatives such as pictures, objects, texts or actions, and demonstrates comprehension by pointing, showing, or speaking.
* *Duplicating*: The listener repeats the message. A variant of this is the telephone chain, during which a message is whispered to one person, who whispers it to the next person, and so on.
* *Answering*: The listener answers the question posed or participates in a face-to-face conversation.
* *Condensing:* the listener takes written notes or makes an outline.
* *Extending*: The listener verbally continues a story or solves a problem.
* *Transferring*: The listener applies the message given orally to a diagram, or a route map, or a chart.

MATERIALS

Teachers in the workplace have the advantage of being able to build activities around actual workplace tasks. Authentic Worksite tasks and vocabulary can be substituted in any textbook exercise written for the workplace to make it relevant for the learner. Teachers in a workplace preparation class, where students are not yet employed, have a harder task. Making listening relevant is sometimes a challenge. A good workplace-oriented text should be helpful in guiding all-around practice. In either situation, teachers will spend time on preparation.

No workplace-oriented textbook will always be relevant to all student needs. Teachers need to listen to their students' needs, and be guided by them. Because of the critical role that listening plays in the acquisition of language, improving listening skills is a challenge that demands both the teacher's and the learner's attention.

Knowledge of the listening process and the factors that affect listening enable teachers to select or create listening activities that meet the needs of their learners. These listening activities must then be woven together with speaking, reading and writing activities to create a balance that mirrors the real world of both the workplace and community.

5

Small Groups Dynamics and Teams

INTRODUCTION

This monograph was developed as a companion to a workshop on group dynamics and team building, presented at the WFH Global NMO Training Workshop May 16-18, 2002, in Huelva, Spain.

The workshop offered two methods of learning:

* Brief talks by the facilitators that described some theory, and
* Structured activities through which the participants experienced and then discussed some of the elements of group dynamics and team building.

In this monograph, as suggested, review some of the theories of group dynamics and team building that were addressed in that workshop. In addition, we have included structured activities that may be used in local group settings. It would be advisable to identify a volunteer who has some experience in managing group dynamics to facilitate the activities. We wish to acknowledge that the content of this monograph is taken from materials and theories developed in the United States. Therefore, it reflects a western European cultural context.

Some human behaviours transcend cultural differences; others do not. The reader will be the best judge of how relevant the material may be for his or her local group. We offer these ideas and exercises as tools to understanding and improving the effectiveness of one's own group; they are not intended to influence or replace readers' cultural traditions. The subjects of group dynamics and team building are broad.

One can study each of these topics for years and still have more to learn. There are many ways to approach each. A simple Internet search will result in thousands of web sites on either group dynamics or team building. These subjects are important because they influence how productive a group or a team becomes. By understanding group dynamics and by doing some team building, a group can increase how much it accomplishes.

UNDERSTANDING GROUP DYNAMICS

The term "group dynamics" refers to the interactions between people who are talking together in a group setting. Group dynamics can be studied in business settings, in volunteer settings, in classroom settings, and in social settings. Any time there are three or more individuals interacting or talking together, there are group dynamics. A great deal can be learned by observation. If one sits back quietly in a group any group one will begin to see certain behavioural patterns emerge. There will be at least one person who tends to take the lead in conversation, offering his or her thoughts and opinions freely.

There will be at least one person who remains quiet, sometimes not even appearing interested in the conversation. There may be someone who tends to interrupt other people, someone who wants the conversation to move along faster, or who wants to focus on a different subject. Another person may be concerned about peoples' feelings and may try to make everyone feel equally welcome. These are only a few of the roles that people assume without even thinking about it when they are in a group setting. Group roles are largely determined by a combination of a person's personality and his or her experience with group settings. A person who is shy is more likely to sit back in a group.

A person who is impatient is more likely to push the discussion ahead. A person who is very confident will offer more opinions. If such roles are more or less pre-determined, how can the group dynamics be improved? The way a group interacts can be improved in several ways. There are training programmes to attend and there are tests one can take to learn about one's communication style.

Perhaps the simplest way to improve a group's dynamics is for one or more group members to learn to *manage* the discussion, and thus help a group accomplish its goals, much as a conductor manages the many players in an orchestra to produce a blended sound. By "manage" we mean respond to and redirect the behaviour or participation of an individual to a direction that is better for the group. Whether or not the group is managed, group roles will occur. By learning about the typical kinds of behaviour that emerge, and how to respond to them appropriately, one can improve the effectiveness of group discussions.

The two most common roles affecting a group's effectiveness are the person who dominates and the person who remains silent. It can be as difficult to get the quiet person to speak as it is to get the talkative person to talk less. To manage the dominant person, one might say something like, "You have a lot of good ideas, Carlos. I have written them down to discuss later. For now, we need to talk about ______." To the quieter person, one might say, "What are your thoughts on this subject, Marie?" It is best to ask the quieter person a question that cannot be answered by a simple "yes" or "no". A broad question "casts a wider net," to use a fishing analogy. In any case, a direct and respectful approach is recommended where possible. There are a variety of other roles that may emerge in a group, and a textbook on group dynamics would be a good resource for learning more about them.

In addition to being influenced by culture, roles are influenced by gender, age, race/ethnicity, religious tradition, and other traits. For most people, though, it is sufficient to know that group settings do bring out certain behaviours, and an effective group is one in which those behaviours are channeled positively to move the agenda forward. Finally, one should be aware that the management of group dynamics can emerge from any group member. The person with the authority to lead may not be the person who is best at actually managing group dynamics.

Any group member who sees an opportunity should *seize* the opportunity to improve the effectiveness of the members' interactions. The entire group is responsible for its own effectiveness and all members share equally in that responsibility. The chairperson or convener has agreed to perform certain duties, but it should not be assumed that he or she is the sole leader.

GETTING ACQUAINTED

Since group dynamics and team building are based fundamentally on the relationships among the people involved, it is both courteous and sensible to assure that the members all are introduced to each other, and that they are offered opportunities to get to know each other and to build relationships. A group or team with members who know each other well is likely to be more effective. People tend to offer more of themselves when they are with people whom they know than when they are with strangers. It is therefore a good idea to spend some time helping people get acquainted with one another. Often we assume people know each other when they do not.

A common feeling among newcomers is that the more senior members of the group are somewhat exclusive. This is because the senior members know each other better and have well-established patterns of communication. They have past experiences in common and they may forget to explain certain references to the newcomers. This can lead to a feeling of exclusion, and if it is not corrected, the newcomers might leave the group. It is the responsibility of the current members to help the newcomers get oriented to the group and to its members. There are many ways to accomplish this.

People have created activities called "Ice Breakers" or "Get-Acquainted Activities." A search on the Internet using either of those terms will produce many examples. These simple games can get people interacting with each other. One popular ice-breaker is to divide the group into pairs, and have one person interview the other for a few minutes, and then switch. Sometimes an outline is given for the interview questions. Then the group is called back together, and each person introduces his or her partner to the whole group.

Individuals learn a bit about the importance of listening when they begin to introduce their partners. They also learn something about the various members of the group. Many find it easier to talk about someone else than to talk about themselves in a large group. The timing for this exercise is about 5 minutes for the interviews, and 30-60 seconds for each introduction. Simpler still is to begin each meeting by asking the members to introduce themselves, and to specify at least part of what they should talk about, with the leader or the chairperson going first to set an example.

A list of some suggested topics for introduction:

* Tell your name, how long you have been involved with the group, and how you became involved with this group.
* Introduce yourself and tell us where you grew up.
* Introduce yourself and tell us a valuable life lesson that you have learned, such as:
  - What you think your greatest strength is;
  - A funny thing that happened to you;
  - When you first learned about our organization;
  - The farthest away you have ever traveled, and why you went there; and
  - One thing you hope we accomplish in the next six months.

The more one gets to know another person, the more he or she will understand that person. The better people understand each other, the more effectively they can work together. Taking five to ten minutes to get acquainted at the beginning of a meeting is a very sound investment of time.

CLARIFYING EXPECTATIONS

Underlying every perception is one's expectation. "Expectation" is that oftenunspoken idea we have of how things are going to be, or how people will behave, or how people will react. Many times people are surprised when something happens that is different from what they expected. They may be so surprised that they are unable to react appropriately to the reality, because they are so caught up in their expectation.

In any group of individuals brought together for a purpose, every one of those participants will likely have a slightly different expectation of what is going to happen and how it is going to happen. This underlying expectation may colour an individual's reactions to the stated agenda. Therefore, it is a good idea to spend a minute or two clarifying members' expectations. It can even become a part of the "getting acquainted" stage. A simple, open-ended question can put the expectations on the table: "What do you expect us to accomplish today?"

GROUP PROBLEM SOLVING

Groups tend to form for one of two reasons: either for purely social purposes or to get something accomplished. In the latter case, there will be some form of problem solving required of the group. It is when a group is trying to accomplish something that the interactions or dynamics become stronger, especially if the group is under constraints in time and resources. There are structured experiences, such as "Broken Squares". This is a fairly simple, straight-forward exercise that can bring out varying styles and skills that can make a group cohesive and effective.

It can help group members learn what helps and what hinders group problem solving. Successful group problem solving depends first on good communication among the members. By "communication" we mean the sharing of information by everyone. Silence does not mean approval. In fact, *we do not know what silence means until it is broken.* We do know that each person has a contribution to make. Members must offer what they know, what they observe, what they think, what they feel for the group to be most effective.

The following are some recommendations for effectively solving a problem as a group:

* Each member should understand the total problem or task. Someone, usually the chairperson or task leader, should summarize the task that is to be done. He or she should seek clarification from the members to assure that everyone understands what the group will be doing.
* Each person should realise how he or she can contribute to the solution. Everyone has talent and skills that they were born with, as well as talents and skills they have acquired. Most of us tend to downplay or minimize what we have to offer. Problem solving is no time to be modest about one's talents. All available skills and talents should be on the table for use by the group in solving its problem.
* Each person should recognize the potential contributions of others. Again, *everyone* has talent and skills they were born with, and those they have acquired through education and experience. Sometimes we recognize a talent or skill in another person that they do not fully realise themselves. It is helpful to give that person encouragement to participate.
* Members should be willing to recognize when other members may need more information or assistance, and to offer their help so that each member can make his or her full contribution to the effort.
* Negotiation is important to success. The very differences that bring many talents into a group also bring in different opinions and perceptions. The best solution is one that everyone finds acceptable. The group should make decisions based on what is in the organization's best interest.
* It is the group's responsibility to help manage the group's dynamics; for example, to help the shy person to contribute, and to help the dominant person make time available for others to speak.
* Everyone operates with assumptions and expectations, and it is important to clarify what those are at the beginning, and whenever it may be necessary.

* Sometimes members lose sight of what the original purpose was and may get sidetracked. These "detours" can waste a lot of the group's time. It is important to keep the purpose, goal, or task in mind, and to bring the discussion back to the stated focus. This is the shared responsibility of all group members.
* Everyone has leadership qualities, and leadership may change depending on the situation or task. Leadership means influence; the person with the most influence is not always the person with the most authority. If a member sees an opportunity that is in the group's best interest, he or she is obligated to call that opportunity to the group's attention.
* Not every task is appropriate for a group. Writing, for example, is best accomplished by an individual. Drafting a budget is better accomplished by an individual. The result or product may be approved by the group, but the actual task of writing or calculating should be performed by an individual.

TEAM BUILDING

What is a team? It is a group that has a job to do, whether as paid participants or as volunteers. It is a group that has spent some time together, whether in smaller increments over a long period of time, or by spending a weekend or more working together on something. It is a group that achieves cohesiveness; a team's strength is found in the relationships among the team members. It is a group with a common objective, whose members are very clear about working towards one purpose. It is a group whose members are *inter*-dependent. Whereas other groups may recognize the strengths of each member, team members *rely* on the strengths of each member to accomplish the objective.

An ideal team has a number of distinct characteristics, and they fall into three areas: their feedback and communication behaviours, their behaviour and conduct courtesies, and their ways of approaching tasks and problems. "Feedback and communication behaviours" describe how the members talk with one another, clarify their expectations, react to each other's ideas and offer their perceptions and opinions.

In an ideal team, the members:

* Ask for help from other members when it is needed and do not waste precious time struggling alone;
* Give positive comments to each other regularly and often, because they know it motivates teammates;
* Give negative observations when necessary, but do it constructively, for example: "Frank, that proposal you wrote is very good, but it's a little weak in the evaluation section. Joe has done a lot of evaluations, perhaps he can help";
* Receive negative observations from another member without becoming defensive, because they know the comments are not meant to be insulting, but are meant to help the team accomplish its goals;
* Support other team members in times of crisis, for example: "Lars, I'm sorry to hear about your family illness. Why don't you go home and I will finish your assignment";
* Offer help to others when their own work is completed.

"Behaviour and conduct courtesies" describe the protocols that the members have agreed to as a responsibility of being a member of the team.

In an ideal team, the members:

* Are ambassadors of that team, and represent the team, not just themselves;
* Remain open-minded and receptive to all ideas, however different from their own;
* Give another member time to get his idea out, and paraphrase the idea to assure they understand the intended message;
* Take turns speaking;
* Encourage full participation by all members;
* Do not have side conversations during a discussion, because participants might miss something important;

* Stay focused on the task at hand, and do not engage in distracting behaviours;
* Call a time-out if they feel another member's behaviour is disruptive;
* Make the team meeting a priority so that attendance is consistent;
* Begin and end meetings on time, so members can use their time most efficiently;
* Obtain closure on topics and get a decision;
* Summarize and clarify the meeting at the end.

Ways of approaching tasks and problems.

In an ideal team, the members:

* Accept every problem as a *team* problem, not one belonging only to one member;
* Never say "we cannot do this," but say "how *can* we do this?";
* Determine the action items that any decision requires, or think through how to carry out decisions;
* Share failures as a team, never blaming only one or two members;
* Look at failures as a way to improve the team functioning, because we can always learn something from failure;
* Share all information, so that everyone is working from the same body of information;
* Use consensus for major decisions, which results in finding the most acceptable decision for everyone, as opposed to voting, in which there are clear winners and losers;
* Stay focused on the purpose of the team, which is to accomplish something together.

A successful team will monitor its own effectiveness and progress. Any member of the team who observes that the team is underperforming has the responsibility to bring it to the attention of the entire group so that appropriate action can be taken to correct the problem. Occasionally, there may be a member of the group who is not really there to advance the group's objective, but perhaps to advance his or her own individual objective. If the person remains unwilling to put the group's objective first, then he or she may have to be removed as a member, or reassigned to a different group that better corresponds with his or her personal objectives. High-performing teams take whatever steps may be necessary to remain focused on their purpose.

TEAM DEVELOPMENT

Teams and groups are living organisms with certain predicttable stages of development. One characterization of the progression of team development has been depicted by a series of steps on a graph. One axis represents success with tasks that are more and more complicated, and the other represents the amount of time and effort that the group has invested in becoming a team.

The graph looks like this:

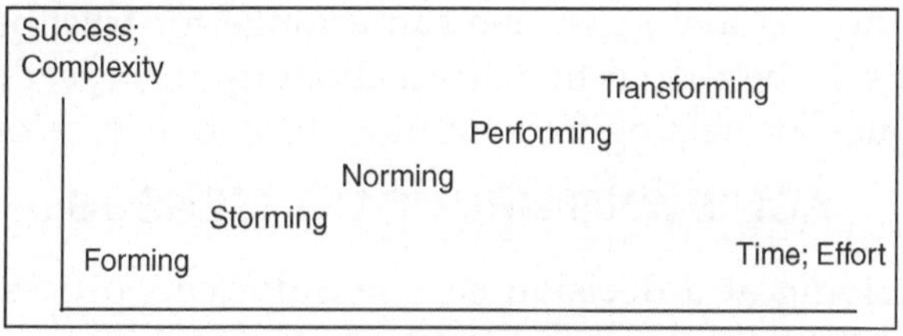

Fig. Team Development

"Forming" is the initial stage of development, when team members may often have differing ideas about purpose. There is relatively little trust. People tend to be careful about what they say, and how they say it. Everyone is on his or her "best behaviour". "Storming" represents the arguing that will likely occur as the team defines itself. There may be conflict about the purpose, leadership, and working procedures. During this stage people often feel the team will never "come together". This stage is similar to the human developmental stage of adolescence.

"Norming" is the stage that occurs when the team members are developing a shared vision and are setting goals and objectives. People are getting to know one another's strengths and are learning how best to work together. The team experiences more stability and productivity. "Performing" indicates that the members now have a clear, shared sense of purpose, high trust, and open communication. The team is effective within the existing paradigm. Camaraderie, relationships, and team spirit are high. "Transforming" occurs when the team is at such an effective level of functioning that it can redefine its shared purpose and respond quickly to change. The leadership within the team is shared, trust is high, and communication is open.

The point of knowing about the stages of a team is two-fold:

* It can be helpful simply to know that there *are* stages, and that it is normal to go through these stages;
* One can identify the stage of development for a given group or team, and can assist the progress through that stage by managing the interactions or dynamics between and among the members.

If there is low trust, one can arrange for trust-building exercises. If the team is in discord about its purpose, there are techniques for helping to determine the common priorities.

ACHIEVING GROUP CONSENSUS

Arriving at a decision can be a difficult process for a group. Many groups resort to voting to decide issues. When possible, it is useful to work to achieve consensus. Consensus differs from voting in that it is more a process of achieving maximum agreement. A topic is discussed until every member is willing to agree. That agreement might be more enthusiastic for some members than others, but all members are on the positive side of agreeing. Like problem solving, consensus requires that everyone share whatever information, opinions, facts, or feelings they may have. It is through this pooling of contributions that the group is able to come to a decision that satisfies everyone. There are a number of activities that can help groups practice consensus building.

Typically they require each member to answer individually some sort of questions or rankorder a list of items. When each has completed the task individually, the group then sets about making one list. Invariably the group rankings are more accurate than the individual rankings. This is because there is greater knowledge in the group than in any single individual. Achieving consensus requires some negotiating. Individual members are usually convinced that their original answers are correct.

Only through listening to someone who thinks differently can one begin to see something in a different way. Explaining the reason behind one's thought can help others to see its merit. Finally, when everyone is committed to a common purpose, the task is more easily accomplished. Commitment to a purpose helps one move past one's own initial thinking, and allows one to listen to a diversity of ideas. Through this the group achieves the best result, by benefiting from the best of all of the members.

ETHNIC COMPOSITION AND ITS DIFFERENTIAL IMPACT ON GROUP PROCESSES IN DIVERSE TEAMS

There was a time in the United States when work teams could be assumed to be composed almost entirely of Caucasians. Not only arework groups becoming more diverse, but the United States is facing a demographic revolution such that even the traditional definition of ethnic majorities and minorities will soon become outdated. Over the next 25 years, minority groups are expected to account for more than 50% of the population in Hawaii, California, New Mexico, and Texas and close to 50% in other heavily populated states such as New York, Maryland, and New Jersey.

This same trend is also reflected in organizations and universities. For example, since 1988, people describing themselves as Caucasian have made up less than 50% of students at the University of California, Berkeley. In fact, as of 2000, self-reported Caucasians made up less than 31% of the total student population. In addition, expanding multinational companies will increasingly involve work teams made up of people from diverse cultures.

As this demographic revolution continues, the important questions become:

* How much will the change in demography affect our workforce? How will different levels of heterogeneity affect individual members of diverse working teams? How will people in the current majority position respond to the changing dynamics of ethnic composition?

Previous studies on ethnic composition primarily compared homogenous versus heterogeneous teams. Some reviewers of the literature suggested that teams homogeneous with regard to ethnicity may be more cohesive than heterogenous teams. On the other hand, ethnic diversity may, in fact, improve the quality of creative brainstorming and may increase group outcome efficacy. This kind of homogeneous versus heterogeneous team comparison, as well as simple cross-national comparisons, is being challenged: Researchers are now being asked to examine situations where people from different cultures interact.

As the demographic revolution within the United States continues, work teams will become increasingly heterogeneous such that the important issues will revolve around the type or degree of heterogeneity and how it affects people from different ethnic groups. For example, a recent study by Earley and Mosakowski looked at different levels of heterogeneity and found that lowand extremely heterogeneous groups outperformed moderately heterogeneous groups. These moderately heterogeneous groups were composed of roughly half of one group and half of another. We propose a typological framework to organize previous research on ethnic composition as well as to guide our own research.

The first set of rows in fig. 5.2 illustrates the simple homo-geneous versus heterogeneous dichotomy typically used in the literature. The second shows how Earley and Mosakowski conceptualized heterogeneity along a three-type continuum. The third example is a more complex continuum of hetero-geneity: In addition to having more categories, some of the categories involve a majority of one group over another. For example, the homogeneous, low heterogeneous, and somewhat low heterogeneous groups involve one ethnicity dominating the team. The moderate category, on the other hand, has equal numbers of both groups.

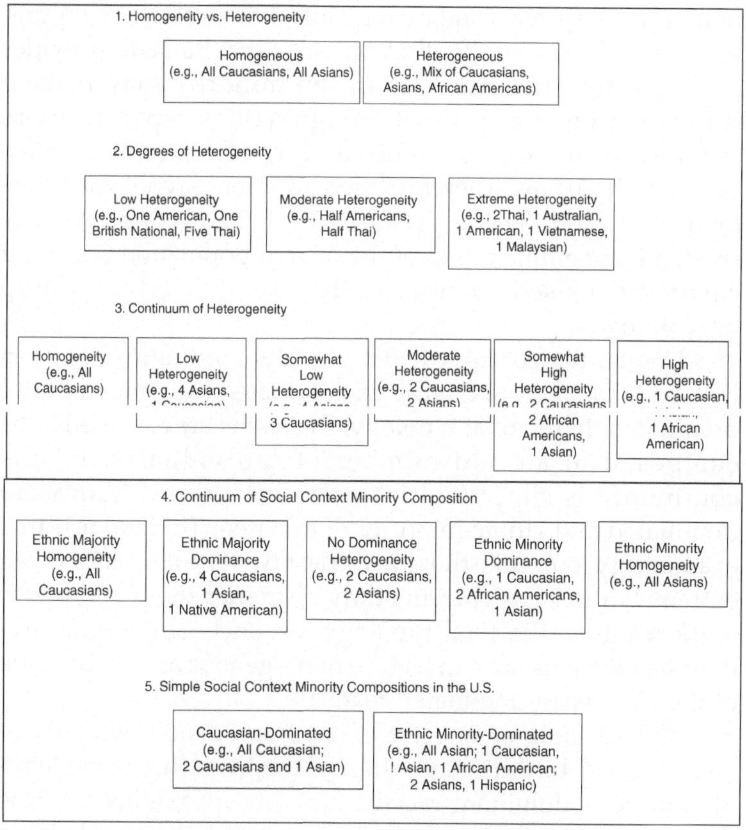

Fig 5.2. Typology of Ethnic Composition.

Both the somewhat high and high heterogeneous groups have a great deal of heterogeneity. In the highest heterogeneous groups, no one group has a numerical advantage or disadvantage. However, these three typologies described so far ignore the issue of the social context: Which ethnic or racial group actually dominates numerically, and is that ethnic group a numerical majority in the population at large? This is going to be an increasingly important distinction: Working groups within the United States will not simply be homogeneous or heterogeneous but dominated by Caucasians or by a mix of ethnic minorities.

Also, a homogeneous group composed mainly of Asian Americans has different implications for group culture than a homogeneous group composed mainly of Caucasian Americans. A recent report by O'Reilly,Williams, and Barsade provides evidence that the ethnicity in the minority may make a difference for group functioning: Whites reported more teamwork in groups dominated by ethnic minorities, particularly Asians. Therefore, two additional typologies have been included. These presume that Caucasians are the predominant ethnic group of the overall population but could easily be revised to assume that another ethnic group predominates.

In one, the complex heterogeneity continuum has been revised to range from Caucasian dominated to ethnic-minority dominated. In the final typology, the teams are assumed to be composed of an odd number of individuals, and the continuum is simplified into two categories: Caucasian dominated and ethnic-minority dominated. To date, research examining groups like those in the last two typologies has been extremely rare. The current study examines the two types of work teams in the final typology. As such, some minority-dominated teams may, in fact, be homogenous as may be some of the Caucasian-dominated teams.

The variable of interest is not homogeneity or heterogeneity *per se* but the proportion of the team that is made up of America's dominant racial/ethnic group. We believe it is important for diversity research to go beyond a simple head count of how many individuals are from different ethnic groups to bring the social/cultural contexts into the study of small group processes. This study addresses the psychological consequences of the different types of ethnic dominance in a small group setting. We also distinguish further the effects of ethnic composition as both group-level and cross-level effects. Ethnic composition is a group-level variable; it can only be measured at the level of the team.

As a group-level effect, ethnic composition can influence group-level outcomes such as team productivity or climate. As a cross-level effect, ethnic composition might influence individuallevel outcomes such as individual productivity or satisfaction. Both of these types of effects are considered context effects because the independent variable is at the group level. However, these context effects may be contingent on variables at the individual level.

In other words, there may be significant interaction effects between individual ethnicity and the experience of team ethnic composition. Some researchers have referred to this sort of effect as a *frog pond effect*; that is, a large frog has a different experience in a small versus a large pond. Frog pond effects are essentially the interaction between a contextual effect and an individual-level variable. In the case of our study, teams composed primarily of ethnic minorities may have certain effects on group dynamics-but only for specific ethnic minorities.

Asian students might have a very different experience in teams composed mainly of ethnic minorities in comparison to Caucasian students. This particular frog pond effect has been found before. Lee, Loeb, and Lubeck found that inequalities in learning between African American and European American children were smaller in classrooms with higher concentrations of African American students. In other words, not only does the context have an effect, but the interaction between the context and the individual has its own effect. Frog pond effects related to ethnicity may be prevalent in diverse, small groups. Therefore, ethnicity may have an effect at the individual level, at the group level and in the interaction between the two. It is possible for these effects to occur independently and/or covary.

The purpose of this study is to examine the effects of ethnic composition on group dynamics. Numerous variables can measure different aspects of group dynamics. Taking the traditional distinction between socioemotional and task dynamics within groups, we are interested in group enjoyment and creative performance. Just as creative performance is a measure of team task success, so is group enjoyment a measure of team social success. These variables may be affected differently by team composition.

In this study, *group enjoyment* refers to howthe individual members of a team rate their interest and pleasure in working with their team. High group enjoyment will also result in more positive emotional experiences and fewer negative emotional experiences. Group enjoyment is different from and more specific than group cohesion. Group cohesion is a more general and complex construct that has been described as *solidarity* or *morale*. Because ethnic composition has not been studied in this manner before, literature on this topic is very limited. To predict the effects of ethnic composition on group enjoyment, it is constructive to use the theoretical dimensions of individualism and collectivism.

Psychological research has often suggested that ethnic differences in the United States follow the prescribed differences by the general framework of individualism-collectivism. Members of collectivist cultures are thought to conform to group norms and have a greater interdependence with others, specifically in-group members. They are often contrasted with members of individualistic cultures who focus more on their independence and individual achievement. Individualism and collectivism have been variously described as opposite ends of a continuum or as two somewhat orthogonal dimensions.

On the country level, many countries have been assessed via their individualism and collectivism: America and the United Kingdom are considered highly individualistic, China is considered extremely collectivistic, and Israel is considered moderately collectivistic. Previous studies have also found differences between different American ethnic groups on individualism and collectivism. In a recent meta-analysis that conceptualized individualism and collectivism as two different dimensions, African Americans and Asian Americans scored significantly higher than European Americans on collectivism.

However, African Americans scored higher than both European Americans and Asian Americans on individualism. Because individualism and collectivism are group-level constructs, teams composed primarily of Caucasian Americans are assumed to be higher on individualism and lower on collectivism than groups composed primarily of Asian

Americans, African Americans, and Hispanics. It is important to acknowledge that the typical categories of Caucasian, Asian, Hispanic, and so on are flawed-particularly as proxies for culture.

Ethnicity should not be defined solely by race, nationality, or geographic location but by psychologically meaningful cultural variables such as values, attitudes, identities, and social experiences. Although we are interested in studying the interaction between different kinds of individual ethnicity and team ethnic composition, we understand that these interactions take place in a wider context that is predominantly Caucasian. What is more important to our research, therefore, is that members of different ethnic minority groups in the United States may share some common experiences. What is more, we are interested primarily in effects at the level of the team rather than at the level of the individual.

Therefore, we consider it appropriate to examine the experience of individuals within teams that are predominantly either Caucasians or a combination of other ethnic groups. The literature on ethnic composition and the socioemotional side of group dynamics is extremely limited. Three studies help shed light on possible connections between ethnicity, individualism/collectivism, and the enjoyment of group work. In one study, collectivists were found to value the relationship maintenance aspects of a work relationship more than individualists.

Another study suggests that Mexican Americans assume that work group success is facilitated by socioemotional factors to a greater degree than do Anglo Americans. It is not that Mexican Americans deny the importance of task-related factors, but "for Anglo-Americans, task success seems dependent on minimizing socioemotional concerns, whereas for Latinos, emphasis on socioemotional aspects is compatible with efficiency and success". Sanchez-Burks and his colleagues attributed these differences to differences in relational schemas regarding work groups.

In other words, attending to relationships is probably part of appropriate working behaviour for Latinos but is considered separate or extraneous for the Anglo Americans. Finally,

O'Reilly demonstrated that Caucasians report more teamwork when in groups dominated by non-Caucasians than in groups dominated by Caucasians. This finding was primarily driven by the experience of Caucasians in groups with proportionally more Asians than non-Asian minority groups.

Taking these disparate studies together, it seems likely that teams composed primarily of ethnic minorities will have greater group enjoyment. Whether because of relational schemas or collectivist values, it seems likely that members of ethnic minority groups such as Asians and Latinos will be more likely to pay attention to the maintenance or socio emotional aspects of group work. Given that the socio emotional aspects of teamwork are inherently tied to how well a group will get along socially, we predict that individuals in teams dominated by ethnic minorities will enjoyworking with their group more.

This enjoyment will also correspond with more positive emotions experienced and fewer negative emotions:

* *Hypothesis 1:* Individuals in teams composed of membersmostly from ethnic minority groups will enjoy themselves more than teams composed mostly of Caucasians as measured by both direct and indirect measures of group enjoyment. This is a cross-level effect of grouplevel ethnic composition on individual enjoyment and emotions.

Much of the past literature focuses on composition differences in performance, particularly team creativity, so we find it important to test this aspect. We chose an interactive, creative task as the focus of our study. Literature on the effects of ethnic composition in terms of Caucasian dominance versus minority dominance is nonexistent. What literature there is on ethnic composition shows that heterogeneous teams outperform homogeneous teams on creative tasks, although moderately heterogeneous teams have been outperformed by somewhat and extremely heterogeneous teams.

The main reason suggested by researchers for these findings is that ethnic diversity is assumed to be correlated with diversity in terms of attitudes, skills, knowledge, and other factors. These different perspectives are theorized to lead to a greater diversity of original ideas. Although the research on heterogeneity versus homogeneity does not directly speak to our types of groups, the theory behind it can still guide our predictions. Diversity in knowledge and skills is likely to foster innovation but probably only when tempered by sufficient group dynamics to allow the team to take advantage of the diversity.

Both minority-dominated and Caucasian-dominated teams can be heterogeneous and diverse; however, we predict that minority dominated teams will have the necessary focus on group processes to allow creativity to develop:

* *Hypothesis 2:* Teams composed mostly of ethnic minorities will outperform those composed mostly of Caucasians on an interactive creative task. Their outputs will be more creative. This is a group effect of ethnic composition on group creativity.

As suggested, also differentiate ethnic composition effects from individual-level ethnicity effects. For example, if Caucasians tended to rate their experiences more positively, then analyses involving ethnic composition would show that teams composed primarily of Caucasians have higher enjoyment. We do not expect individuallevel ethnic differences on the dependent variables of interest; effects due to ethnic composition are not simply due to an aggregation of individual-level ethnicity effects but are true group-level effects. Therefore, as suggested, test these effects with individual race/ethnicity as an independent variable.

We predict that there will be no mean differences between individuals of different ethnicity on the dependent variables of interest:

* *Hypothesis 3:* There will be no mean differences between participants of different racial/ethnic backgrounds *on the individual level* for group enjoyment or creative performance. This hypothesis does not contradict those above that predict differences based on overall ethnic composition.

We are also interested in frog pond effects for individual ethnicity. In addition to there being an effect for context, there could be an effect for the interaction between the individual and the context. This means that the experience of an Asian American in a minority-dominated team could be different from a Caucasian in a minority-dominated team. Given the finding that disparities in test scores are smaller in classes where African American children are in greater numbers, it is likely that ethnic minority individuals will enjoy being in teams dominated by ethnic minorities above and beyond that explained by the team effect. However, significant frog pond effects are often difficult to discover when the interaction covaries with the main effects.

* *Hypothesis 4:* We expect to find evidence for frog pond effects such that the findings due to team ethnic composition will be especially pronounced formembers of some ethnic groups compared to others. In other words, we predict an interaction between individual race/ethnicity and ethnic composition for the different group-process variables.

METHOD

Participants

The participants were 108 undergraduates at the *University of California* (UC), Berkeley, who took part in the study to fulfill a partial course requirement. They worked together in teams of 3 per session to give a total of 36 teams. These teams were small, but the creative task they performed required interdependence and mutual awareness-two qualities necessary for a group. The participants signed up to be in the study with no knowledge of its purpose. Ethnic composition of teams occurred naturally. Seventy-five per cent of the participants were female, and 25% were male. In terms of ethnic composition, 70% of the teams had two or three ethnic minorities, and 25% had two or three Caucasians. One team in each category was homogeneous and the rest were heterogeneous.

Overall, only two of the teams were homogeneous in terms of ethnicity, so analyses comparing heterogeneous and homogenous teams were not possible. The analyses comparing group ethnic composition, therefore, examine differences primarily between different types of heterogeneous teams. Individually, the participants were 43% Asian or Asian American, 34% Caucasian, 5.6% African American, 5.6% Hispanic, and 10% a combination of two or more ethnic identities. Two per cent did not report their ethnicity. Five per cent of the teams were not classified in terms of ethnic composition because of the 2% of participants who did not report their race/ethnicity and were dropped from the analyses. The overall gender and ethnic proportions were typical of the UC Berkeley participant pool.

Procedure

We chose an interactive creativity task to provide an appropriate setting with both task and socioemotional outcomes. The participants worked together to write a creative ending to a short story, "The Boy Who Sang for Death," by Jane Yolen. The story as published has two endings and, therefore, has a natural stopping point where it needs to be resolved. We instructed the participants to make their ending as creative as possible but warned that it had to flowlogically from the story.

This task can be generalized to the common practice for television and movie scriptwriters to work on story elements in small teams. After writing down their story ending, the participants then individually filled out a questionnaire that asked them to rate their enjoyment of the task and working with the team. The survey also asked the respondents to indicate which of several emotions they felt during the session. Participants were asked for their racial/ethnic identity in an open-ended question, and these data were coded according to U.S. Census categories. The questionnaire data were treated as individual-level variables, as each participant filled out the questionnaire without input from the others.

Measures

Creativity

Each team came up with one story ending, whichwas

evaluated for its creativity. The story endings were rated for creativity by six English literature graduate students who were familiar with assessing writing and were themselves diverse in terms of both gender and ethnicity. The coders used the Amabile consensual assessment technique to make their judgements on a scale of 1 to 5. With this technique, coders work independently to rate the story endings relative to each other for creativity. Interrater reliability was satisfactory: Cronbach's alpha, which is what Amabile generally used, was.79, and the intraclass correlation using the means of the raters' assessments was.76.

Group Enjoyment

How well the participants enjoyed working with their team overall was operationalized as three specific variables: group enjoyment, more positive emotions experienced, and fewer negative emotions experienced. Here, group enjoyment was formed from a composite of three specific questionnaire items: enjoyment of working with the group, how interesting it was to work with the group, and willingness to work with the same group again on a similar task in the future. The emotion data, which were initially binary were grouped into two composites: all the positive emotions and all the negative emotions.

The emotion checklist was based on a list used in previous emotions research for participants to assess a dyadic interaction but modified for breadth and applicability to a creative team project. The positive emotion composite included feeling amused, engaged, attractive, excited, happy, joyful, playful, effective, interested, hopeful, loving, proud, and sympathetic. The negative emotion composite included feeling afraid, angry, annoyed, anxious, bored, contemptuous, cynical, distracted, disgusted, embarrassed, envious, exhausted, frustrated, guilty, lonely, painful, sad, and tired. The alpha of the negative emotion composite is low because the responses for negative emotions were idiosyncratic with many of the emotions listed chosen by fewer than six respondents.

The negative emotion composite was significantly negatively correlated with the positive emotion composite, although negative and positive emotions may be weakly positively correlated in interdependent cultures. The group enjoyment composite was positively correlated with the composite of positive emotions and negatively correlated with the composite of negative emotions. It was also necessary to create dummy variables for individuallevel race/ethnicity and for ethnic composition.

Groups composed mainly of ethnic minorities were coded as 1, and groups composed mainly of Caucasian students were coded as 0. There were two dummy variables for individual race/ethnicity. For the first race/ethnicity dummy variable, Caucasian participants were coded as 1 and all other students were coded as 0. For the second race/ethnicity dummy variable, Hispanic, African American, and all other non-Asian ethnic minorities were coded as 1 and Asian American and Caucasian students were coded as 0. The coding of the race/ethnicity variables allowed the intercept to be the mean of Asian and Asian American participants when both race/ethnicity variables were entered.

Analyses

Researchers realise that analysing multilevel data using normal regression methods can be fraught with problems. For example, the individual-level data are interdependent and analysing the data at the individual and/or group level alone is both mathematically and conceptually inaccurate. Unless otherwise mentioned, the data were analysed using hierarchical linear modeling via the hierarchical linear and nonlinear modeling programme, HLM5. This is considered the best method for analysing multilevel and cross-level data as well as data with unbalanced groups.

In our case, our data are both unbalanced and have dependencies within the different groups. Given that HLM uses maximum likelihood estimation methods, it is quite robust in analysing unbalanced data. Frog pond effects here are analysed as group-level effects that influence individual-level effects. All non-dummy variables were standardized for the HLM analyses.

CONCLUSION

More can be accomplished with groups than can be achieved by individuals alone, but to be productive a group must remain focused and healthy. One analogy is to liken a group to a motor vehicle. A group, like a vehicle, can get someone to a place faster. Most of us are more interested in our destination than we are in the vehicle that carries us there. However, if we do not pay attention to the vehicle, it will fall into disrepair.

A group, too, needs fueling and maintenance. Another analogy is that of a garden. One plants a garden and then tends to it, giving it water and nutrients, removing the weeds, and with sufficient time and attention the garden flourishes. A group, too, needs nourishment, and to have its "weeds" removed. One cannot take a group for granted, any more than one can take a garden or a vehicle for granted. To do so invites problems. It is far better to give some time and attention to the group's dynamics from time to time. By doing so, a group can sustain its forward development and achieve its full potential.

6

Motivation

MEANING OF MOTIVATION

Motivation is one of the most frequently used words in psychology. It refers to the factors which move or activate the organism. We infer the presence of motivation when we see that people work towards certain goals. For example, we might observe that a student works hard at almost every task that comes to him/her; from this we infer that the person has motive to achieve.

All human behaviour appears to arise in response to some form of internal (physiological) or external (environmental) stimulation. The behaviours, however, are not random. They often involve some purpose or goal. It is often held that behaviours take place as a result of the arousal of certain motives. Thus motivation can be defined as the process of activating, maintaining and directing behaviour towards a particular goal.

The process is usually terminated once the desired goal is attained by the person. The process of initiating action is technically called 'motivation'. Directing behaviour towards certain goal is the essence of motivation. Motivation is not always directly observable. It is inferred and used to explain behaviour. When we ask "What motivates a person to do a particular task?" We usually mean why does she behave as she does. In other words, motivation, as popularly used, refers to the cause or why of behaviour. Interestingly, we are not aware of all our motives. Behaviour can be governed by unconscious motives too.

If our understanding of motives is correct, we have a powerful tool for explaining behaviour. We explain our everyday behaviour in terms of various motives. Motives also help us make predictions about behaviour. We may tell what a person will do in future. Motives may not tell exactly what will happen but they give us an idea about the range of activities a person will do. Thus a person with a need to achieve in academics will work hard in school, an individual with a strong need to excel in sports will put in a lot of hard work in that field; similarly in business and in many other situations.

KEY CONCEPTS OF MOTIVATION

NEEDS AND MOTIVES

A need is a condition of lack or deficit of something required by the organism. In order to maintain homeostasis or balance the organism finds it necessary to satisfy the needs. The needs are of different types. The need for food or water is a physiological need, which arises out of lack or deficit of food or water in the organism.

The needs for excretion and urination are also physiological needs. They are due to the organism's necessity to eliminate waste matter from the body. The need for contact with other persons is a social need. The other social needs include need for prestige, status, affection, self-esteem, and so on. A person becomes more aware of his needs when they are not fulfilled.

In other words, when you are hungry, you need food, and, when you are thirsty you need water. In these cases you are in a state of deprivation and your bodily system suffers from some kind of imbalance. The needs may be broadly categorised as, primary or physiological needs and secondary or social needs. Needs for food, water, sex, sleep and rest, and elimination are primary needs.

Needs for achievement, affiliation, power are examples of social needs. The term 'motive' refers to goal directed behaviour and energising conditions within the organism that drive behaviour. It is generally used to refer to certain conditions which, besides arousing, predispose a person to respond, or behave in a way appropriate to that motive. Motives direct the activity of the individual towards person's goals.

GOALS

Thinking about the goal motivates a person to organize his or her action. If hunger is a need, eating food is a goal. Thus goal is related to the need state. However, in certain cases, behaviour is also guided by intrinsic goals. It means behaviour does not always need external goal. It may be satisfying and enjoyable in itself. Some people may like to sing, dance or play just for the sake of singing, dancing or playing. They like such activities. Thus goals can be intrinsic or extrinsic.

INCENTIVES

Incentives refers to the goal objects which satisfy the needs. Incentives vary in quality and quantity which make them less or more satisfying and attractive. Thus one can put in greater amount of effort to attain a more attractive incentive. As a matter of fact many incentives assume considerable significance in the lives of people and they do every thing possible to attain those incentives.

INSTINCTS

Instinct is an old concept in the field of motivation. It is defined as an innate biological force that predisposes the organism to act in a certain way. At one time all behaviours were supposed to be results of certain instincts. Some of the instincts identified by early psychologists are fight, repulsion, curiosity, self abasement, acquisition etc. It was thought that instincts were inherited and compelling sources of conduct, but can be modified by learning and experience. This term is no more used in relation to human behaviour. Animal behaviour is sometimes explained using this term. In current usage 'instinct' is reserved for innate response tendencies found among animals.

TYPES OF NEEDS

It is difficult to classify needs into distinct categories because the behaviour displayed by an individual at a given time is not the outcome of a single need. Many needs or motives contribute to it. But on the basis of information gained through the analysis of human behaviour, psychologists have attempted to classify human needs into two broad categories.

These categories are as follows:

* Primary or physiological needs, and
* Secondary or socio-psychogenic needs.

The primary needs are rooted in the physiological state of the body. They are innate and include bodily conditions such as hunger, thirst, sex, temperature regulation, sleep and pain. These needs are of recurring type becaue they can be satisfied for short periods only. The secondary or socio-psychogenic needs are unique to human beings.

Many of them are learned and they drive the individual towards special kinds of behaviours. Since these needs are learned, their strength differs greatly from one individual to another. Some of the important socio-psychogenic needs are power, affiliation, achievement and approval. Psychologists have developed a number of standardized tests for the assessment of these needs. They may also be assessed through non testing procedures as well.

HIERARCHY OF NEEDS

Abraham Maslow, who was a humanistic psychologist, argued that needs are arranged in a ladder-like steps. He proposed a rising order of needs from the level of physiological to self transcendence. The order of needs starts from basic survival or lower order needs to higher order needs. As one level of need is satisfied another higher order need will emerge and a ssume importance in life. The hierarchy is shown in Fig. 6.1.

creating many problems in personal and social lives of the people. It is therefore important to plan activities and organize relationships in such a manner that the task remains in the center of interest.

SELF-EFFICACY

People hold beliefs about their competence to undertake some task and such beliefs influence the level of their performance. The self-efficacy beliefs are the subjective standards held by the people that inform judgements about choosing specific goals. Introduced by Bandura, the concept of self-efficacy has been used to motivate people in a variety of settings. By learning appropriate or realistic self-efficacy beliefs one can plan behaviours and perform at a higher level. Self-efficacy beliefs are found to play significant role in adjustment and physical health. It is what people believe they can do with their skills under certain conditions. Self-efficacy beliefs develop over time. They reflect development of understanding that actions produce results and one can produce action that causes results. It may be noted that efficacy beliefs also operate at collective levels. Thus, collective efficacy involves a group's shared belief in its joint capabilities to organize and execute the courses of action required to produce the given level of attainment.

VALUES

Values work as important motivators. They are considered as desirable and cherisliable goals that serve as guiding principles in people's lives. Values help to make choices. Values prioritize needs. It is only because of values that people take purposeful long range actions. Pleasure and pain connected with specific behaviours have momentary effects. In the analysis of values, moral values are given special significance. These values guide choices and actions. Moral values differentiate between good and bad.

In a recent study based on data from several countries, some values have been noted which are given below:

* *Power*: This includes social status and prestige, control and dominance over people and resources

* *Achievement:* This includes personal success by demonstrating competence according to social standards.
* *Self-direction*: This includes independent thought and action, choosing, creating, and exploring.
* *Universalism:* This includes understanding, appreciation, tolerance and protection for the welfare of all people.
* *Benovelence*: This includes preservation and enhancement of the welfare of people with whom one is in frequent personal contact.
* *Tradition:* This includes respect, commitment and acceptance of the customers and ideas that are given importance in the traditional cultures or religions.
* *Conformity:* This includes restraint of action, inclination, and impulses likely to upset or harm others and violate social expectations or norms.
* *Security:* This includes safety, harmony and stability of society, of relationships and of self.

In the Indian context the framework of Dharma provides a set of values which are considered central to the sustenance of life.

They include:

* Truth,
* Non stealing,
* Keeping tolerance,
* Intellect,
* Knowledge,
* Non-anger,
* Forgiveness,
* Purity,
* Control of sense organs and
* Self control.

These values provide basis for maintaining and promoting life at the individual and the social levels. It maintains a the view that holds entire universe into account.

FRUSTATION AND CONFLICT

You must be aware that it is not always easy to satisfy the needs. You must have a variety of needs at a time. We all face certain difficulties in our attempts to satisfy the needs. We sometimes meet with failures. Also many obstacles prevent us from reaching the goals. When our needs are not satisfied, we get frustrated. Frustration is the feeling within an individual of being blocked in the attempts to satisfy needs which one considers significant.

Frustration refers to the blocking of behaviour directed towards a goal. An individual displays some sort of disturbed behaviour when he or she is prevented form fulfilling the desired goals. If motives are frustrated or blocked, the person may feel anxious, depressed or angry. For example, if you want to go to a movie or want to play and your parents refuse permission, you may show some kind of disturbed behaviour such as anger and shouting. Frustration often leads to aggression directed towards to source of frustration. Generally there are three main sources of frustration.

These are as follows:

* *Environmental Forces*: The environmental factors can frustrate the satisfaction of motives. The obstacle may be physical such as lack of money or a road block. They may be social. For instance, yours parents, teachers or classmates may prevent you from doing something what you want to do.
* *Personal Factors or Limitations*: They make goals unattainable and produce frustration. The personal inadequacy may be either physical or psychological. The personal characteristics of individual like personality or intelligence affect performance. The limitations of ability frustrate individuals because they do not let him or her to achieve very high goals. At times we have conflicting goals which create frustration.
* *Conflict*: A conflict is a situation in which an individual is required to act in two or more incompatible ways to achieve two or more exclusive goals. It occurs when an individual is unable to choose between two or more goals.

We all confront some degree of conflict in every stage of our life. We sometimes face a situation where we are supposed to choose between two or more alternatives. For example, we may have to decide whether to buy a book or go to a movie. On the one hand, you may like to play and get company of your friend, and on the other, if you study for the examination you may be successful in the exams. The motive to play and get the company of the friend is thus in conflict with the motive to be successful in examination.

THE MOTIVATION TO MANAGE

An Understanding Of The factors which contribute to the low proportions of women in administrative library positions can provide the library profession with a theoretical basis from which to initiate change. A number of factors previously have been suggested to explain the under representation of women in the administrative ranks. In particular, recent psychological research on the scarcity of women in management tends to focus on personality characteristics and behaviour patterns of women as probable explanations for low job status. Women are seen to be unable to function adequately in the administrative positions from which they are excluded. Obstacles are seen as residing within women themselves, *i.e.*, their own attributes and lack of motivation may impede high levels of achievement.

Several studies address this issue. Findings of these studies support the notion that females are socialized to aspire towards work activities that do not emphasize managerial skills. O'Leary,' for example, illustrates that women as a group describe themselves as different from or even opposite to men as a group on presumed requisite managerial traits. Both O'Leary and Terborg discuss the existence of a "male managerial model."

As McGregor describes it:

* The model of the successful manager in our culture is a masculine one. The good manager is aggressive, competitive, firm and just. He is not feminine, he is not soft and yielding or dependent or intuitive in the womanly sense. The very expression of emotion is widely viewed as a feminine weakness that would interfere with effective business procedures.

This model is supported by research which suggests that there are a number of relatively consistent personality differences between males and females. Brenner and Greenhaus report on studies which show that males tend to be more aggressive than females, and that females are more nurturing than males. The studies also find males to be more dominant and more achievement-oriented than females.

These studies offer support for identification of distinctive roles for males and females in the workplace. For example, a 1973 study by Schein finds a clear difference between the particular characteristics, traits, and attributes that middle-line managers perceive to be commonly held by women in general and those characteristics held by managers. A follow-up study by Schein in 1975 finds that both successful managers and men are perceived to possess the characteristics of leadership ability, competitiveness, self-confidence, objectivity, aggressiveness, forcefulness, and being ambitious and desirous of responsibility. Female managers as well as male managers identify these characteristics as basically "male" in nature. In other words, for both male and female respondents, "to think manager, means to think male."

Perhaps the most noted recent research on women's motivation to manage is that reported by Horner. Horner takes the motivation model of achievement developed by Atkinson and Feather and McClelland, Atkinson, Clark, and Lowell and hypothesizes that women do not achieve because of motivational conflict over achievement. Horner defines this motive as the fear that success in competitive achievement situations will lead to negative consequences, such as unpopularity and loss of femininity. While sub-sequent psychological research into fear of success fails to find consistent relationships between fear of success and sex of respondent, the concept continues to be the impetus for much related research One related research trend examines the depressed educational aspirations of women.

Cantor suggests that women's expectations about their personal competence may lower their aspirations:

* Having been exposed to general expectations of feminine incompetence, women may come to share

their expectations and avoid achievement situations since achievement situations or cues should signal failure to persons who view themselves as incompetent.

Consequently, at a time when discrimination against women in the library profession is gaining increased attention, it is important to know to what extent females actually have the motivational requirements to perform effectively in managerial positions. The question is of equal significance to employing libraries and to women who may be contemplating careers in library administration.

Over the past twenty years a number of studies have been conducted-primarily using the *Miner Sentence Completion Scale* (MSCS) - which have demonstrated the construct as well as concurrent and predictive validity of the concept of the motivation to manage in highly structured organizations of an essentially bureaucratic form. The motivation-to-manage concept has shown itself to be predictive both of movement up the hierarchy and of effective management performance.

Much of the research concerning gender effects on motivation to manage has involved individuals already in managerial positions. Such research may prove misleading because those studied have already chosen a managerial role, and consequently are likely to have a higher motivation to manage than those not in managerial ranks. For example, a Miner study done in 1974 shows no consistent differences in the managerial motivation of male and female managers in a department.

Studies among student populations from which managerial talent is drawn are another approach to examining motivation to manage. Miner finds substantial gender differences in motivation to manage among several samples of college students, including two samples of business students. Bartol also finds significant differences between male and female business students on motivation to manage, although the amount of variance accounted for according to gender is less than 10 per cent.

One point to be made in evaluating most motivation-to-manage research is that it traditionally has focused on male-intensive, for-profit organizations. It may be that significant differences in motivation-to-manage results can be found in a female-intensive profession such as librarianship. Personality characteristics of librarians have been recently examined by Sukiennik. She summarizes a number of studies which show that the typical librarian is more deferential than the general population, and possesses to a greater degree a set of qualities that Sukiennik characterizes as "endurance". She points out that male and female librarians are less likely to be affiliative, dominant, or aggressive than the population at large.

A separate study by Rainwaters and reported by Sukiennik examines the personality characteristics of male and female library science students. Using the Edwards Personal Preference Schedules, the men in the experimental group rated significantly higher than the male norm in the subscales on Achievement, Deference, Order, and Endurance. The women's scores were higher than the female norm in the subscales on Deference, Order, and Endurance, and lower in Exhibition, Affiliation, Dominance, and Aggression. A 1957 study by Douglass and discussed by Sukiennik supports the notion that librarians lack the characteristics associated with managers. Douglass's most significant finding is that those librarians tested lack ascendancy, drive, leadership qualities, and motivation.

The major purpose of our study was to identify motivation-to-manage levels among one segment of the population of practicing librarians-academic librarians-and the student population from which academic librarians come. The results of the various studies reviewed here support the notion that females are socialized to aspire towards work activities that are not considered managerial in nature. Librarianship emphasizes such activities. Consequently, we hypothesized that women who work as librarians, as a group, are not motivated to manage. However, inasmuch as men are socialized to aspire to management positions, we further hypothesized that male librarians' motivation to manage, while low will be higher than that of women.

POPULATIONS

Inasmuch as our hypotheses were derived from previous

research carried out using a population of academic librarian, that same population was used in this study. In order to compare the managerial motivation levels of individuals at various levels of experience in librarianship, the population of students preparing for work in academic libraries was selected for inclusion in the study as well. The presence of individuals who possessed no experience, but who had already declared a preference for academic librarianship, offers a test of the hypothesis that levels of motivation to manage vary with amount of professional experience.

Using estimates of population parameters derived from the authors' just-cited previous research, a sample of approximately 250 academic librarians was indicated. In reality, a determination of the true population of all academic librarians in the United States was not possible: the actual population was dictated by the presence of a convenient sampling frame, the latest edition of the American Library Association's membership directory.' The total population of students pursuing the first professional degree in librarianship who further could be identified as intending to work in academic/research libraries, was much more difficult to determine. Lacking a frame that could enumerate this population, it was decided that students in MLS pro-grams would be sampled.

The other piece of information needed-the type-of-library preference of students pursuing the MLS-was not available either. However, since one of the study's aims was to compare students' responses by academic library preferences vs. other type-of-library preferences, a type-of-library preference item was included in the student survey. Seven library science programmes were sampled and matched according to geographic region and size. Each school's cooperation was obtained by assuring confidentiality in data reporting, with the further cooperation of one faculty member from each programme who oversaw the administration of the survey to students who were enrolled in a required course.

INSTRUMENTATION

Because of its validity, reliability, amount of previous use, and development of a close-ended form of question-asking, the Miner Sentence Completion Scale was chosen as the device to determine the degree of a respondent's motivation to manage. The Miner Sentence Completion Scale, multiple-choice version, is a set of forty statement stubs, each stub followed by six multiple-choice alternatives. The forty statement stubs or items include five that are not scored, but are included to assist in disguising the intent of the scale.

The thirty-five scorable items, organized randomly, and unknown to the respondent, represent seven subscales:

* Authority Figures
* Competitive Games
* Competitive Situations
* Assertive Role
* Imposing Wishes
* Standing Out From the Group
* Routine Administrative Functions

The six alternatives for each item include two positive responses, two neutral responses, and two negative responses. The alternatives are organized randomly: there is no pattern of listing the six alternatives. Following is an example of one of the statements in the multiple-choice version of the Miner Sentence Completion Scale:

Being interviewed for a job:

* ( ) is necessary
* ( ) is a pain in the neck
* ( ) you should tell the truth
* ( ) is very interesting
* ( ) makes me nervous
* ( ) I am confident

This item, according to the Miner scoring key, is part of the Competitive Situations subscale. The key indicates that the two positive responses are "is very interesting," and "I am confident." The two neutral responses are "is necessary" and "you should tell the truth." The two negative responses are "is a pain in the neck" and "makes me nervous."

Although each subscale offers interesting opportunities to investigate individual components of the motivation to manage, this study used a simple summed score across the subscales, a typical application of the Miner scale.

As a result of pre-testing the multiple-choice version of the Miner scale during the summer of 1983, it was determined that three of the scale's forty multiple-choice items elicited undesirable responses, and worse, these three items lowered the participants' probability of completing the scale at all. With the permission of the scale's author, the three troublesome items were modified to increase neutrality according to gender. Although the internal consistency of this present study is not diminished, the comparability of our results to other results based on the Miner scale can be questioned.

Separate sets of additional questions were also pre-tested among the academic librarians and the students. Both students and practitioners were asked to indicate sex, age, marital status, and education. The student instrument also elicited information concerning the expected date of completion of the master's programme and the student's employment goal. Beyond the shared-background variables, the professionals were asked to indicate degree of budgetary authority, category of job activity, number of employees supervised, and total years of professional experience.

DATA COLLECTION

During the time period spanning fall 1983 through spring 1984, data were collected from both academic librarians and MLS students. A first and second wave of packets sent to 300 academic and research librarians yielded 262 usable responses, for an effective response rate of 87.3 per cent. Analysis of each variable in the data set against a variable reflecting date of return indicated no significant relationships. From this analysis, it was concluded that the assumption of no non-response bias could be entertained: the data supplied by the responding academic librarians were assumed to be representative of the population of all academic librarians holding membership in the American Library Association.

During the same period, appropriate faculty members at each of the seven library schools sampled were contacted, cooperation was obtained, and packets were sent. Each packet contained the number of data collection sets requested by the faculty member and a set of instructions for the faculty member. Inasmuch as the students filled out the questionnaire during a class period and thus represented a captive audience, the response rate was as would be expected-100 per cent or 291 cases.

The assumption that the ninety-three students who identified themselves as pursuing a goal of academic/research librarianship are representative of all such students rests on the representativeness of the seven institutions that were chosen. In all, data reflecting the responses of 355 individuals were analysed. Responses were coded and keyed into a floppy disk data file using a microcomputer and locally written input-and-data-checking programme. Data were uploaded to the University of Oklahoma's mainframe system to be analysed through SPSS, although data analysis also took place concurrently on a microcomputer.

MOTIVATION AND PRODUCTIVITY

Employee motivation is important in libraries, as in any other organization. This object attempts to identify the place of motivation in developing human resources in the library. This attempt begins with the need to define human resources, human resources development, and motivation, and to discuss theories of motivation and the literature of motivation as they pertain to libraries.

THE CONCEPT OF HUMAN RESOURCES

The UNECA conceptualizes human resources as the body of knowledge, skills, attitudes, physical, and managerial efforts required to manipulate land, capital, and technology, to produce goods and services for human consumption and welfare.

Human resources includes:

* Technical skill and abilities acquired from education, training, and experience. It indicates the ability to use knowledge, methods, and techniques in the performance of library tasks.

* Human skills, which is the ability to work with and through people. It includes the understanding of motivation and the application of effective leadership.
* Conceptual skill, which incorporates the ability to understand the complexity of the overall organization.

Human resources includes two major activities. The first is recruitment, selection, compensation, discipline, appraisal, and welfare of employees. The second is working with employees to improve their efficiency and productivity. The activities that enable individuals and groups to acquire new knowledge and skills and assume new roles and responsibilities are usually referred to as human resources development.

HUMAN RESOURCES DEVELOPMENT

Researchers defines human resources development as a "series of organized activities conducted within a specified time and designed to produce behaviour change" in individuals and organizations. The key point is learning. The "organized activities contained in the definition provided above embraced a carefully developed learning activity with identifiable components of objectives, actions, and evaluation. These conditions must exist in all forms of human resources development." Ideally, human resources development should provide solutions to problems such as a shortage of employees, employees who are inadequately skilled and efficient, high turnover, organizational expansion, career planning, and training needs.

UNDERSTANDING MOTIVATION USING THEORIES

Theories of motivation can help us understand why people behave as they do. No theory has a universal approach to explain human behaviour, because people are too far complex. Two important groups of theories are content theories and process theories. Content theories are concerned with identifying what factors in an individual or the work environment that energize and sustain behaviour. Process theories try to describe how behaviour is energized, directed, and sustained. Process theories first attempt to define variables in choice, *i.e.*, Should I work hard? (Choice); How hard do I work? (Persistence). Two content theories and two process theories will be discussed.

MASLOW'S HIERARCHY OF NEEDS

Maslow's hierarchy has had widespread acceptance since it was introduced. The theory posits that behaviour at a particular moment is determined by the strongest need. Maslow hypothesized five levels of needs: physiological, safety, social, esteem, and self-actualization. He placed them in a framework referred to as the hierarchy of needs because of the different levels of importance. Maslow states that, if all needs are unsatisfied at a particular time, satisfaction of the predominant need is most pressing. Those that come first must be satisfied before a higher-level need comes into play.

HERZBERG'S TWO-FACTOR THEORY

Frederick Herzberg advanced another content explanation of motivation in 1959. His theory was based on a study of need satisfaction among engineers and accountants. The theory is referred to as the two-factor theory of motivation. Herzberg and his associates asked the subjects to think of times both when they felt especially good and when they felt especially bad about their jobs. Each employee was then asked to describe the conditions that led to these feelings.

Based on the study, Herzberg reached two conclusions:

* Some job conditions operate primarily to dissatisfy employees when they are not present, but the presence of these conditions does not build strong motivation. Herzberg called these "maintenance factors" and he identified ten:
  - Company policy and administration
  - Technical supervision
  - Interpersonal relations with the supervisor
  - Interpersonal relations with peers
  - Interpersonal relations with subordinates

- Salary
- Job security
- Personal life
- Working conditions
- Status

* Some job conditions build high-level motivation and job satisfaction, but if they are not present, they do not prove highly dissatisfying. Herzberg described six of these "motivational factors":
    - Achievement
    - Recognition
    - Advancement
    - The work itself
    - Responsibility
    - Growth

EQUITY THEORY

Equity theory was made popular by Adams. It posits that perceived inequity is a motivational force. Workers evaluate equity using a ratio of inputs to outputs. Inputs include qualification, experience, effort, and ability. Outcomes include benefits. Inequities occur when workers feel that outcomes are not comparable to inputs.

EXPECTANCY THEORY

Expectancy theory was presented by psychologist Victor Vroom in 1966. Vroom asserts that employees are motivated to make choices among behaviours. If employees believe that effort will be rewarded, there will be motivated effort, that is, they will decide to work harder to receive a reward. Variables in expectancy theory are choice, expectancy, and preference. Choice is the freedom to select from a number of behaviours. Expectancy is the belief that certain behaviours will or will not be successful. Preferences are the values a person attaches to different outcomes.

MOTIVATION IN THE DEVELOPMENT OF HUMAN RESOURCES IN THE LIBRARY

A library is an organization whose mission is to provide

information to its users. The library staff are the human resources, who provide information services using library resources. How well the services are provided depends on how well the human resources are motivated and developed.

Motivation is crucial to the development of human resources in the library in the following ways:

* Maslow's hierarchy of needs is apparent in library employment. Acquiring a job and looking for job security help satisfy physiological and safety needs. When those needs are satisfied, employees look to their need for belonging and self-esteem. The need for self-esteem and self-actualization are represented in library human resources development efforts that focus on training, creativity, problem-solving, and so on.
* The maintenance and motivational factors of Herzberg's two-factor theory play important roles in the development of human resources in the library. Herzberg's believed that motivators must be build into the job. These include responsibility, autonomy, respect and recognition from superiors, a sense of wellbeing, and the opportunity to have one's ideas adopted.
* Equity theory indicates likewise has a place in the library. Workers compare their pay, work schedules, benefits, or any reward with what is being received by other employees. Unless the reward system is carefully administered, it could result in problems of perceived or actual inequity.
* Expectancy theory can be used in the development of human resources in libraries. The logic of expectancy theory is that individuals exert effort for a performance that results in preferred rewards. Expectancy can be influenced by selecting individuals with particular skills and abilities, providing training, and providing support to achieve a particular level of performance.

STRATEGIES FOR INCREASING MOTIVATION

Job Enrichment

The idea of quality work life has received attention for several decades. Workers become increasingly dissatisfied and frustrated by routine tasks. The result may be lower output, poor attitude, lower quality, absenteeism, high turnover, and pressure for better conditions and greater participation in decision-making. Herzberg contributed the theory of job enrichment as a motivational technique. Job enrichment provides employees with an opportunity to grow psychologically and mature in a job.

Job enrichment attempts to make the job itself motivational. Research indicates that jobs higher in enrichment factors result in higher satisfaction; however, research also indicates that enriched jobs require more training time and result in slightly higher anxiety and stress. Job enrichment increases a job's range and depth, which refers to the number of activities and the autonomy, responsibility, discretion, and control.

Merit Pay

The money that employees receive is actually a package made up of salary, and other fringe benefits such as transport, housing, furniture, medical allowance. Others include meal subsidy and utility allowances. The motivation theories discussed, suggest that and fringe benefits can have some influence on effort and persistence. The money that employees receive is actually a package of salary and benefits. Theories of motivation suggest that salary and benefits have influence on effort and persistence. Pay has the potential to satisfy each of the five needs in Maslow's hierarchy.

In Herzberg's two-factor model pay is a maintenance factor that should not contribute significantly to motivation. In expectancy theory, pay can satisfy a variety of needs and influence choice and behaviour, while in equity theory, pay is a major outcome that one compares with other employees. A number of studies reveal that, in order to motivate, a salary plan must demonstrate that good performance leads to higher levels of pay, minimize any negative consequences of good performance, and relate other rewards to good performance.

Flexible Working Hours

Libraries are faced with an increasingly diverse workforce that includes nursing mothers, single parents with young children, employees with very different responsibilities, and those taking classes or pursuing degrees to improve skills and abilities or for self-improvement. The concept of flexible working hours has motivational appeal to many library staff. Flexible time is intended to ensure that the work of the organization is accomplished and, at the same time, to permit library staff and their supervisors to establish work schedules that recognize individual and family needs. Research indicates that flexible scheduling can be motivational in that job satisfaction is improved and absenteeism reduced. The ability to accommodate employee needs is a healthy and positive approach to motivation.

CONCLUSION AND RECOMMENDATIONS

It is the responsibility of the library management to discover the potential in each library staff member, and to apply the appropriate motivational strategy. Motivation is an individual matter and one needs to know and understand the individuals that are to be motivated. Individuals have their own goals and aspirations. Individual employees are being asked to make the library succeed. One cannot hire only the hand and the brain; the owner of that hand and brain must always come along.

7

Conflict: The Unavoidable Connections

DEFINITION

A team is a small group of people with complementary skills who are committed to a common purpose, performance goals, and approach for which they hold themselves mutually accountable. Although student teams may not satisfy all the requirements of the definition, the degree to which they do often determines their effectiveness.

RATIONALE

"Students do not come to school with all the social skills they need to collaborate effectively with others. Therefore, teachers need to teach the appropriate communication, leadership, trust, decision making, and conflict management skills to students and provide the motivation to use these skills in order for groups to function effectively." Faculty must take responsibility to help students develop their skills to participate on and lead teams.

Students bring different ideas, goals, values, beliefs and needs to their teams and these differences are a primary strength of teams. These same differences inevitably lead to conflict, even if the level of conflict is low. Since conflict is inevitable, one of the ways in which faculty members can help students improve their abilities to function on multidisciplinary teams is to work with them to develop their understanding of conflict and their capabilities to manage and resolve conflict.

To this end, this document addresses the following questions:

* What is conflict and conflict management?
* Why learn more about conflict and conflict management?
* How do people respond to conflict?
* What modes do people use to address conflict?
* What factors can affect our conflict modes?
* How might you select your conflict management style?
* How might you apply this information?

WHAT IS CONFLICT AND CONFLICT MANAGEMENT

Conflict may be defined as a struggle or contest between people with opposing needs, ideas, beliefs, values, or goals. Conflict on teams is inevitable; however, the results of conflict are not predetermined. Conflict might escalate and lead to nonproductive results, or conflict can be beneficially resolved and lead to quality final products. Therefore, learning to manage conflict is integral to a high-performance team. Although very few people go looking for conflict, more often than not, conflict results because of miscommunication between people with regard to their needs, ideas, beliefs, goals, or values. Conflict management is the principle that all conflicts cannot necessarily be resolved, but learning how to manage conflicts can decrease the odds of nonproductive escalation. Conflict management involves acquiring skills related to conflict resolution, self-awareness about conflict modes, conflict communication skills, and establishing a structure for management of conflict in your environment.

WHY LEARN MORE ABOUT CONFLICT AND CONFLICT MANAGEMENT

Listening, oral communication, interpersonal communication, and teamwork rank near the top of skills that employers seek in their new hires. When you learn to effectively manage and resolve conflicts with others, then more opportunities for successful team memberships are available to you.

If we can learn to manage this highly probable event called conflict, then we are less apt to practice destructive behaviours that will negatively impact our team. Although conflict may be misunderstood and unappreciated, research shows that unresolved conflict can lead to aggression. Most of us use conflict skills that we observed growing up, unless we have made a conscious effort to change our conflict management style. Some of us observed good conflict management, while others observed faulty conflict management. Most of us have several reasons to improve our conflict-management skills.

Faculty members should help students develop their conflict management skills. Most people do not resolve conflicts because they either have a faulty skill set and/or because they do not know the organization's policy on conflict management. All team members need to know their conflict styles, conflict intervention methods, and strategies for conflict skill improvement.

HOW DO PEOPLE RESPOND TO CONFLICT? FIGHT OR FLIGHT

Physiologically we respond to conflict in one of two ways—we want to "get away from the conflict" or we are ready to "take on anyone who comes our way." Think for a moment about when you are in conflict. Do you want to leave or do you want to fight when a conflict presents itself? Neither physiological response is good or bad—it's personal response. What is important to learn, regardless of our initial physiological response to conflict, is that we should intentionally choose our response to conflict. Whether we feel like we want to fight or flee when a conflict arises, we can deliberately choose a conflict mode. By consciously choosing a conflict mode instead of to conflict, we are more likely to productively contribute to solving the problem at hand. Five conflict response modes that can be used in conflict.

WHAT MODES DO PEOPLE USE TO ADDRESS CONFLICT

* Compromising
* Collaborating

* Competing
* Avoiding
* Accommodating

Each of these modes can be characterized by two scales: assertiveness and cooperation. None of these modes is wrong to use, but there are right and wrong times to use each. The following sections describe the five modes. The information may help each team member to characterize her/his model for conflict management.

HOW TO DISCERN YOUR CONFLICT MODE

The *Thomas-Kilmann Conflict Mode Instrument* (TKI) is a widely used assessment for determining conflict modes. The assessment takes less than fifteen minutes to complete and yields conflict scores in the areas of avoiding, competing, compromising, accommodating, and collaborating.

COMPETING

The competing conflict mode is high assertiveness and low cooperation. Times when the competing mode is appropriate are when quick action needs to be taken, when unpopular decisions need to be made, when vital issues must be handled, or when one is protecting self-interests.

Competing Skills:

* Arguing or debating
* Using rank or influence
* Asserting your opinions and feelings
* Standing your ground
* Stating your position clearly

AVOIDING

The avoiding mode is low assertiveness and low cooperation. Many times people will avoid conflicts out of fear of engaging in a conflict or because they do not have confidence in their conflict management skills. Times when the avoiding mode is appropriate are when you have issues of low importance, to reduce tensions, to buy some time, or when you are in a position of lower power.

Avoiding Skills:

* Ability to withdraw
* Ability to sidestep issues
* Ability to leave things unresolved
* Sense of timing

ACCOMMODATING

The accommodating mode is low assertiveness and high cooperation. Times when the accommodating mode is appropriate are to show reasonableness, develop performance, create good will, or keep peace. Some people use the accommodating mode when the issue or outcome is of low importance to them. The accommodating mode can be problematic when one uses the mode to "keep a tally" or to be a martyr. For example, if you keep a list of the number of times you have accommodated someone and then you expect that person to realise, without your communicating to the person, that she/he should now accommodate you.

Accommodating Skills:

* Forgetting your desires
* Selflessness
* Ability to yield
* Obeying orders

COMPROMISING

The compromising mode is moderate assertiveness and moderate cooperation. Some people define compromise as "giving up more than you want," while others see compromise as both parties winning. Times when the compromising mode is appropriate are when you are dealing with issues of moderate importance, when you have equal power status, or when you have a strong commitment for resolution. Compromising mode can also be used as a temporary solution when there are time constraints.

Compromising Skills:

* Negotiating
* Finding a middle ground
* Assessing value
* Making concessions

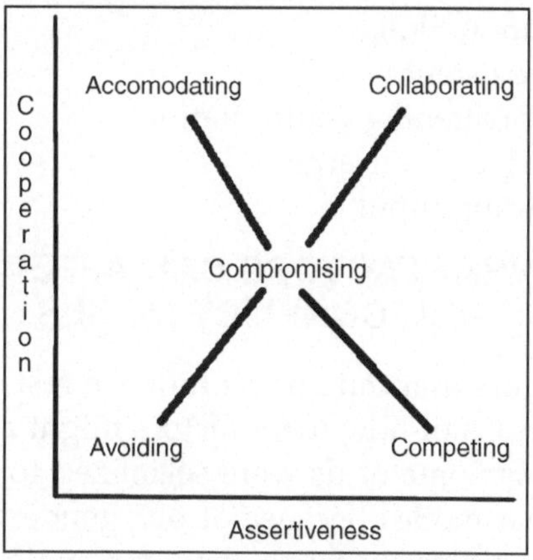

Fig 7.1. Five Modes of Conflict Management.

COLLABORATING

The collaborating mode is high assertiveness and high cooperation. Collaboration has been described as "putting an idea on top of an idea on top of an idea . . . in order to achieve the best solution to a conflict." The best solution is defined as a creative solution to the conflict that would not have been generated by a single individual. With such a positive outcome for collaboration, some people will profess that the collaboration mode is always the best conflict mode to use. However, collaborating takes a great deal of time and energy. Therefore, the collaborating mode should be used when the conflict warrants the time and energy. For example, if your team is establishing initial parameters for how to work effectively together, then using the collaborating mode could be quite useful. On the other hand, if your team is in conflict about where to go to lunch today, the time and energy necessary to collaboratively resolve the conflict is probably not beneficial.

Times when the collaborative mode is appropriate are when the conflict is important to the people who are constructing an integrative solution, when the issues are too important to compromise, when merging perspectives, when gaining commitment, when improving relationships, or when learning.

Collaboration Skills:

* Active listening.
* Nonthreatening confrontation.
* Identifying concerns.
* Analysing input.

WHAT FACTORS CAN AFFECT OUR CONFLICT MODES

Some factors that can impact how we respond to conflict with explanations of how these factors might affect us:

* *Gender:* Some of us were socialized to use particular conflict modes because of our gender. For example, some males, because they are male, were taught "always stand up to someone, and, if you have to fight, then fight." If one was socialized this way he will be more likely to use assertive conflict modes versus using cooperative modes.
* *Self-concept:* How we think and feel about ourselves affect how we approach conflict. Do we think our thoughts, feelings, and opinions are worth being heard by the person with whom we are in conflict?
* *Expectations:* Do we believe the other person or our team wants to resolve the conflict?
* *Situation*: Where is the conflict occurring, do we know the person we are in conflict with, and is the conflict personal or professional?
* *Position (Power)*: What is our power status relationship, (that is, equal, more, or less) with the person with whom we are in conflict?
* *Practice*: Practice involves being able to use all five conflict modes effectively, being able to determine what conflict mode would be most effective to resolve the conflict, and the ability to change modes as necessary while engaged in conflict.
* *Determining the Best Mode:* Through knowledge about conflict and through practice we develop a "conflict management understanding" and can, with ease and limited energy, determine what conflict mode to use

with the particular person with whom we are in conflict.

* *Communication Skills*: The essence of conflict resolution and conflict management is the ability to communicate effectively. People who have and use effective communication will resolve their conflicts with greater ease and success.
* *Life Experiences:* We often practice the conflict modes we saw our primary caretaker(s) use unless we have made a conscious choice as adults to change or adapt our conflict styles. Some of us had great role models teach us to manage our conflicts and others of us had less-than-great role models. Our life experiences, both personal and professional, have taught us to frame conflict as either something positive that can be worked through or something negative to be avoided and ignored at all costs.

Discerning how we manage our conflict, why we manage conflict the way we do, and thinking about the value of engaging in conflict with others are important. With better understanding we can make informed choices about how we engage in conflict and when as suggested, engage in conflict.

HOW MIGHT YOU SELECT YOUR CONFLICT MANAGEMENT STYLE

There are times when we have a choice to engage in or avoid a conflict. The following six variables should be considered when you decide whether to engage in a conflict.

HOW INVESTED IN THE RELATIONSHIP ARE YOU

The importance of the working/personal relationship often dictates whether you will engage in a conflict. If you value the person and/or the relationship, going through the process of conflict resolution is important.

HOW IMPORTANT IS THE ISSUE TO YOU

Even if the relationship is not of great value to you, one must often engage in conflict if the issue is important to you.

For example, if the issue is a belief, value, or regulation that you believe in or are hired to enforce, then engaging in the conflict is necessary. If the relationship and the issue are both important to you, there is an even more compelling reason to engage in the conflict.

DO YOU HAVE THE ENERGY FOR THE CONFLICT

Many of us say, "There is not time to do all that I want to do in a day." Often the issue is not how much time is available but how much energy we have for what we need to do. Even in a track meet, runners are given recovery time before they have to run another race. Energy, not time, is being managed in these situations.

ARE YOU AWARE OF THE POTENTIAL CONSEQUENCES

Prior to engaging in a conflict, thinking about anticipated consequences from engaging in the conflict is wise. For example, there may be a risk for your safety, a risk for job loss, or an opportunity for a better working relationship. Many times people will engage in conflict and then be shocked by the outcome or consequence of engaging in the conflict. Thoughtful reflection about the consequences, both positive and negative, is useful before engaging in or avoiding a conflict.

ARE YOU READY FOR THE CONSEQUENCES

After analysing potential consequences, determine whether you are prepared for the consequences of engaging in the conflict. For example, one employee anticipated a job loss if she continued to engage in the conflict she was having with her boss over a particular issue. After careful consideration, the employee thought and believed strongly enough about the issue that she did engage in the conflict with her boss. Her annual contract was not renewed for the upcoming year.

Because this individual had thought through the consequences of engaging in the conflict, she was prepared to be without a job for a while and able to financially and emotionally plan for this outcome. Most consequences of engaging in conflict are not this severe, but this example illustrates the value of thinking through consequences.

WHAT ARE THE CONSEQUENCES IF YOU DO NOT ENGAGE IN THE CONFLICT

To avoid losing a sense of self, there are times when you must engage in conflict. Most people have core values, ideas, beliefs, or morals. If a person is going to sacrifice one of their core beliefs by avoiding a conflict, personal loss of respect must be considered. In such cases, even if a person is not excited about confronting the conflict, one must carefully consider the consequences of evading the conflict. When the personal consequences of turning away from the conflict outweigh all other factors, then a person usually must take part in the conflict.

HOW MIGHT INDIVIDUAL STUDENTS APPLY THIS INFORMATION TO IMPROVE THEIR CONFLICT MANAGEMENT SKILLS

Applying the preceding information about the five different modes of conflict management, factors affecting models of conflict management, and processes for selecting one or more approaches to conflict involves both self-awareness and an awareness of the others involved in the conflict.

In terms of self-awareness, reflecting on the following questions would provide useful information in selecting how to approach a conflict situation:

* Am I in conflict?
* With whom am I in conflict?
* Why am I motivated to resolve the conflict?
* What conflict mode am I going to use to manage this conflict?

Since conflict involves at least two people, improving awareness of the other party involved in a conflict might also be useful in choosing how to approach a conflict situation.

Reflecting on the following questions might improve awareness of the other party involved in a confliction:

* What is the nature of the conflict, that is, what is the conflict about?

* What might motivate the other person(s) involved to resolve the conflict?
* What conflict modes is the other person using?
* How might I Intervene to resolve/manage the conflict?

Learning more about conflict allows greater intentionality in selecting a conflict response. Most people have set reactions to conflicts. By learning more about principles of conflict, conflict modes, and reflection on the above questions, we can be more intentional in deciding on a conflict response. Greater intentionality will likely lead to more effective conflict management. The following examples provide additional suggestions that individuals might use to improve their conflict management skills.

INDIVIDUAL REFLECTION EXERCISE

In addition to reflecting on the preceding questions, Karl Smith suggests that the following exercise might provide individuals with valuable information about their perspectives on conflict.

Exercise

Write the word conflict in the center of a blank piece of paper and draw a circle around it. Quickly jot down all the words and phrases you associate with the word conflict by arranging them around your circle. Review your list of associations and categorize them as positive, negative, or neutral. Count the total number of positive, negative, and neutral associations, and calculate the percentages that are positive, negative, and neutral. Did you have more than 90% positive? Did you have more than 90% negative? What do your associations with the word conflict indicate about your views about conflict and your approach to conflict?

LEARNING ABOUT YOUR CONFLICT MODES

Review brief descriptions of the five modes and choose your primary conflict mode. Supplementing individual reflection on conflict modes, you might find out more about your modes of conflict using instruments that are available. Karl Smith in his book provides a copy of a questionnaire based on the Blake and Mouton conflict model· Completing the questionnaire, scoring your responses, and reflecting on your answers might provide valuable information about your approaches to conflict.

The TKI is a more recent instrument that is based on the Blake and Mouton conflict model and provides information about your conflict modes in terms of the modes. Taking the TKI assessment would provide information about your primary conflict modes. Equipped with this information, additional individual reflection would help you to determine your current level of comfort with your conflict resolution styles. Then, you might decide whether you want to make changes.

CREATING AN INDIVIDUAL CONFLICT MANAGEMENT PLAN

Create a conflict management plan. A conflict management plan is a thought and behaviour process one can follow when in conflict. A person creates a list of steps she/he can follow when a conflict comes up so that the person can productively manage/solve the conflict. These steps have to be thoughts or behaviours that can be realistically done. The literature shows that, if we can identify we are in conflict and can then implement a conflict management plan, our opportunity for resolution of the conflict increases significantly. We identify we are in conflict by identifying our physiological responses when in conflict and by identifying thoughts and feelings we are having that trigger us to realise that we are experiencing a conflict.

There are three steps to making a conflict plan. First, write down what physiological responses you have when you know you are in conflict (*e.g.*, my palms are sweaty, my heart is racing). Second, write down what thoughts you typically have when in a conflict (*e.g.*, "I want to hurt him"; "I want to just get away from her"). Finally, list 4–8 steps you can follow to help you manage your thoughts and emotions in a productive way to manage/solve your conflict (*e.g.*, 1. I will take a deep breath; 2. I will think about how I want to respond, etc.). Refer to Algert and Watson to learn more about creating a conflict management plan.

LISTENING

Improving listening skills is one approach to improving conflict management skills. Eugene Raudsepp states that "Studies show, however, that only about 10% of us listen properly."

HOW MIGHT A STUDENT TEAM APPLY THIS INFORMATION TO IMPROVE ITS APPROACHES TO CONFLICT AND/OR SKILLS IN MANAGING CONFLICT WITHIN THE TEAM

Applying the preceding information about the five different modes of conflict management, factors affecting models of conflict management, and processes for selecting one or more approaches to conflict within the context of a student team involves increasing the awareness of the each of the team members about the way the other team members view conflict and how the other team members approach conflict.

There are two basic types of team activities:

* In the first type of team activity, individual team members learn more about their perspectives and approaches to conflict through either individual reflection or appropriate instruments. Then, the individuals share with their team members what they have learned.
* In the second type, the team engages in an activity that simulates a hopefully low level of conflict. Then, the team reflects about its actions, learns from its experiences, and develops ways to address conflict more constructively in the future.

COLLABORATING WITH DIFFERENT INDIVIDUAL CONFLICT MODES

Ask each member to complete the exercise on the preceding page in which she/he identifies their primary mode of conflict management. Then, ask each individual team member to share her/his own primary mode of conflict management and to provide examples that illustrate that mode.

Next, ask the team to identify potential strengths for the combination of different styles and potential problems that might arise with the combination of conflict management modes. Finally, ask the team to develop strategies to minimize potential problems and build on their strengths.

DEVELOPING A POSITIVE TEAM PERSPECTIVE ABOUT CONFLICT

Start with the individual reflection exercise on the preceding page in which each member writes the word conflict and associates different words or phrases with conflict. Then, ask each member to share the insights she/he learned through the individual reflection. Next, ask the team to take all of the positive associations with conflict and combine them together to construct positive ways in which the team might view conflict. Finally, ask the team to take all of the negative associations with conflict and devise ways in which the negative associates might be eliminated or minimized.

DEVELOPING A CONSENSUS DECISION

In this book on Teamwork and Project Management, Karl Smith asks teams to rank fifteen causes of death in the United States in terms of their frequency of occurrence. These types of exercises can stimulate team development in several ways. One of the ways is to provoke a low level of conflict within the team and to learn from its experience. After completing the exercise, the team can debrief its performance. The team might address several questions. What were the positive aspects in the way we handled conflict? How did our various modes of conflict management help our performance? How did our various modes of conflict management hinder our performance? How might we improve the ways in which we managed conflict within our team?

INTRATEAM COMMUNICATION

Improving intrateam communication can reduce the likelihood of conflict and increase the chances for faster, more effective management of conflict when it occurs. The Foundation Coalition has prepared a summary on Effective Interpersonal/Intrateam Communication that may provide helpful information and activities.

HOW MIGHT A FACULTY MEMBER APPLY THIS INFORMATION IN HER/HIS COURSE

Your learning objects and activities will depend on the maturity of your students, their prior experience and knowledge of conflict management skills, and the amount of class time you choose to invest in conflict management. The following paragraphs provide three examples of possible learning objectives and classroom activities.

EXAMPLE NO. 1

If you are teaching a class in which you will be using student teams and have about twenty minutes for conflict management, you might set the following learning objective and use the following class activity.

Classroom Activity

Discuss the first page of this document. Ask your students to work in teams and discuss what they think about conflict. Have they had positive or negative outcomes when they have engaged in conflict at work or school? Next, have the students identify their physiological response to conflict: fight or flight. Has the initial conflict response, fight or flight, had positive or negative outcomes? Let the students know, regardless of their physiological response, they can intentionally pick a conflict mode they want to use when in conflict. They do not have to just fight or flee when a conflict arises. Finally, ask students to identify positive outcomes that can occur from engaging in conflict (peace, relief, improved relationship, stronger team, understanding, better communication, greater productivity, etc.). Through identifying how we engage in conflict and recognizing that engaging in conflict can be positive, we are more likely to engage in conflict when necessary.

EXAMPLE NO. 2

If you are teaching a class in which you will be using student teams and have an entire class period to help your students develop their conflict management skills, then you might select the following learning objectives and use the following classroom activities.

EXAMPLE NO. 3

If you are teaching a class in which you will be using student teams and choose to invest a homework assignment and an entire class period in helping your students develop their conflict management skills, then you might select the following learning objectives and use the following classroom activities.

TIPS ON HOW TO MANAGE CONFLICT

If you are in conflict with someone and you don't know how to deal with it, some of these tips may be helpful. If there is no threat of physical violence, talking it out is the best solution. Face-to-face contact is better than letters and messages-and a good deal better than banging on walls, throwing things, or complaining about it to everyone else. Choose a good time to approach the other person so that neither of you is rushed. Don't start when the other person is on the way to work, or you've had a terrible day, or you're just about to cook dinner. That will only add to the frustration. Find a place where you can both sit comfortably and quietly for a while.

Explain that the conflict has been worrying you and you'd like to sort it out. Think beforehand about what you want to say. It's important to state clearly what the problem is and how you feel about it. Don't blame the other person for everything or begin with your opinion of what should be done. Avoid name calling—it only makes it harder for the person to hear what you are saying. Don't be tempted to interpret the other person's behaviour. Don't say 'You're blocking my driveway on purpose, just to make me angry'. Instead, say 'When your car blocks my driveway I get angry because it is difficult to get in or out'. Give the person a chance to tell you the other side of the story.

Be prepared to relax, listen and take everything in. Let the person *know* you are listening. You may not agree, but there's nothing more frustrating than trying to talk to someone who doesn't appear to be listening. Say that you're glad you're talking about the problem. This helps to ease the tension and is a great help in moving things towards an agreement. When you've reached this point, try working on the dispute cooperatively. Work out what you both have to do to resolve the problem. Two or more people working on a problem together can get further than one person telling the other to change. Since you're taking the time to work on a problem, take the time to get it right.

Get the whole problem out in the open. Don't leave out the part that seems less important or is the hardest to talk about. Those are the things that will ruin the solution you come up with. Agree to check with each other at a specific time in the future to see how things are going—and don't forget to do it. If things have gone too far for you to handle it by yourself, there is help at hand. The Dispute Resolution Centres provide a free, confidential and impartial mediation service throughout Queensland. Trained mediators are available to guide discussion and help you reach a solution.

CONFLICT, LEADERSHIP AND CHANGE

CONFLICT AND CHANGE

We live in constant change. Businesses have to continue to evolve and change in order to compete, to keep up with new technologies, to recruit and retain the best employees. Individuals have to change, learn and grow professionally just to stay current with the requirements of their jobs, let alone move up in their organizations and chosen careers. One of the inevitable facts of being in a transition is that it evokes conflict.

This is as much the case for individuals as it is for organizations. Change and transition create friction and conflict. But this is not the problem most of us take it to be.

In fact, conflict is a wonderful gift—it is the engine that drives evolution. There is nothing inherently wrong with conflict. This is good news, because conflict appears to be inherent in the structure of the universe, so there is no escaping it. As any physicist would tell us, if there were no conflict among forces there would, quite simply, be no physical universe as we know it. Instead we would have a steady state, with no change of any kind, nothing new (and nothing old), no evolution.

The great gift of conflict is that it carries within it the seeds of something new and potentially better than what has been. As Albert Einstein noted, "The significant problems we face cannot be solved at the same level of thinking we were at when we created them." Conflict serves as the messenger telling us we that can no longer fruitfully remain at the current level, that is time to evolve. More importantly, it is by successfully harnessing the generative energy of conflict that we can find our way to the next level.

CONFLICT, PAIN AND FEAR

Conflict drives evolution and change, whether it is the evolution of our planet, our species, our cultures, or the changes each of us undergo as individuals. Yet many of us look on conflict as uncomfortable at best, if not dangerous, painful, and frightening. This is not so difficult to understand, considering that human history has been rife with conflicts that have resulted in pain and even death—sometimes for one or two people, sometimes for tens of thousands.

Other assessments and feelings that often arise around conflict include competition, antagonism, anger, aggression, winning and losing, power and powerlessness. *The Argument Culture,* Deborah Tannen notes that in our society we tend to look at the world from an either/or, win/lose perspective. For us, conflict is seen primarily through the either/or lens. In this simplistic view possibilities for the future are limited to just three: my way, your way, or some kind of compromise way that can be formed by each of us giving up some of what we want, a kind of lose-a-little/lose-a-little solution.

Viewed through this lens, conflict is clearly something to be avoided. And, if we can't avoid it, we should fight to win. We certainly don't want to lose, and compromise is only marginally better. This approach to conflict makes it almost impossible to recognize and capitalize on its gift. As long as this is going on the individual or organization stays stuck in the conflict and stuck at the current level. They fail to evolve towards something better.

THE TWO GIFTS OF CONFLICT

On the surface level change evokes conflict between individuals and groups. When we view conflict from this level it is threatening. At a deeper level, however, change offers us two great gifts. One is that conflicts between people, groups, systems, processes, and ideas signal the need for change. For a leader tuned into this level conflict can serve as a clear message that some change needs to occur. The other great gift of conflict lies in how it can be used to determine what changes are best to make.

Making a practice of creative conflict will lead to better ideas, systems, processes, and relationships. Using conflict creatively, a company can direct its energy towards creating a new, better approach to a situation, a process or an idea. The best solutions almost always arise out of a conversation that includes creative conflict. Powerfully generative energy is born out of the tension of holding seemingly opposing forces, ideas, directions, wants and needs with openness, compassion, and authentic exploration. When people in conflict are willing to do this, what eventually happens is that they find a way to transcend the old, opposing stories they held and emerge together into a new, larger story that is much more than the old stories.

The result of using conflict in this way is a new and better solution. This doesn't mean it has to be radically different than what came before. But the understanding that emerges will offer new, different possibilities for more effective action. And it is critical that the "new way" contains room to include the key interests expressed in the old, opposing views. It is not a "compromise" solution in which each party gives something up. What all parties do have to give up is their old stories. They must be willing to explore the possibility of something new and better.

The key to creative conflict is that its focus is on ideas, processes, interests, and outcomes. In the destructive process most people understand as conflict the focus is on winning or, failing that, finding a tolerable compromise. Conversation is primarily about different positions and personalities. It is also about the past: what happened, who did what, who was to blame. With creative conflict, on the other hand, people are concerned primarily with the outcome. They are engaged in a search for the best answers, the most effective ideas for the future.

CONFLICT AND LEADERSHIP

A great leader is one who recognizes that conflict comes bearing gifts. Instead of avoiding it, they welcome conflict as an indicator that change is necessary. And they foster creative conflict as an ally on a journey to something better. Rather than seeking simply to "win" a conflict at the current level, they to use it as a tool to uncover better possibilities and evolve to a new level from which the problems created at the lower level can be solved.

In his landmark book *Good To Great*, Jim Collins and his researchers identified a group of eleven companies that, by their rigorous standards, had become and remained "great". Based on exhaustive research, reading and personal interviews, they then identified what those eleven great companies do differently from all the rest.

One key difference Collins notes is how the leadership teams in those companies foster creative conflict as a way of setting their courses and navigating their way to greatness. He captures how they use conflict Collins this way: " . .. all the good-to-great companies had a penchant for intense dialogue.

Phrases like 'loud debate,' 'heated discussions,' and 'healthy conflict' peppered the objects and interview transcripts from all the companies." These companies don't avoid conflict, and they aren't employing win/lose strategies or seeking compromises. They are harnessing the immense power of generative conversations around conflicting ideas to continuously evolve themselves into the best companies they can be.

PRECONDITIONS FOR CREATIVE CONFLICT

Creative conflict doesn't just happen. We human beings have had extensive practice at destructive conflict, so it takes both *specific intent* and a *particular set of communication skills* to manage a conversation that uses conflict creatively. The good news is that the skills can be readily learned. We at Insight Communication are among many who have been successfully teaching and coaching people in skills for creative conflict and problem solving for many years.

Equally important, however, is having a clear, explicit intent to use the two great gifts conflict offers. When they do, leaders will recognize when conflict in their environment is telling them that something needs to change. They can then use creative conflict as a powerful tool to identify the best changes to make, the ones that will bring the greatest benefit to everyone involved. Great leaders use conflict in just these ways.

8

Librarians Perform Sacred Functions

If libraries are imagined as heavenly, it stands to reason that librarianship is likewise a spiritual profession. As proof that this is so, I offer the following job description taken from the Encyclopedia of

Career and Vocational Guidance:

* Individuals entering this field need to be outgoing and friendly and have a strong desire to help others. They need to be able to get along with people from a wide variety of backgrounds. They need patience, sympathy and open-mindedness to be able to listen to the problems of others, while maintaining a discreet and sincere respect. They must possess a strong feeling. . . of service, which means giving material success a lower priority.

Does this sound like a job description for a reference librarian? I believe it does. But the profession being described is that of a Protestant minister. I took the liberty of omitting the requirement that individuals feel "God is calling them" to service. Secular librarians may not feel called by God, but they may feel called to serve by Something or Someone they cannot describe.

LIBRARIANS IN MINISTERIAL ROLES

I am not the first to equate libraries and librarians with holy work. Charles Curran called librarians high priests in the early 1990s. A book about Indiana's Carnegie libraries is titled

Temples of Knowledge. Library historian Matthew Battles noted that the proliferation of the book in the nineteenth century transformed the library "from temple to market, from canon to cornucopia." The library, almost more than the church, had become the people's temple.

Nor is this the first writing to equate librarians and ministers. In 1953 the librarian at the Yale Divinity School, Raymond Morris, wrote "Theological Librarianship as a Ministry." For him, just walking up and down the stacks was a mystical experience. "Theological librarianship is at its best a ministry," he claimed. Morris was addressing work in a religious library, but his theological reference could easily be applied to secular libraries.

Two major social changes since the 1950s have allowed the closer parallel between librarianship and the ministry:

* First, the secularizing trend has changed the role of the clergy.
* Second, secular professions-including librarian-ship-have assumed functions once exclusively held by religious authorities.

Especially in recent years, the role of clergy in many American denominations has evolved from high priest to religious authority to counselor. In years gone by, clergy were viewed as holy emissaries, possessing what appeared to believers to be a monopoly on divine intercession. Over time they lost this exclusive domain, becoming more earthly religious authorities than heavenly agents. Though they continued to wield power among the faithful, it was unmistakably a diluted mightiness.

Now clergy in many denominations are but one of many sources congregants turn to for advice and counsel. Many still turn to their clergy in times of trouble, but they can just as easily take their troubles to a marriage counselor, social worker, psychotherapist, or television talk show host Oprah Winfrey. A variety of other secular professions have assumed functions once exclusively held by religious authorities. Doctors, nurses, and hospice workers, among others, have supplanted their role as comforters. A myriad of help dispensing professions-psychiatric social workers, family therapists, marriage counselors, and the like—have sprung up to fill the void. Librarians have also garnered their share of ministerial roles.

HISTORY OF LIBRARY/CLERGY RELATIONSHIP

Before we look at the ministerial functions of librarianship, it may be useful to examine underlying historical explanations of the similarity. Originally librarians were members of religious orders, serving the dual functions of copying and maintaining book collections. Librarians used to be called *scriptores.* Catalogers at the Vatican today who collect and compile catalogs still carry this title, making the inhabitants of these jobs arguably the possessors of one of the oldest continuing job descriptions.

The *scriptorium* where they worked was known to be a busy, active place, but along with the bustle of the work it still exuded a religious aura. "There you will find all that God has sent down to earth from heaven . . . and all the worldly wisdom that has been known to the world in various ages," proclaimed one description of a book copying scene. As late as the 1800s, the library profession continued to draw its practitioners from among the religious.

The practice had become so common that Justin Winsor, the first American Library Association president, stated that he no longer wanted the profession filled with "clergymen whose only merit was that bronchitis was a demerit to their original calling." Rather, he sought "positive individuals who had entered their calling by choice." It is interesting to note Winsor's wording; after discouraging the religiously affiliated from the field, he encouraged others to enter this secular "calling."

LIBRARIANS AS MINISTERS

Many librarians are uncomfortable seeing their work as a divine calling, more often approaching it as a secular activity. And most of the praying librarians engage in at work tends to be for the end of the day. Middle school librarians-the truly sainted among the profession-are known to pray exceptionally hard! Joking aside, a profound commitment to be of assistance can be found in all librarians. So passionate is the drive, it could even be interpreted as a secular manifestation of a religious sentiment.

The desire to be of service has been, and continues to be, a major draw to the profession. Ninety five per cent of librarians said the service orientation of the profession motivated them to become librarians. Another study found that the satisfaction derived by serving people is what new librarians thrive on. "Interacting with the public, dealing with appreciative patrons and seeing people smile" were what new librarians found most fulfilling about the profession. Library historian Christine Pawley claims that, throughout the history of the profession, librarians have been passionate advocates for their institutions, though sometimes their tone borders on being "celebratory," if not "selfcongratulatory."

Service more than money has in the past and continues to draws librarians to the field. As Pawley puts it, "Ideological and emotional involvement is essential in a service occupation, especially one where the financial rewards are poor." Librarians render their service in a secular setting, but the same activity performed in a different setting could be considered religious. One dictionary definition, ministers give service, care, or aid and contribute to people's comfort or happiness. This beautiful description of ministerial service could perfectly apply to librarians. In his major study of American Christian thought, religion scholar Stephen Prothero highlighted the religious dimension to service. American Christians believe God is served in serving man. After all, as he puts it, "Jesus was the supreme illustration of Godly service." No one has claimed that librarians are similarly divine but some may see librarians as the secular, human version of service here on earth.

LIBRARIANS AS ASCETIC, SELF-SACRIFICING MONKS

Considering their conjoined history, it should come as no surprise that librarians, just like monks, are often imagined as impoverished and cloistered. The librarian, just like the monastic, is often pictured toiling away over stacks of books, all the while doing it on behalf of the community. Because of the librarian's contemplative, serene nature and duties that require communing with the world of words and ideas, he or she is imagined to know more than most people. Because librarians remain separated from humanity, they have a more direct line to God, working selflessly for the community and God's sake.

The high moral standards for librarians are apparent through the requirements originally proposed for the profession: "a college degree, a high moral character, an intrinsic sense for order and [what else?] a love for books." Though not richly rewarded in financial terms, librarians have often been pictured as "high-minded" and rich in serenity and peace. To borrow a phrase from columnist David Brooks, for librarians the holy dollar holds no divinity. Of course, as librarians are well aware, the profession has historically been associated with low salaries.

One salary survey from 1928 revealed that hod carriers made almost one-third more than librarians, though catalogers came close by commanding $0.83 per hour salary. Naturally, plumbers beat them all at $1.29 per hour. In what may be one of the best understatements about the library profession, a 1929 report summarized that "improvement in these conditions has not yet reached a point where librarianship may be said to receive proper recognition and compensation." Though improvement of salaries remains a priority, money is not the overriding motivation for those entering the profession.

One study of seasoned librarians noted that, "surprisingly, for a profession as notoriously underpaid as librarianship, not a single respondent mentioned salary" as a negative feature of the profession. Still, librarians did express frustration over the lack of funding for library services. Other studies have shown that for new librarians salary continues to be of lesser importance than sharing in an altruistic profession and making a difference in people's lives. Another contemporary image of the librarian similar to religious hermits-though granted less severe than that of monks-depicts librarians as sexless, strict, and serious.

A ponytailed male librarian joked at a conference: "You know the image. The one with the bun, glasses, sensible shoes. Some librarians take exception to it, but personally, I think the image is great. Just look at me," he said, pointing to his ponytail. "It describes me perfectly." Frequently this image of the librarian is paired with that of the cold, stern, no-nonsense old maid. "I remember the librarian when I was growing up as being so severe, you were afraid to even cough," remembered one elderly patron. A perfect depiction of the sexless ascetic librarian can be seen in the movie *It's a Wonderful Life*. The main character regretfully imagines that his untimely death destines his wife to becoming a librarian.

Music Man shows Marian the Librarian as an uptight spinster dedicated exclusively to the moral uplift of the community. Those who attended Catholic schools in a much earlier era may remember nuns who fit the severe, frightening image so familiar to the old-fashioned librarian stereotype. Since the beginning of the profession, librarians have been depicted as self-sacrificing. Saint Lawrence the Librarian, the Catholic Church's official saint of librarians and archivists, epitomizes the selfless giving of oneself for a grand cause. In 258 BCE, when Roman imperial guards demanded that Lawrence surrender the Church archives, he hid them, refusing to divulge their location. Even after being lashed to an iron grid and dangled over a charcoal fire, he refused to reveal their whereabouts. "I am roasted enough on this side," he is rumored to have said. "Turn me over and eat."

LIBRARIANS AS NOT-SO-SAINTED

Of course librarianship, like all professions, has had its share of both saints and scoundrels. One reason the first ALA president stressed high standards for new entrants to the profession may have been the less-than-virtuous history of those choosing the career. Though librarians are fond of trumpeting their goodness, vice rather than virtue motivated at least some of those involved in the establishment of libraries.

Many ancient libraries were founded by stealing and copying books. When the Alexandrian library was created, the

Ptolomies ordered the confiscation of any books visitors possessed. Though the stated purpose was for making copies for the libraries, sometimes the originals were kept as well. Librarians can take a perverse pride in the fact that one of the stated purposes of collecting the books was to corner the ancient market in intellectual capital. Though less than virtuous, the motivation is an acknowledgment of the power books can convey. When the Medici family established what has been called the first modern public library in 1444, some believe the "public" access was in essence a "vehicle of publicity".

Though it is true the library benefited society, historian Lisa Jardine believes that its establishment added up to a "recognisable programme of self-promotion and public commemoration" for the Medici family name as much as for the public good. Thomas Bentley, the librarian of Cambridge's Trinity College, lost his job in 1728 because of unauthorized extended trips to the Continent.

Despite his claim that his sole motivation was to "study and acquire books"-central activities, he explained, for any librarian to serve his community-he was duly fired. Among the reasons given for the action was that his presence was needed in the library. As was noted in his dismissal, a chief function of a librarian is to be in the library and "watch each library reader, and never let one out of his sight," unfortunately remaining as central functions for the profession ever since.

LIBRARIANS AS RESPECTED PRIESTS

Librarians are not usually referred to with the honourific title of Reverend, but they are a revered population nonetheless. A librarian from the northern portion of the country recounted a minor car accident she had in a rural part of the Deep South. When the young man driving the other car looked at her insurance information, he learned of her place of employment and therefore her profession. "I cain't believe I hit a li—brarian," he said in a classic southern accent. "I'm so sorry," he said sincerely. "I had no idea you were a librarian. I cain't believe what I just did. Shaking his head, he repeated, "I hit a librarian." The southern drawl of that word continued ringing in her ears throughout her trip, as did his deferential tone. "I felt just like a priest or something, the way he acted when he found out what I did."

Both clergy and librarians are imagined to have a direct line to a higher authority. For the religious, the authority may be considered divine, with God bestowing special access, abilities, or knowledge. For the secular, the source more likely derives from the sum total of civilization's written record. As living representations of traditions, librarians inspire reverence because of the long and glorious history of the institution, along with all the accumulated knowledge it represents. Perhaps it is this reverence that explains why trial attorneys favour librarians on their juries.

Not only do they command the respect of their fellow jurors, they also are trusted for their good judgment and intelligence. From the beginning librarians have been among the most educated of the population by virtue of their literacy. The librarian-scribe was often one of the few people in a town who could read and write. So respected was the profession that Jews in ancient times were not allowed to live in a town that did not have a scribe. The deference due librarians bears similarities to that of funeral directors, another profession that bestows upon its members a community's trust, value, and respect.

One funeral director's brochure proclaimed all members of that profession to be philosophers automatically because they "have caught a glimpse of death and the Force... responsible for existence." Librarians are also intimately involved in the Force, but for them it is the Force of Knowledge. Librarians, like funeral directors, come in contact with the dead daily. Though they deal with the corpus of the written word rather than the corpse of a person, perhaps the similarity lends respect to both professions.

At a recent college committee meeting, I was reminded of the respect our profession automatically garners. After introducing myself as the assistant library director, one committee member repeatedly addressed me as "Madam Librarian" throughout the meeting. His tone implied both respect and mocking but revealed what I assumed was an underlying deference for members of my profession.

Other librarians have noted that, upon learning of our occupation, some people immediately try to impress us with their literary and intellectual prowess. "I love the library", "I am a big reader", "I use the library all the time" are all frequent rejoinders from those who learn they are in the presence of a librarian, which brings to mind another similarity between libraries and religious institutions. Surveys respondents frequently overreport both church attendance and library use.

LIBRARIANS AS RECEIVERS OF CONFESSIONS

Both librarians and clergy must be able to keep secrets. Because people come to the library and to a house of worship to seek help with serious personal problems, both institutions must guarantee a high level of confidentiality and trust. Indeed, it could be argued that the scandal experienced within the Catholic Church over child abuse accusations was virulent not only because of the abhorrent charges but also because of the perceived violation of this trust. Alfred Kazin noted with appreciation how librarians protected his privacy: "No matter what I posed to a librarian, no one behind the information desk ever asked me why I needed it." The centrality of patron privacy to librarians is evident in the ALA policy on confidentiality and the Library Bill of Rights. Librarians continue to defend the right of patron privacy, as demonstrated recently by the profession's opposition to the U.S. PATRIOT Act.

LIBRARIANS AS PROPHETS FOR SOCIAL JUSTICE

The goal of Habitat for Humanity is "to solve the nation's housing problem one house at a time." For librarians this goal could be stated as "to improve the condition of humanity one person at a time." Regardless of their religious persuasion, all librarians share a faith: belief in the power of the written word to uplift humanity. Librarians see their role as helping not just individuals but society at large.

Reference librarians are key to this social salvation, for they are the ones on the front lines helping one person at a time.

Perhaps that explains why throughout history librarians have been likened to other helping, healing professions. "Intellectual physicians," "apostles of culture," and "social workers of the mind" have all been used to underscore the librarian's role in improving, uplifting, and healing both the individual and society. This emphasis on societal improvement is evident in such organizations as the ALA Social Responsibilities Round Table.

Biblical prophets also raised their voices to bring justice and righteousness to their societies. Wielding the authority of God's power, they beseeched members of the community to uplift and improve the living conditions of their day. The power associated with these prophets is not usually seen among librarians, who have historically been pictured as meek and mild. Yet in an interesting twist to the classic image of librarians, recent depictions show librarians as zealous and even violent protectors of good against evil. Batgirl, a librarian by profession, is the classic comic book heroine battling evil and fighting crime with information power.

The television show *Buffy the Vampire Slayer* also depicts a librarian fighting injustice and standing on the side of right. The controversy over the U.S. PATRIOT Act, resulting in librarians being dubbed "hysterical Ruby Ridge–type radicals," has added to this image as defenders of the public good. An Iraqi librarian even became a cultural hero in her country for valiantly rescuing 30,000 books just days before the library was burned in 2003. Two children's books, *The Librarian of Basra* and *Alia's Mission: Saving the Books of Iraq,* recount her triumphant work. As a character in one of these books proclaims, "It's not necessary to see through walls or fly or have any superpowers to be a real-life superhero." Evidently being a librarian and acting on one's professional convictions is heroic enough.

LIBRARIANS AS SEERS AND GURUS

On a recent trip to Miami, the Dalai Lama drew a crowd of several thousand, many of whom had come seeking divine guidance. One such seeker shouted from the audience, "What is one's purpose on earth?" The Dalai Lama lowered his head and silently reflected for several seconds. He slowly raised his head, studied the face of the questioner, waited dramatically, then stated flatly, "I don't know." Perhaps the Dalai Lama and the questioner should stop by their local library to find their answers. William Cole once said, "The library is the place where I ask questions I can't get answers to." Susan Allen Toth put it, "When I enter a library... I still have a reassuring sense that it is going to tell me all I need to know."

The Episcopal Book of Common Prayer, God is the one unto whom all hearts are open, all desires known, and from whom no secrets are hid. But Harvey Cox noted that people act as if the stock market, rather than God, knows the deepest secrets and darkest desires of our heart. Just like God and the stock market, librarians must possess—or at least appear to possess-the gift of divination and the ability to see into an individual's soul. When perplexed, people have been turning to the library as long as there have been libraries. In 1690, politician and diplomat Sir William Temple wrote that people sought out books as guides, searching for a hand "pointing out the straight upon the road," as well as resolving their doubts.

Even Henry VIII consulted the books of his rapidly growing library to seek guidance and justification for his political and personal actions. Many patrons approach the reference librarian with a confession. Because their inability to use the library is a source of embarrassment and shame, their stated desire may not match their actual need. "Where is the fiction section?" may mean "I'm looking for Stephen King's latest novel." "I need something on U.S. history" translates into "My son needs to do a report on the Spanish-American War." The art of the reference interview, as taught in basic library science classes, enables librarians to rephrase the question tactfully and reexamine the patron until the hidden truth is revealed.

As library historian Matthew Battles puts it, "Readers read books; librarians read readers." This process can be challenging when the patron needs a book on economic history, but when the need is for information on impotence, spouse abuse, or personal bankruptcy, skills far beyond those taught in school are required. When dealing with these types of problems librarians, like men and women of the cloth, must "reach down into the soul" of the person standing before them and help. Ancient high priests had an advantage contemporary librarians and clergy lack.

As library activists put it:

* In days of old, seers entered a trance state and then informed anxious seekers . . . whether this was an auspicious time to begin a journey, get married or start a war. The prophets of Israel repaired to the desert and then returned to announce whether Yahweh was feeling benevolent or wrathful.

Because their apparent source was the divine, priests supposedly had an inside track to God's omniscience. After peering into a person's heart and knowing their deepest secrets and darkest desires, holy seers could tap holy information. But today psychology and intuition are about all librarians have to work with to know what people really need. Even catalogers who work behind the library scene are expected to possess this ability to see into the soul of others. They must do so only from the printed word in front of them. The Dewey decimal classification rules instruct librarians that if a book can be classified under two subjects, catalogers should "determine the author's purpose" before issuing a call number.

LIBRARIANS AS MAGICIANS

Magic and religion have had a complex, at times competitive relationship. Magic is the art of producing a desired result through the use of techniques such as incantations to control supernatural forces. Some would argue that this perfectly describes religious rituals as well. The Bible frequently inveighs against sorcerers, soothsayers, those who cast out spells and work marvels, warning that these are "abhorrent practices" performed by other people and other nations.

At the same time, ancient high priests supervised sacrificial offerings and performed acts that surely would have appeared as magic to members of those other nations. Exactly what made one act religious and the other magical is a fascinating topic but beyond the scope of this book. What is relevant to the library context, however, is the unknown, secret element of both magic and religious practice. Audience members are not privy to all the information possessed by priests or magicians. Words are intoned in secret, hands waved and items manipulated by way of knowledge and techniques not generally shared by all.

In the same way, librarians produce information that can seem magical-and even miraculous-to library users. My cousin remembered seeing a silly television show years ago about a New York socialite forced to live on a farm, but she could not remember the name of the show. It took me approximately five minutes to locate the name of the show for her-*Green Acres*. "God, I don't know how you do that!" she said with such enthusiasm that I did not know if she meant "God" as in "Gosh" or was thinking of me as divine at that moment. Other librarians have their own stories of patrons dazzled and amazed by their ability to produce information seemingly out of thin air.

To many it can appear "as if sprung from the brow of Zeus," says Matthew Battles. This is especially true now that so much library information is produced from a computer rather than a printed book. Library users approach the librarian, state what they need, and, poof, from the depth of the machine emerges exactly what they seek. After producing five articles in less than a minute for one patron, Library of Congress reference librarian Thomas Mann explained, "We can show people things they don't ask for." Library historian Arthur Bostwick reminds us that the modern public library was founded on the dual purpose of finding a reader for every book on its shelves and a book for every reader in a community.

"In all cases it should bring book and reader together." "There is a book for every person," claims Ranganathan's Five Laws of Librarianship. Implicit in this union of person and book is an understanding that, by applying a bit of library magic, the librarian can bring about a desired result. Perhaps no supernatural forces will be controlled, but every person touched by her magic will gain access to the universe within the walls of a library.

LIBRARIANS AS TEACHERS

Just like in Jesus's parable, librarians prefer to teach library users to fish rather than serve up fish on demand. Library literature constantly reminds librarians that their instructional role is central to the profession. Along with giving patrons the answers they seek, they are encouraged to teach users the research process so they can learn to find information on their own. A *New York Times* article on the changing role of library research, many librarians have found that the new reliance on electronic resources makes their role as guides more important than ever.

Though librarians originally feared that technology would replace them, they now see themselves needed more than ever because of the difficulty of conducting research electronically. As one pundit put it, information overload is an important new emotional, social, and political problem. "Almost anybody can *add* information. The difficult question is how to *reduce* it." Library users being overwhelmed by vast library resources is nothing new.

EXPLAINING LIBRARIAN/CLERGY SIMILARITIES

PERSONALITIES

Besides the religion-like functions of the library profession, similarities can also be found in the personalities of clergy and librarians. One online career planning tool, the preferred personality types and skills for members of the clergy are nearly identical to those optimum for librarians. The Myers-Briggs Type Indicator, a well-known personality test that categorizes people according to stated preferences in thinking and perceiving, provides an excellent demonstration of similarities between the two. Generally acknowledged as the most popular self-insight psychological test in use today, at least a million people take Myers-Briggs every year. By assigning people to one of sixteen different categories, and combining four subscale ratings for each, people can be categorized according to their supposed personality traits. As the chart on this page reveals, librarians and clergy have remarkably similar test results.

Clergy	Librarians
INFJ	INFJ
INTJ	INTJ
ENFP	INFP

Notes: (Traits represented by abbreviations; E = Extraversion; I = Introversion; S = Sensing; N = Intuition; T = Thinking; F = Feeling; J = Judging; P = Perceiving)

Similarly, the online career planning tool Bridges Choices Planner helps students compare their skills to those needed in various occupations. By ranking basic skills such as mathematics and reading comprehension from 1 to 5, individuals can easily plot their own abilities with different careers. As with the Myers-Briggs instrument, the planner on this page shows many similarities between the required abilities for clergy and librarians.

Basic Skill	Clergy	Librarians
Reading comprehension	level 5	level 5
Active listening	level 5	level 4
Writing	level 5	level 4
Speaking	level 5	level 4
Critical thinking	level 4	level 3
Active learning	level 4	level 4
Mathematics	level 1	level 1
Science	level 1	level 1

In his 1950 classic *The Lonely Crowd*, sociologist David Riesman identified three major personality types, which religion professor Stephen Prothero summarized as "tradition-directed people who follow rules written by ancestors; inner-directed people who follow rules laid down by their parents; and other-directed people willing to bend the rules in order to win the approval of their peers." One would assume that both religiously inclined individuals and librarians would qualify for the first personality grouping.

Religion by its very nature includes dictates for living that have been inherited from ancestors. Librarians not only serve as the recipients of past traditions but are governed by cataloging and classification rules that accompany them. Though it is difficult to pinpoint personality traits common among librarians, similar characteristics can be identified among well-known librarians of the past. According to library historian Dee Garrison, Melvil Dewey, the father of modern library science, exhibited "the classic obsessive compulsive personality: order, perfectionism, detail, intellectualization and commitment to work." Many librarians will squirm reading these symptoms, for many of these negativesounding traits are helpful, and even required, to perform certain functions of the profession.

In summarizing the life of the first librarian of the Library of the British Museum, library historian Matthew Battles claims that Antonio Panizzi's progressive ideology and esoteric knowledge prefigured him for a career as a librarian. Panizzi was also a devotee of secret societies, liberal politics, and mysticism, but whether these are librarian predilections is open to debate. Hypothesizing about librarian traits from history may be a shaky way to unearth the personality characteristics of the profession. One can, however, assume that most librarians today are readers.

A survey by the National Endowment for the Arts sheds light on this population group:

* People who read for pleasure [and one would assume librarians figure largely among this group] are many times more likely than those who don't to visit museums and attend musical performances, almost three times as likely to perform volunteer and charity work, and almost twice as likely to attend sporting events. Readers, in other words, are active, while nonreaders—more than half the population—have settled into apathy.

BACKGROUNDS AND DEMOGRAPHICS

Along with certain personality traits, demographic factors may explain the librarian/clergy similarity. The preponderance of women among the profession has been much discussed and need not be rehashed here. Still, it is interesting to note that, like libraries, organized religion is and has been heavily women dominated. As early as 1691, Cotton Mather complained that "there are far more godly women in the world than there are godly men." One study of American religious history found that in "virtually every religious group in every era in U.S. history, women have outnumbered men."

Since Melvil Dewey's original call for women in the profession, librarianship has been dominated by the "fairer sex." In an oft-quoted lecture on the qualifications of librarians, Dewey said librarians should possess such virtues as "a clear head and a good heart. When I look into the future, I am inclined to think that most men who will achieve this greatness will be women." Female dominance was not a given in the early years of U.S. librarianship, especially because of concerns about women's potential "questionable health."

"The inability of many 'woman assistants' to do the year's work without breaking down, even when a month's vacation is allowed, brings up the question of the employment of women in libraries," reported a 1929 survey of the American Public Library. Potential concerns were, however, allayed by the medical officer of the New York Public Library, who found that woman assistants were in better physical condition than the men.

Another population group that seems to be over represented among librarians is the "religiously related," though I am the first to admit that my experience working in a religion-affiliated library may have skewed my observation. But even in my various secular work settings, such as public libraries and publicly funded college libraries, I found many librarians who were former clergy, nuns, or others who had considered joining the clergy sometime in their lives.

Likewise, the number of librarians in these settings who

were spouses or children of clergy appeared to far exceed that found in other professions, though, again, I stress that this is simply conjecture. Eager library science students should take note: I believe this subject is ripe for research. There also seems to be a preponderance of librarians deeply fascinated by the topic of religion. Though of course people from all walks of life could be called "religious" and show an interest in the subject, in my experience librarians are especially attracted to religious study. No studies I know of provide the religious breakdown of the profession, though the racial/ethnic demographics of American librarians is well documented.

Because of the tradition of separation of church and state, statistics on religious affiliations are not routinely asked by the government and tend to be avoided by professional associations. When I tried combining statistics from the ALA and the National Jewish Population Survey, it revealed a guesstimate that 16 per cent of U.S. professional librarians are Jewish, though they constitute less than three per cent of the country's population. Additional statistical analysis is needed to verify this estimate and determine the percentages of other religious traditions within the field.

RELIGIOUS INFLUENCE ON LIBRARIANS

Without surveying librarians for their religious affiliations, it is difficult to surmise what, if any, influence religion has had on librarians throughout history. It is true that the very first issue of the *American Library Journal* reported the journal's founders to have "an *intense faith* in the future of libraries." Tidbits from history reveal that religion played a large part in the lives of many of these individuals. Harvard College, which "began its life as library," was founded by Puritan minister John Harvard.

Reflecting his theological interest, three-quarters of the books were on theology, and the library remained a theological library for at least a century. John Cotton Dana, who led a successful attempt to democratize the electoral machinery of the ALA, was a "religious radical". Ranganathan's classification scheme emerged from his background in mathematics and belief in Hindu mysticism, both of which led him to attempt to connect separate pieces in a systematic way. Religious influences can be seen in Melvil Dewey, who came upon the idea for his famous classification system while in church and referred to the education of librarians as "the suburbs of the holy field."

The Victorian demand of duty to God and work, along with a sense of right and duty to authority, was a forceful part of his upbringing. A near-death experience early in life led to what later became an evangelical call for time-saving efficiency and a devotion to the cause of simplified spelling. Dewey was such a crusader against drink and tobacco that a friend remarked, "It is not enough for you to do your duty, but you must make others, as far as possible, see your duty in the same light."

Judith Krug, director of ALA's Office for Intellectual Freedom, partially attributes her tireless efforts in the field of intellectual freedom to her Jewish roots. Though she did not consciously choose her field of interest because she was Jewish, "the values I hold dear made me ideal for this job." And from whence did she develop these values? "From my mother—a Jewish mother, of course—and from my Jewish background, which made it a perfect fit." Another well-known librarian influenced by the Jewish religion was Golda Meir, who worked at the Milwaukee Public Library before becoming prime minister of Israel. The influence her earlier profession had on her political success can only be guessed at.

RELIGION-LIKE LIBRARIANSHIP VALUES

Similarities can be found not only in the personalities of librarians and members of the clergy but in the values that undergird both professions. A case could be made that librarians subscribe to the basic tenets of liberal Protestantism, whether they are adherents of this faith or not. Librarians will recognize the following underlying beliefs of this faith, summarized by Stephen Prothero. For comparison, these basic tenets are juxtaposed with Ranganathan's Five Laws of Librarianship:

Liberal Protestantism	Ranganathan's Five Laws
The goodness of humanity	Every reader his book
Inevitability of progress	Books are for use
	Save the time of the user
Necessity of good works	Every book its reader
Immanence of God in nature, culture, and the human heart	Library is a growing organism

In much of this book I discuss how each of these values is supported and enhanced by library usage. It can be noted briefly here that librarians embrace a belief in human goodness every time they strive to connect a person with a book. Likewise, progress is implied, either through personal self-improvement or societal uplift, through reading. Belief in the necessity of good works is evident in librarians' mission to service. Finally, viewing the library as a growing organism-perhaps not as God but as a living force that will continue in the future as it has in the past-can be seen as a expression of the immanence of the divine.

9

Librarians and Libraries Organize Chaos

Public speaking is feared by more people than death. Comedian Jerry Seinfeld quips, "That means that at a funeral, people would rather be *in* the coffin than delivering the eulogy." But there is another fear people dread even more than speechmaking, snakes, spiders, and heights combined. People fear chaos. "People want order to be able to control their lives," observes David Brooks. Especially when we are surrounded with so much material wealth, stuff can suffocate us.

According to market research, the three most important amenities desired by home buyers are extra counter space in the kitchen, storage space in the basement, and plenty of closets, all features that help organize the possessions of everyday living—or at least that give the appearance of an organized life. In a critique of American consumption patterns, Brooks noted how products allow people to spin tales about themselves. By purchasing a Sears utility closet, one imagines attaining that elusive fantasy of an organized and therefore orderly and peaceful life.

Home builders feed the fantasy by providing places to put the Cuisinart, the winter sweaters, the extra rolls of toilet paper. But organizing possessions is just part of the human need to control chaos. Especially in the electronic era, people drown in the sea of information, unable to drop anchor on any solid ground. The deluge of information ironically results in no information. As I noted in an object about the drawbacks of library technology, "It was better to have four books on genealogy than 1,736,388 hits on Google." With so much information available, the sea of bits and bytes engulfs you. It is revealing that, along with the "information highway" metaphor, surfing the ocean is often used to characterize the limitless Internet.

The ocean can seem an uncontrollable force—the ultimate expression of disorder. Water and chaos were prominent features in ancient myths. Evidence of creation and deluge myths have been found inscribed on Sumerian cuneiform tablets of 2600 BCE. In polytheistic religions, ocean gods were imagined as all-powerful behemoths reigning over the seas. Lake gods, on the other hand, were rarely imagined. Indeed, lakes often seem peaceful and calming because their boundaries are visible. Limited and controlled by the shore, there is no need to imagine a comforting presence for a lake. And so it can be for knowledge and existence.

TAMING CHAOS BY NAMING AND ORGANIZING

In many religions God is and has the power to make something out of nothing and nothing out of something. God accomplishes this divine creation through the twin activities of naming and organizing. God, as divine omnipotence, is and has the capacity to define what is real. God can create the boundaries to calm and control chaos, thereby turning an ocean into a lake. The Hebrew bible, which forms the basis of Judaism, Christianity, and Islam, begins with God creating and bringing order out of chaos.

By classifying and naming, existence comes into being—first separating light from darkness, day from night, water from sky and dry land. Even man gets separated from woman. When a couple learns they are going to have a baby, they immediately begin the enjoyable tasks of selecting a name and determining the sex of the baby. Both activities help create the child in the mind of the parents as it forms in the body of the mother. Mentally giving their offspring a name and placing that individual in the category of either male or female are the first steps to arranging them in the universe of humanity.

According to anthropologist Mary Douglas, all ethnic groups create and enforce social boundaries by separating, dividing, and classifying. The culprit leading people to categorize is not necessarily animosity towards others. Rather, a sense of order results through the religious stories, rituals, traditions, and myths people tell to distinguish themselves from other people. Americans excel at organizing. Many believe our ability to organize to "get the job done" characterizes the national personality.

LIBRARY AS ORGANIZED WISDOM

In ancient biblical tradition, God was depicted as wisdom. According to Proverbs, wisdom was the first of God's creations and "was there when He set the heavens into place and when He fixed the foundations of the earth". Like the Greek goddess Sophia, wisdom was likened to a woman walking among the people, bringing enlightenment to those open to receiving her insights. Wisdom was frequently referred to not merely in the modern sense of information but rather as a way of thinking, the search for meaning and order, the path to right living.

Wisdom could be found in texts, but it was also found in people, sages, nature, folktales, and experience. It is easy to imagine such a divine being as—or at least living in—the library. In an imaginative rethinking of how people think of God, Harvey Cox describes how the concept of the stock market—which he refers as The Market—has been attributed to comprehensive wisdom. The Market, like God, is able to determine human needs.

Humans can tap divine revelation by learning to read when The Market is apprehensive, relieved, nervous, or jubilant. Much like Cox's reimagining of God as the stock market, one could substitute The Library for The Market. Though no one library could claim to contain all human knowledge, at least until the advent of the Internet libraries were the only place one could find the accumulated wisdom of mankind.

Indeed, one could construct a syllogism:

* God is all wisdom.

* All wisdom is the accumulated knowledge of the library.
* Therefore, God is the accumulated knowledge of the library.

If God is wisdom, the library has surely been his exclusive domicile throughout history. As early as the year 800 CE, the library was described as the place where you find all that God has sent down to earth from heaven, containing all the worldly wisdom that has been made known to the world in various ages. When he is in the stacks of a library, says library historian Matthew Battles, "I have the impression that its volumes contain the entirety of human experience. That they make not a model for, but a model of the universe." But the library is more than simply the warehouse of wisdom–it is the organized, systematic world of knowledge.

Since the beginning of the written word libraries have not only collected knowledge but structured and therefore controlled access to it. One frequent symbol of this imagined organized universe was, and continues to be, the tree. Among the various religious symbols and metaphors representing the chaotic universe at peace—a rainbow, a sunset, a ray of light shining through clouds—the tree represents the orderly, organized, knowable universe. With branches outstretched, the tree shows how life stretches upward while remaining grounded.

With its height, the tree conveys an overarching hierarchy. Like a rainbow it joins sky and earth, but it continues to develop and grow without losing its shape. The tree conveys a continuing dialectic of one piece forming from what exists below—knowledge and the universe unfolding in an orderly, systematic fashion. Unlike the overwhelming, limitless ocean of information, the tree of knowledge is finite and easily grasped. Even children can climb a tree, exploring from branch to branch, slowly ascending at their own speed rather than being engulfed and drowning.

CATALOGUING AND CLASSIFYING

Librarians are intimately familiar with the tree as a metaphor for controlling the chaos of the world of information.

But the library tree is not imagined as a maple or oak; rather, the tree of library knowledge is the standardized classification system. No matter which system is used–the Dewey decimal classification, Library of Congress, or National Library of Medicine system–all libraries employ a treelike system to control the chaos of knowledge. Those learning cataloging according to the Dewey decimal classification system are taught the essence of this simple but profound plan.

"The subject matter and notation are hierarchical, so that what is true of a given whole is true of all its parts," explains the preface to the abridged Dewey classification system. A book classifier preparing to use the decimal schedule must understand the principle of hierarchy: each entry is a part of and governed by every entry superior to it. "To understand the full meaning and force of 621.3888, must view it as a part of 621.388, which in turn is a part of 621.38, which is a part of 621.3, which is a part of 621, which is a part of 620, which is a part of 600."

Catalogers take those "miserable things"—square pegs of knowledge that don't fit anywhere—and place them carefully into a grand, organized scheme. Without this placement and structure, the knowledge being classified would never be found, its existence obliterated. Bookstores are good examples of generalized groupings of information that lack the tender touch of the cataloger. A study that compared bookstore and library arrangements concluded that "libraries are systemically superior to bookstores."

Though many requests for information can be found in bookstores, libraries do a better job of leading to specific information needs. Especially effective, noted the study, was the fact that libraries "are arranged to allow patrons to locate information effectively and to utilize that information from one library to the next." One of the best ways to see the importance of the classification and cataloging functions of libraries is to look at the Internet, where these functions are by and large missing. Frustration runs rampant when searching the Web for specific information.

Indeed, many people come to the library after hours of fruitless computer searching on their own. I remember a student asking me for information on an obscure American poet. As I headed to the closest computer, she grabbed my arm and physically restrained me. "No", she insisted. "I have already used the computer at home and couldn't find anything. I need something besides that". The information I located for her-which she gratefully acknowledged as exactly what she needed-was obtained through the computer. I had, however, been able to locate and retrieve it thanks to the organized system of periodical databases created by librarians.

Few realise the power librarians wield when they categorize and classify information. Mothers and fathers, gods and God create by naming and organizing. Librarians do so as well when they order knowledge. Rather than fashion their world with clay or earth, librarian-gods breathe life into existence by providing structure. A world of random objects without context is nothing more than uncontrolled chaos. But librarians create connections by naming knowledge and placing it within an organized scheme.

Becoming intellectual demiurges, librarians act as supernatural beings, creating and fashioning the world of knowledge as they please. Librarians' vital but frequently unacknowledged systematic approach to knowledge was brought home to me when my husband's picture appeared in a regional health magazine. Having benefited from a new surgical procedure, he literally became its poster child when the magazine included his picture in an object about the benefits of the operation. A friend noticed his photo, cut it out, and sent it to me. She did so, however, without noting any bibliographic information about the source of the magazine.

No librarian would have sent such a photo without at least some bibliographic reference. With our intrinsic sense of order, librarians know that in the future this unidentified photo will be like an isolated tidbit. Without any context to the person or source, in no time this picture will be unidentifiable and useless. It will be as if it never existed. What makes the librarian's power even more awesome is the comprehensive nature of the organized system libraries have created. Thanks to the voluntary standardization librarians have assumed for their craft, a higher authority legitimizes their pronouncements.

National, even global submission is demanded to their proclamations of placement within this comprehensive system. "Class here," "Class elsewhere," "See," or "See also," declares the voice from on high, directing their actions as they place every bit of knowledge in its place within the universe. The actions—and thinking processes—of millions of library users forever are affected by their work. Like gods, catalogers look into people's hearts. If a book has two subjects, they must determine the author's purpose. A Phoenix schedule gives librarians the power to destroy by retiring subject headings no longer needed. Librarians can mercilessly obliterate entire bodies of knowledge from the face of the earth and from civilization entirely.

HISTORICAL ROLE OF LIBRARIANS AS KNOWLEDGE ORGANIZERS

Librarians have been representing the universe of knowledge through organized systems for thousands of years. As Matthew Battles reports in his excellent library history, as far back as the seventh century BCE the 25,000-tablet library in the city of Nineveh was highly organized. In this ancient library, the tablets were tied together, marked with a label, and cataloged with the titles of works and the number of tablets in the group.

The famous Alexandrian library was also systematically organized, with scroll tags including author and title information. Because the scrolls would not stand up on shelves, they were heaped together into precarious piles. When one scroll was removed, the others would all need to be shifted, so only a kind of generalized order was possible. Eventually cards were employed to help locate physical items. Because the original cards were playing cards, the contents of those much-beloved card catalogs approximated the size and shape of a deck of cards. Before the days of Melvil Dewey, the order of library books was primarily location-based, with books shelved by accession number.

As late as 1929, one survey of U.S. libraries found that arranging books on the shelves in the order received was still in vogue, especially in small libraries. The card catalog provided numerical information about the book's location. The innovation for which Dewey is most often credited is arranging books both by location and subject. He "married two systems—one epistemological and one numerical." The numbers in his system were not just designations of a shelving system; they also showed the relationships among the fields of knowledge. This idea, which Dewey claims came to him while sitting in church, was to place all human knowledge into "ten tight holes."

Within his system, any book's "subject matter and the notation are hierarchical; so that what is true of a given whole is true of all its parts." Dewey believed that virtually any given set of objects could be classified by placing together objects with certain characteristics in common and separating them from objects without these characteristics. At the very core of this system is the belief that the disorganized, confusing tumult of our world can be tamed and transformed into an orderly, systematic arrangement. When imagined within such a framework, where a book is classified reveals not simply information about its contents but also its place within the hierarchy of all human knowledge.

Implicit in this arrangement is a belief in the rational order of the universe. "The schedules are developed according to logical principles." The logic of the universe is reflected in the logic of the system. Classification of books assumes an idealized overarching structure of knowledge and truth. Catalogers using the Dewey decimal classification system are urged "to make correct decisions" concerning the placement of material with the scheme, assuming there is a right way to classify not only that one book but the world at large.

As Battles puts it, one could imagine that rearranging the books on the shelves "would reveal mysteries of the universe, a sacred logos tantamount to the secret name of God." Whether godly or not, providing order to knowledge remains a vital service. Antonio Panizzi, nineteenth-century librarian at the

British Museum and one of the founders of modern cataloging, saw the very future of humankind at stake through the act of cataloging. The library catalog, he claimed, is "more than a list, more even than a guide to knowledge: it could be the means to transform society itself." By providing what he described as easy access to the works of a library collection, the catalog throws open the doors of knowledge. The humble card catalog provided "the poor student the same means of indulging his learned curiosity . . . as the richest man in the kingdom."

ORGANIZING KNOWLEDGE: MISSION IMPOSSIBLE

Lest we get carried away with these notions of librarian organizing power, the limits of this ability must be admitted. First and foremost among the obstacles is the rate of information pouring forth. Knowledge is doubling at the rate of 100 per cent every twenty months. "What you know now will be obsolete by Christmas," claims Frank Ogden. Especially with the Internet, the flow of information is overwhelming. The idea that this tidal wave of inundating information can be harnessed, captured, and controlled for even a millisecond seems quaint at best.

Foolhardy seems a more apt description. Though librarians have made valiant attempts to treat Internet sites like books—describing and organizing them with controlled vocabulary and structured hierarchies-to date these efforts have met with limited success. Though technological developments may improve such efforts in the future, for the time being it does not appear that librarians will be able to locate, describe, categorize, and arrange the totality of electronic information.

Some have argued that librarians never have been able to control the flow of printed information because the task of organizing knowledge itself is impossible. As anyone who has pursued academic study recently knows, belief in a purely rationalistic, ordered universe with universally applicable rules and standards is distinctly out of fashion. One of the only definite laws governing the postmodern academic world is that there are no definite laws. Belief in an overarching reality-one that purports to be the same for everyone regardless of perspective or personal stance—is no longer accepted on face value. When rationalist thought itself is called into question, belief that any structure can adequately organize knowledge also grows suspect.

If there is nothing absolutely the same for all, how can one organizing principle universally apply? Attempting to organize all of human knowledge into ten categories-or even ten thousand categories-seems a futile, even impossible task. According to this theory, if every person on earth has a legitimate way of viewing and organizing the world, there must be at least that many organizing systems. Even without calling the process of organizing knowledge into question, it could be argued that libraries never managed the task adequately in the first place.

Even the revered Dewey decimal classification system is decided by a committee. After the publication of the fifteenth edition of this national classification standard, the editors solicited criticism so that successive editors could "bring out the perfect book." Despite their optimism, no future editions have claimed perfection. And perfect or not, many classification systems are simply too complicated for many libraries. Dewey's first decimal classification system, published in 1873. By 1894 it had grown but was too complicated for many small libraries.

An abridged edition was published that year to remedy the problem, but recurring complaints insisted that even the shortened version had become "too detailed and complex for the small collections for which they were intended." Though most libraries struggle to contain the information on their shelves through some organizational structure, the effort can be daunting. Just like the scrolls heaped into precarious piles, some small and large libraries today manage to maintain "only a kind of generalized order."

Despite these limitations on their ability to organize knowledge, a perception still exists that libraries manage the task well enough. With the "generalized order" they offer, library users can locate the information they are seeking or stumble upon that which they need but did not know existed. Linda Weltner believed that having access to the library's world wisdom was all she needed in life. "As long as I can read, nothing human is beyond my understanding." Anne Lamott extolled the virtues of stumbling upon unknown treasures. She credits her mother with teaching her how to use a library when she was a child.

"If you insist on having a destination when you come into a library, you're shortchanging yourself." Instead, to find small miracles and truth, one must "wander, letting the book take you where it will." Lamott poetically described the pleasures that await one who follows this advice. Finding and reading library books "is like breathing fresh ocean air," or eating homegrown tomatoes. In the space between words, in the margins, she found the "juicy moments of life and spirit and friendship."

10

Librarians and Libraries Give Immortality

Tibetan monks are required to spend one week sleeping in a cemetery. Christians must put ashes on their foreheads once a year to remind them that they are but dust. Jews annually recite in unison the most horrific list of disasters that could possibly befall them.

Religions force these rituals upon their adherents because of the inherent tendency in all of us to forget our mortality. As theologian Harvey Cox noted, by ensconcing themselves into gated communities and purchasing expensive health insurance policies and retirement plans, people fool themselves into thinking they are beyond mortal danger; even so, disaster can strike at any moment.

Often it takes a life-threatening illness or other tragedy to awaken the fragility of life. A woman who worked with cancer survivors came to see the world divided into two kinds of people: those who have been in contact with their own fragility and those who have not. Those who face death squarely in the face never leave the experience unchanged. Religion is vital in helping people confront their mortality.

For some an everlasting heaven triumphing over the finality of life is imagined and embraced. Other religions offer faith, works, and grace as hoped-for avenues to everlasting life. Still others imagine their good deeds on earth and loved ones' memories granting them eternal satisfaction. Along with these religious paths to immortality, secular pathways also lead to an imagined life beyond life.

CONSTANT CHANGE AND NEED FOR PERMANENCE

As librarians and library users are painfully aware, the rate of technological change is unprecedented. So fast are things changing that in 2003 an international "Accelerating Change Conference" was held to examine, not the changes swirling about us, but only their dizzying pace. One of the frightening questions addressed at the meeting was whether runaway technological advances are outstripping our ability to even comprehend them. The reasons behind this oxymoronic "permanent change" are varied.

Consumerism may be one culprit. Alexis de Tocqueville noted that Americans seemed spiritually adrift in their land of plenty because they did not know how to orient their lives. "Material goods are the sole fixed point, the sole incontestable value amidst the uncertainty of all things." Henry Steele Commager believes the excessive nervous vitality of Americans is the reason for our sense of instability and rootlessness. There is an "air of impermanence to almost everything Americans undertook." I once observed an example of confusion wrought by constant consumer product impermanence when I overheard an old man muttering to himself in the grocery store cereal aisle: "Darn it, where is it? Where is it?" he repeated as a mantra.

After several minutes of frustrated searching, he shouted "Damn it, they don't make Toasted Frosties anymore!" He walloped his cart with a punishing blow, sending it spinning into the Quaker Cream of Wheat cartons. I understood his frustration all too well. The discontinuation of the onepound can of Maxwell House Colombian Supreme has produced my own incidents of shopping cart assault. Missing cereals and coffee cans are not the only victims of capitalism's continuing changes. "No manufacturing plan is permanent... against competition," claims urbanist W. Rae Douglas.

"No system of transportation withstands disruptive change, no corporation is immune to takeover or bankruptcy." Jobs are no longer permanent. Neighbours come and go. With the rate of divorce, even spouses can seem impermanent fixtures in people's lives. When times are unsettled as they arenow, people long to identify with something that will not disappear or change before their very eyes.

The constant, frenetic pace of change reminds us that nothing lasts. No product, service, place, or thing is guaranteed to be here in the future. And, of course, neither will we. And so we long to unite with something or some institution that will stay the same, or at least give the appearance of permanence in our very impermanent world. The problem is that any institution that manages to remain unchanged will become obsolete and be replaced—because institutions, just like people, must adapt to survive. Yet those very adaptations that guarantee an institution's continuation weaken its historical continuity.

A precarious balancing act is required for any institution to provide a sense of permanence in this temporary world. Organizations that survive must constantly change to remain relevant, while appearing to be unchanged in the process. There are two institutions that appear unchanging as they change, that remain current in people's lives while continually blending past, present, and future. Religion is one. Libraries are the other. Standing like a rock of ages, a mighty fortress, both libraries and religions appear to live on without changing, though in truth both experience change continually.

INSTITUTIONS AS LIVING ORGANISMS

For an institution to appear to live on indefinitely, it must appear to be alive. Religious institutions liken their communities to living beings. The Catholic Church refers to the community of the faithful as the Body of Christ, reflecting the ability of the populace to keep on living beyond the life of any one individual member. Jews call themselves Israel in the plural, not referring to the country but rather to the idea of a continuing community. Libraries, too, have been seen as living institutions.

"The library is a growing organism," states Law Five of Ranganathan's basic guideposts for the modern library. Library historian Matthew Battles poetically sees the library breathing, "exhaling at the start of the term and inhaling at the end, when the books fly back." Perhaps it is this sense of a living, breathing library, alive with some indescribable life force, that draws people to the library.

People are attracted to libraries for reasons far more profound than simply needing information. Many come to immerse themselves in the library's energy. Inspiration–from the Latin term for "to breathe"–seems to occur within the library walls. Simply sitting among the books, one feels immersed in an aura of living spirit. One reason libraries feel so alive is that each book on the shelf seems animated. Books have often been referred to as living beings, described through references to birth, death, and life everlasting. "A book is as close to a living thing as you could get without being one," said Bill Harley.

Books are sometimes imagined as living people transformed into paper. Ralph Waldo Emerson felt surrounded by "many hundreds of dear friends" when in a library. Alfred Kazin said that every time he was in a library, press into every single mind right there on the open shelves." Writers often refer to the act of writing as giving birth. "The joy of working on a manuscript," claims publisher-turned-agent Betsy Lerner "is not unlike the midwife's joy." At the other end of the life span, unwanted library donations are often called "book graveyards."

Jews historically had, and continue to observe, strict regulations governing the disposal of sacred books. A special graveyard for books called the Genizah provides a permanent resting place for books no longer needed. They must be buried because "the contents of books go to heaven like the soul." But the fact that religious institutions and libraries seem to be alive and contain living beings does not in and of itself grant immortality.

To convey a sense of life everlasting effectively, the institution must also provide a way for the individual to feel a part of the collapsed past, present, and future of the institutional thread. Religions and libraries attain this through communal memory, history, and the printed word.

COMMUNAL MEMORY

Shared communal memory is like a river, said Bill Moyers, "dynamic and changing, bearing the heritage of the past to water the fields of the present." The waters of the river feel comforting and refreshing. When one stands in the river of religious heritage, one feels immortally immersed in and surrounded by the past, present, and future. Religious traditions constantly repeat their shared history—their communal memory-to enable the faithful to stand in the past and present simultaneously. By enacting the remembered history through narrative, myth, and ritual, people are encouraged to bring to mind and identify with those who came before them. The word "remember" is used on 169 occasions in the Bible.

Even God is told to remember and can be reprimanded should he fail to do so. Psalm 44 scolds God for not remembering, suggesting that he may have fallen asleep on the job. For religious communal memory to seem legitimate, it must be steeped in history. The regalia of the clergy, décor of the house of worship, and religious artifacts convey the historical message of the religion. The words repeated in the liturgy, holiday rituals, and communal myths all bring to mind imagined historical moments. Life cycle events frequently evoke the memories of those who came before, bringing a sense of continuity and history to everyday lives. But remembering is just the first part of the process.

The person approaching a tradition does not do so objectively but comes with a desire to join with it, own it-"commune with it," to use the religious term. By doing so, people can vicariously gain a sense of immortality. To believers, this unending tradition seems somehow good, complete, and holy. Enmeshing oneself in a historical tradition seems melding into an aspect of God. The narrative history of a people can take on divine characteristics.

Even if parts of the remembered history are tragic, violent, humiliating, and better left unremembered, participating in the continuing historical experience can feel like a holy experience. The act of remembering may even strengthen the religion itself. "To belong to a tradition is to become part of a chain, and the longer the chain, the more secure each individual link." Obviously libraries capture and preserve communal memory; indeed, it is their reason for being.

As Goethe put it, libraries serve as "the memory of mankind." The library does not require 169 biblical commandments to remember. Preserving the written record of civilization is the purpose of the institution's existence: "Libraries should provide materials and information presenting all points of view on current and historical issues," proclaims of the ALA's Library Bill of Rights. In fulfilling this directive, libraries are preserving the memory of the past and present for generations to come. In his book on library history, Matthew Battles speaks of a "universal library," imagined as the totality of knowledge gathered, organized, and preserved for all time.

Longfellow said libraries contain it all, both "the ruins of an antique world, and the glories of a modern one." The Internet has been referred to as the sea of information. Others may see it as the river of knowledge, evoking the same image Moyers used to describe a religious tradition. Francis Lieber saw libraries not as the water but as "the bridges over which civilization travels from generation to generation." When imagined this way, the act of checking out a book from a library can be seen as dipping into or crossing over the river of accumulated, historical knowledge.

Whether one checks out *The Prince* from the 1500s or *Men Are from Mars, Women Are from Venus*, library users interact daily with the accumulated record of humankind. Cognizant of their special role in preserving printed history, librarians have a special reverence for history. I saw a demonstration of this one day when I visited the journalism office at my college, hoping to make a copy of an early issue of the school newspaper. I asked the editor if I could borrow the original-the only known copy-and take it to my office. "Normally I would say no," he said. "But since you are a librarian, it's okay."

IMMORTALITY THROUGH WORDS AND BOOKS

As the newspaper editor knew, librarians revere the written word. They do so because words pack a powerful punch. "In the beginning was the Word, and the Word was with God, and the Word was God," begins the New Testament's Gospel of John. In traditional Judaism even the name of God cannot be written because of its power; it is shown in print only as an abbreviation. Even in secular language, some words are associated with great power. The word "abracadabra" is the rendered version of a religious incantation, which supposedly created matter with its utterance. Simply saying certain words can bring disaster. "Break a leg" is offered to actors rather than "Good luck" because the latter said aloud will evoke long-sleeping theater spirits.

Especially when committed to paper and gathered together as a book, words become potent. Christian and Jewish worship services ritually incorporate books. In the central part of Jewish service, the Torah is brought from the ark and shared among the people. Catholic worship services include a Bible with other holy religious objects as part of the religious ritual. By incorporating books into their worship, religions demonstrate the central place of their revered written text. Here, they announce to the congregants, is the written story of our people and our faith.

Individuals, too, use books to record and proclaim their own stories and faith. Intellectual historian Warren Susman noted that historians cannot claim for themselves a monopoly on history: "Everyman–and every woman and child–is in some fundamental sense his own historian." This desire to record one's presence on earth leads some to carve their initials on trees, drives others to press their hands into soft sidewalk cement, and inspires some to create or sell books. Books, according to John Milton, are a means to achieving "life beyond life."

A character in a Jonathan Rosen novel contemplated this immortal aspect of books when planning his suicide. After gathering the drugs and scotch that would accomplish the task, "he stood for a moment in front of the vast bookshelf that formed one whole wall of his study. There were many books in several languages. Poetry. Novels. Histories. Prayer books. Somehow, they would have to speak for him. Part of him would live in those books."

According to writer/publisher/agent Betsy Lerner, immortality affects not just authors but others in the book trade:

> * Just as the author hopes for immortality through publication of his book, most people in publishing hope to work on a book that touches people, entertains them, enlightens them, or changes them, a book that shapes the national dialogue or becomes a part of the lexicon. Publishing people, along with the author, believe that a book can still be a force of nature.

The desire to conquer immortality drives others to embark on the arduous task of writing a book, acknowledged by authors everywhere as a laborious undertaking.

"Writing a book is horrible," said George Orwell's:

> * An exhausting struggle, like a long bout of some painful illness. One would never undertake such a thing if one were not driven by some demon whom one can neither resist nor understand. For all one knows that demon is simply the same instinct that makes a baby squall for attention.

While in the process of producing a manuscript, philosopher and cultural critic Walter Benjamin claimed the book was more important than he was. Whether driven by demons or inspired by angels, people continue to write books. Imagining a descendant generations from now discovering one's writing in a dusty attic is a heavenly thought. Likewise, eternal damnation could be defined as seeing one's magnum opus buried under chicken bones in the garbage can. And so we write books. Bill Moyers reported his delight when asked to write a book.

"Few things flatter a broadcast journalist more than the prospect of even the briefest half-life between hard covers," he says. "Like ice, we melt into the milieu. We're lucky if someday a grandchild or a graduate student is curious about what we once said. Writing a book allows you to connect the dots between past and present."

LIBRARY IMMORTALITY

If writing a book offers an author a "half-life" of perceived immortality, getting that book onto the library shelf seems to extend the period eternally. It is imagined that the words of one's soul, if not one's soul itself, can live forever in a library. Schopenhauer clarified Goethe's characterization of the library as "the *papered* memorial of mankind". Authors clamor to have their words included among these library papers. Librarians are well aware of the pull of the library shelves. Imagining generations to come reading their words drives authors to dump their manuscripts and self-published books on libraries.

Others empty their attics and basements of once-beloved books, offering up these overstuffed Burdine's bags and brimming Tide boxes in the hopes of winning a place on a library shelf. Here on a library bookshelf their words will live on everlasting. The library offers a link with an anonymous public that no attic can match. The appeal of the library stacks was demonstrated to me firsthand when, as a college library director, I instituted a formal ceremony called "Barry Authors Reception."

Any college faculty, student, or staff who had penned a book during the year would be allowed to ceremoniously present their book to the library. Throughout my thirty-year library career, few other programmes or services have been as successful. During the wine and cheese reception that followed, I was thanked repeatedly for initiating this programme. As one faculty member put it, "People don't realise what goes into writing a book." Evidently the creation of the authors programme had tapped an unrecognized fact that, as Battles put it, "inclusion in the library represents a landmark in a literary life."

A study of the history of the Charleston Library Society revealed that local churches had donated books about their religious congregation to the local library, even though the materials were freely available to parishioners through the church. Apparently the presence of these books in the library legitimized their organization.

As described in a short story by Max Beerbohm, one fictionalized author even made a deal with the devil to live eternally in hell in exchange for an opportunity to visit the British Library's reading room one hundred years later to see his books amid the library collection. Ironically, Battles mused in the pages of his book on library history where it would be in the library. "Where will I find the book you are reading now?" Will it be "history, memoir, or fiction?" I must confess to having the same thoughts as I typed this work. It is one thing to have one's book written and published, but the pinnacle of publishing lies in securing the placement of one's words on a library shelf.

IMMORTAL CITATIONS

Having your words placed for perpetuity on the library shelves is only part of the process. For future generations to find one's noble words, access to these writings must be organized, classified, located, and retrieved. Here it should be mentioned that citing a source in MLA format, though it may seem devilish work to the nascent student, is actually a heavenly act. When done right, the "Works Cited" page grants immortality to both the writer of the paper and the source cited. Citations are so important that they have even been credited with creating the Internet as we know it today. The desire to improve the existing academic system of citation led Tim Berners-Lee to create the World Wide Web.

The desire to reverse the process led Larry Page and Sergey Brin to create what later became Google. As John Battelle notes in *Wired* magazine, "The needle that threads these efforts together—the practice of pointing to other people's work . . . is the citation." Citations are critical because, as both religions and librarians acknowledge, great truths can emerge from the written word, but so can dire consequences from misstatements and falsehoods. To protect against this, both religions and libraries employed elaborate systems of quality control.

In religions this was attained through rules governing the copying, distribution, public reading, and treatment of holy texts. Libraries relied on the sacred system of citations. Anthropologists have found that in oral, nonliterate cultures a person's word takes on special meaning. Examples of the importance of the spoken word can be seen in the frequent instances in the Bible of bestowing a blessing or swearing an oath. So important was the latter that men uttered them, not by raising their hand, but by placing it on their genitals, graphically demonstrating that future generations would abide by what was being sworn. When literacy spread, the reliance on accuracy remained an important concern. The scribes who copied manuscripts were under strict requirements to duplicate their material accurately.

During the Middle Ages Christian monasteries, which were the setting for *scriptoria*, instituted elaborate quality control measures to certify the fidelity of text copies. A *precentor* who also sometimes served as the librarian supervised the copying of texts. The *precentor* would choose and present a text to each scribe. If the scribe refused to copy the selected text, the *precentor* could "deprive him of his wine." After being copied, texts were examined by at least one and sometimes two correctors. Because accurate copying required extreme concentration, after silent reading became the norm around the ninth century scribes were required to work in silence. When they needed a certain book for reference in their work, they pantomimed hand signals.

Placing the hands on the head in the shape of a crown referred to King David and meant "pass the psalter." "I need the missal" was communicated by making the sign of the cross. In those pre–politically correct times, scratching the body like a dog referred to pagan works. St. Jerome required his scribes to transmit a formula attributed to St. Ireneus that threatened "the Lord Jesus Christ in His glorious Second Coming, will come to... compare what you have copied against the original." Sometimes scribes were allowed to sign their work and add a personal expression in the text. "So be it," "Peace," and "Amen" were written. Often the words "Thank goodness it's finished!" were added.

Modern-day librarians will be heartened to learn that one scribe ended his manuscript with the complaint that his work was fruitless since nobody reads books today. Judaism established elaborate rules for the public reading of the Torah to ensure its accurate recitation, with many of these ritually incorporated into the current worship service. In some synagogues on Monday, Thursday, and Saturday when the Torah is read aloud, a *gabbai* must be present to look over the reader's shoulder to guarantee that every syllable is chanted correctly. As nervous bar and bat mitzvah boys and girls know, the *gabbai* is obligated to correct the slightest mispronunciation made by the chanter.

When the Torah is lifted from the lectern to be wrapped and returned to the ark, it is mandatory that several columns of text be shown to the public, ensuring that everyone in the congregation can see the text personally. The Talmud, a massive compilation of biblical commentary, meticulously credits the source of quotations and arguments. A heavenly reward is promised to those who cite accurately. "One who recalls a teaching in the name of its author brings redemption to the world," claims Rabbi Elazar in the name of Rabbi Haninha. Naturally, the quote includes a citation.

Footnotes are the *gabbais* of the academic world, or, as Princeton University historian Anthony Grafton put it, the high whine of the dentist's drill inflicting random but necessary pain. Though students may experience footnotes as a pain in a different part of their anatomy, Grafton says they absolutely matter. "Arguments... stride forward or totter backward" solely through these funny little asterisks and elevated numbers. Writer Mary Gordon knows firsthand the power of citations to bring the dead back to life.

As she recounts in the biography of her father, *Shadow Man*, by following citations to his writing, Gordon was able to reconstruct the life of her father, who died when she was seven. As she recounts dramatically, with the help of tireless librarians and the interlibrary loan system she was able to locate the "anti-Semitic articles and pretentious literary journalism" her father wrote. Ultimately her search of archives and libraries revealed the "bombshell truth" that her father was not the Catholic Harvard graduate of family lore but rather a Jewish high school dropout from Vilva, Lithuania.

LIMITS TO LIBRARY IMMORTALITY

Mary Gordon was lucky. She was able to assemble the facts of her father's life because Brown University still had a copy of *Hot Dog: A Monthly for Regular Fellows* in a cardboard box. This archive, along with an elaborate trail of indexes, microfilm, and print resources, enabled her to piece together the story of her father's life. But as Nicholson Baker made painfully obvious in his scorching book on library print withdrawals, *Double Fold,* fewer and fewer libraries are able to maintain print collections at the levels they once did. Given shrinking libraries and electronic resources, immorality through the library shelves may be more myth than reality.

When pressed, most people-and librarians-will acknowledge the cruel fact that even the vast holdings of all the libraries of the world cannot contain and preserve the complete written record of human knowledge. But as with religious practice, we wink about ourselves and continue as if we had not recognized that fact. Librarians are aware of the extensive winking that is needed. Because publishers cannot afford to warehouse lowdemand books, they rely on libraries to provide access to these titles.

Calvin Trillin quipped that the life of a book is somewhere between that of milk and yogurt. Libraries are, however, less and less able to fill the need for permanent book conservatories. Administrators with budgetary control over libraries believe, like so many people, that "everything is on the Internet." Therefore, they are reluctant to commit scarce funds to construct buildings to house substantial print collections. Without the promise of more space, librarians must painfully withdraw existing materials in order to make space for the new.

Though collection weeding has long been a standard of basic librarianship, the pressure to withdraw, withdraw, withdraw to make room for the new has grown to what in some libraries is crisis level. What happens to all of those weeded books is always a powder keg problem for librarians. "I sneak out to the dumpster at night," confesses one librarian, "so no one will see me throwing away books." Many librarians resort to this tactic, knowing that the sight of unused, discarded books can inflame the public like little else.

Perhaps the sight of books in trash cans affects the soul because of the imagined end of the immortality of the books' authors. Or maybe the thought of a useful resource going to waste, like the sin of throwing away food, is troubling. Boxes of college textbooks are dragged from apartment to condo to house for no known reason. The same reluctance to toss a book means that librarians must either conceal the fact that they discard books or try to find them loving homes, which sometimes is easier for unwanted cats than books. After all, if the books were useful in the first place, the library would not be getting rid of them. Because books are physical objects, they are also perishable.

Mold, deterioration, fires, disintegration all threaten the immortality of the library book. Though an idealized library triumphing over time, space, and mold spores is imagined, it is just that—an ideal rather than a reality. Even in those libraries where space and physical deterioration are not problems, ever-changing electronic resources make the permanent recording of information challenging. Ownership versus access remains a central concern for libraries. Given the unstable corporate environment of many information providers, librarians are rightfully skeptical about entrusting the commercial world with their sacred duty to maintain and preserve their written legacy.

But in some subject areas there are few realistic alternatives. The print versions may be exorbitantly priced. Space may not be available to house these resources, even if they can be physically acquired. Accelerating price increases also keep libraries from purchasing and owning many key titles. The sheer amount of information being produced limits the ability of libraries to adequately acquire, organize, preserve, and disseminate the written knowledge of civilization.

Thomas Cahill said, "History proves nothing because it contains everything." Referring to religions' directives to remember, Harvey Cox observes that "to remember everything is to remember nothing in particular. One would be better off to forget." Underscoring the problem of too much information coming in, Jorge Luis Borges wrote a story titled "Funes el Memorioso" in which a riding accident causes a man to remember every minute of every day, all conversation and all his thoughts, even remembering remembering.

The act of remembering comes to consume him, leaving time for nothing but remembering. And so it seems that libraries must spend an inordinate amount of time, effort, and money controlling the overwhelming production of information. Still, in reality, they do accomplish this task. Though by no means a perfect system, libraries are still able to acquire books, organize them, share information about their holdings, and provide the materials to those who need them. If they didn't, no one would lug boxes of books to donate them to libraries.

Whether real or imagined, authors still seek their immortality through library shelves, and they do so for good reason. Libraries provide them, if not immortality, at least longevity beyond their physical years on earth. An analysis of the 1800s Charleston library collection found several books still on the shelf today. And when the temples and royal palaces of the Tigris and Euphrates valleys were excavated, "Houses of Tablets" were found attached to these ancient religious and governmental seats of power. Even with the ability to ensure their legacies through pyramids and mummification, the written word still was seen as one of the best methods to provide life everlasting.

11

Librarians and Libraries Uplift Individuals and Society

Ask any librarian what is the first thing they hear when approached at the reference desk, and they will tell you it is a confession. "It's been a long time since I have used a library," or "I know I should know how to do this," are murmured by library users before they dare even ask where the restroom is. Haughty librarians of yore exploited these penitential offerings by following each confession with a sneer, which may explain why libraries used to be so quiet. People were too ashamed to speak. But now modern librarians indoctrinated in the dogma of customer service immediately absolve the guilt-ridden with an understanding, "Of course," or "That's okay," resulting in a more relaxed, if noisier, library patron.

One need not even come to the library to suffer library guilt. Like religious service attendance, survey respondents consistently exaggerate library usage. If all the people who say they attend church "daily or weekly" and those who report using their local libraries "often or frequently" actually did so, both institutions would exceed the "Maximum Capacity" signs posted in their buildings several times over. People may enter the library already feeling guilty, but librarians inadvertently perpetuate their shame through the ubiquitous "READ" posters plastered on library walls.

In these graven images, bigger-than-life movie icons sit serenely with books splayed upon their laps and dispense beatific smiles to all who pass below. Where churches place a picture of Jesus and the Bible, libraries display a photo of Britney Spears with her copy of *Harry Potter and the Sorcerer's Stone*. "PRAY," demands the felt banner on the wall in a church. "READ," implores Oprah Winfrey in the reference room. One different fourletter word spells the path to salvation in both locales.

"Develop Yourself" is a recent variation on this theme. From superimposed photos of friendly faces and camera film on posters and bookmarks, the implied message is that personal fulfilment will come in the library through exposure so to speak-to books. Operating in a secular environment, librarians may not realise the subtle religious message of these campaigns. But there is no doubt about it; the "READ" campaigns are part of an underlying redemptive mission that is nothing short of the secular version of evangelization. The word "evangelical" comes from the Greek word for the good news of the Gospel.

The primary obligation of evangelicals is to save as many souls as possible. Librarians also want to spread the "good news," but theirs is not the word of the Gospel but rather the words of all gospels. Or, more specifically, they bring the gospel of words. Fundamental to librarians is the assumption that one will be "delivered" to a better place through reading. The use of guilt in libraries to encourage individual self-improvement is part of a larger redefinition of the concept of sin and salvation.

Organized religions once held the monopoly on redeeming individuals from sin by employing what Harvard theologian Harvey Cox dubbed "moral terrorism." Religious institutions would frighten people with threats of everlasting punishment.

Attending church, eating certain food, performing ritual acts, uttering magical incantations could bring blessed redemption, while failing to do these things or doing them incorrectly could spell dire consequences. No matter what someone had done wrong, religion was the authority setting and enforcing the rules for salvation.

RETHINKING SIN AND SALVATION

The traditional understanding of sin and salvation no longer characterizes the mind-set of most people; a different version has arisen in its place. Indeed, one minister quipped that, "when we use words 'redemption' or 'conversion,' people think we're talking about bonds." Belief that sinners will be eternally damned, or that they must repent in order to be eternally redeemed, describes the religious outlook of few Americans. According to surveys of religious thought, among all major American religions the hell-and-damnation sense of sin no longer holds sway.

"Any religion that demands you believe in human depravity won't make it in America," concluded religion scholar Alan Wolfe. The de-emphasis of sin and salvation has not been limited to the major liberal Protestant and Jewish denominations. Even fundamental denominations have changed their stance on this once-central doctrine. One survey found that only 16 per cent of Southern Baptist Church sermons included the classic image of fire and damnation. The Lord to whom most Americans, including many born-again Christians, turn today rarely gets angry.

Within American Christianity, the formerly central traditional teachings about heaven and hell, sin and the devil have lost their saliency for many and fallen away entirely for others. Within American Catholicism there has been a noted decrease in the rite of confession. Indicative of the changed perspective, even the Catholic Church has softened its fire-and-brimstone vision of hell. Pope John Paul II referred to hell as a symbol of spiritual isolation. Rather than flames and demons with tridents, the pontiff equated eternal damnation with the pain of realizing that one is cut off from what makes life livable.

FREE CHOICE

Fear of eternal damnation may no longer influence religious believers as it once did, but a deeply held belief in individual free choice remains strong. Central to the belief system of most Americans is the notion that an individual can alter his or her station in life—be it financially or morally—by what they do here and now. The idea of predestined fate holds little attraction within American thought. The bootstraps mentality stressing individual control is alive and well. As the ad slogan puts it, "Just Do It." Those who "do it" will be rewarded, those who don't have only themselves to blame.

Cox reminds us that Christianity and Judaism insist that human beings are created with the freedom to examine their lives and, with the help of God, mend their ways. Though we are bound by our time, place, and genetic inheritance, what we do is up to us. Americans fervently believe that individuals are responsible for their actions and will be rewarded or punished because of them. It is up to us—and not a religious organization—to improve ourselves. Replacing the former belief in divine intercession, self-fulfilment and self-improvement are now the true avenues to contemporary salvation.

As Northwestern University media professor Laura Kipnis puts it, "Once brimstone and hellfire kept populations in line, now there's sudsy self-improvement." The contemporary emphasis on self-improvement brings to mind the biblical Hebrew word for sin, *chait,* which was derived from the archery term meaning to miss the mark. Human frailty was understood as the individual striving for perfection but not quite hitting the target straight on every time. Today both the creation of the target and one's progress towards it are up to each person.

PSYCHOLOGY OF SIN

When the pope refers to hell as a symbol of spiritual isolation rather than a fiery pit, obviously a profound change in the religious imagination is at work. Like the pope, people have retreated from the former notion of sin, adopting instead nonjudgmental language of wrongdoing. Religion experts call this transformation the "psychologizing" of American religion. People today seek "well-being" rather than deliverance. Cultural historian Jackson Lears sees the trend as a switch from Protestantism to secularity, salvation to self-realization.

Wolfe sees it as blending the themes of personal recovery with spiritual regeneration. Ever since the days of Freud there has been a complicated relationship between religion and psychology, at times complementing and at times competing with each other. Throughout most of history, the prescription for curing what we now call psychological problems would have been ascetic prayer, fasting, or religious commitment. But now the source of salvation would more likely be found by making an appointment with a mental health counselor or checking out the latest Wayne Dyer book.

Many theologians have speculated on the reasons for the demise of the previously held doctrine of hell and damnation. The Enlightenment, widespread literacy, increased education, and technological and scientific advances have been proposed as reasons that fear of eternal punishment no longer inspires people's behaviour. One hypothesis posits that fewer and fewer Catholics go to confession because they are not as inclined to think of themselves as sinners in the first place.

PERVASIVE GUILT

Ironically, though the pathway to paradise appears easier, its attainment is more complicated. When salvation required believing in a saving Jesus and going to church on Sunday, the actions one needed to perform were straight-forward. But now both the actions and thoughts needed to bring deliverance are murkier. Some believe that this amorphous sense of sin has heightened people's underlying sense of guilt. We aren't quite sure what we should be doing but are vaguely aware that, whatever it is, we're not doing it enough, or correctly, or with the appropriate mind-set.

The result is pervasive guilt, which can be manifested in a variety of ways, including an overwhelming desire to confess. Scholars of religion and popular culture have noted an increased fascination with public television confessions, taking the form of debasing, self-effacing revelations on talk shows. Why someone would come before a nationally televised audience to reveal one's infidelity with their mother-in-law seems incomprehensible.

But when seen as a substitution for the rite of confession, it seems at least a bit more understandable, though still bizarre. Likewise, there has been an explosion of television shows that elicit a confession of guilt after intense, belabored police interrogations. The popularity of *The Apprentice* with the thunderous Donald Trump pronouncing the death sentence of "You're fired!" may be seen as a secularized version of a divine decree of damnation, eternally banishing the sinner from the corporate Garden of Eden.

REDEFINED CONTEMPORARY SINS

We no longer worry about saving our eternal souls. Rather, generalized anxiety about obesity, health, love, and money bedevil us today. The American obsession with fat is a prime example of the conflagration of consumer culture, therapeutic remedies, and reimagined sin. Fat has been demonized, claims Dinitia Smith in a *New York Times* article. Historians and cultural critics are beginning to see that the American obsession with obesity is based less on science and more on morality. We feel guilty about the abundance of food and excesses of our consumer culture. Some social critics claim dieting fads are a new kind of puritanism, with dieting becoming a way to express virtue and self-control.

Not only is dieting virtuous but, in the extreme, abstaining from food becomes The Way to ultimate salvation. "Control of your destiny lies in your spoon," proclaims one diet ad. An exercise programme promises that by transforming your body you can transform your life. "Only a layer of cellulite stands between and bliss," observes Judith Wright, author of *There Must Be More Than This*. "If only I could get thin," the average overweight American thinks, "then I'll feel good about myself." And feeling good about oneself is required for—if not the definition of—personal salvation.

Closely allied to the cult of thinness is the contemporary obsession with health. Rather than praying, fasting, belonging, or believing, the blessing of a long, prosperous, happy life is attainable through diet and exercise. To ensure longevity you must eat the right foods, avoid "sinful" temptations, and take care of your body. People used to go to Mass to ward off evil; now they eat tofu and work out at the gym. Certain foods have even taken on an aura of sanctity, while others convey depravity.

"Sinful" rich desserts are guaranteed to bring punishment later, while abstinence ensures a blessed long life. David Brooks noted a near-holy feeling in a Whole Food grocery store where he fantasized setting off alarms by smuggling in a bag of Doritos. The state of medical care is an excellent example of how people become simultaneously more empowered and more confused by relocating both the path to salvation and salvation itself from organized religion to the individual. Individuals are urged to take responsibility for their own health. Not only must you get a second opinion on any medical treatment, but with the "help" of television ads and commercials you must also select your own doctor, decide which hospital is best for you, know which drug to ask your doctor about, and inform yourself about treatment options. Love with just the right person will also bring about personal salvation.

As Kipnis explains, "Just as earlier strivers and pilgrims sought grace and afterlife salvation... we subjugate ourselves . . . hoping for similar payoffs here on earth: the salvation of a better relationship." The attainment of financial success operates as the yardstick of judgement for many people. "Success means what salvation once meant," claims religion historian Peter Gardella. "Millions who practice no organized religion call themselves to regular internal judgments on the basis of their standards for success." In our consumer culture, money—or the lack thereof—often becomes the measure of an individual's success.

Much like obesity, poverty becomes a moral failing because the individual is imagined to be in control. If you fail to attain the expected level of financial well-being—the right kind of house, car, or college for your kid—surely you must have done something wrong. Even those who refuse to equate their balance sheet with personal success can create other demons with which they torture themselves. Gardella admitted that the production of published books became his own driving ambition. Though he was not proud of it, it became the measure of that man.

As a fellow writer, I well understand his torment. My obsessive preoccupation with this writing project is wreaking havoc with my family, but I am bedeviled to persevere. Perhaps this is what demonic possession feels like. When sin was governed by organized religion, the path to personal redemption was more straightforward; what an individual needed to do, say, or believe was known. Whether they did so or not, at least the road to redemption was obvious. With salvation more a psychological failing, and guilt pervasive, the way out seems less clear. Many seek the mental health route and consult a shrink. Others go on yet another diet or join yet another health club. Some, however, head to the library as their source of salvation.

LIBRARIES AND SALVATION

The previous brief detour into redefined sin may seem far removed from librarianship, but it is not. Librarians receive confessions of guilt continually. Exactly what the library penitent feels guilty about, and what exculpatory expression is expected from the librarian, is not clear. Perhaps library users, like many in our society, are plagued with a generalized guilt because of this diffused religious path to salvation. They know they should be improving themselves but are not sure exactly how to go about it. They feel guilt at their ignorance yet at the same time vaguely aware that the library holds the source of their salvation.

It is hard to think of any difficulty plaguing a human being that could not be lessened with the help of a reference librarian. With the plethora of selfhelp books in existence, most likely a book has been written to help people deal with whatever troubles them, whether the problem be real or imagined. The library is an excellent resource for self-improvement, self-fulfilment, and self-help of all types. Of course, the library is not the only place people seek help.

An entire self-help industry including psychologists, counselors, and mental health services has emerged, each promising their own version of deliverance. Likewise, the consumer market has been more than willing to fill the void by developing aids in the form of books, videos, and products that offer salvation. All of these stand ready to redeem and save people, albeit at a price. Libraries are unique dispensers of self-help because library assistance is free. Libraries are one of the last bastions of free service. At no cost–if they return their materials on time–library users from the affluent suburban housewife to the homeless drug addict can seek self-improvement without laying out even one penny.

The dispensation of library self-help takes various forms: books, online resources, support group meeting space, social service directories, information and referral services. Regardless of the form or format, all library help is free. But beyond providing self-improvement in the form of self-help guidance, libraries also support those with more philosophical questions. When people need answers to those eternal questions–the reason for suffering, the meaning of life, why bad things happen to good people and *vice versa*–the library stands ready to help. Books can provide the deep questions and the answers people have asked and answered for thousands of years.

Even when the search to answers leads nowhere, solace may be found in knowing that throughout human history people have grappled–sometimes unsuccessfully—with the same questions. But at least they tried. One book not only offered philosophical pondering, it even spared a life. While being held captive by an accused killer, hostage Ashley Smith began reading from the book *The Purpose-Driven Life*, concentrating on the section that discusses how life is meant to be spent in service to God and others. Her captor asked her to read it again and shortly thereafter set her free.

LIBRARY "FLASHLIGHT" GOD

Those with a religious predilection may see these life-affirming aspects of library usage in spiritual terms. For them, a library-dwelling God could be imagined as the divine force that helps one find his or her proper destination. God as Guide, God as Light, or God as The Way all point to this side of the divine that helps people go from the dark place where they are to a brighter spot. In his survey of contemporary religious thought, Wolfe found this notion so prevalent he came to call it the "flashlight" God, the sense that the divine gently guides people towards their individual salvation.

By having their paths illuminated, people are provided at least one way towards their individual courses of action. If God is a "flashlight", for many the source of that shining light is knowledge. It is no coincidence that the scientific revolution was called the Enlightenment, for knowledge and understanding have often been referred to as illumination. When Lady Wisdom walked among the people she carried a torch, bringing light to humanity. Libraries are both the source and storehouse of enlightened knowledge.

LIBRARY GOD AS THE FORCE

Along with God as a Guide, others imagine God as the source of individual initiative. "God helps those who help themselves" approximates this expression of this divinity. Not only does God guide, God also inspires. "God only gives you what you can handle" is familiar to many. Or, as Nietzsche put it, "What does not kill me, makes me stronger." In contemporary theology, God becomes the *ability* to handle what is put before you, the spiritual presence that inspires and supports action. For Christians this aspect of holiness can be found in the Holy Spirit or grace; for Jews, the Torah; for Eastern religions, karma.

Described succinctly in popular theology as "God is a verb," the ability to deal with life's triumphs and failures is imagined as divinely inspired, if not divine itself. Moviegoers will recognize the *Star Wars* sort of God: "May the force be with you" is a prayer of inspiration and hope. Poet Ruth Brin beautifully describes this divine force as "the strength of life, the power moving us to do good, the source of love." Especially important for American society, which emphasizes the individual over community, God can also be seen as the force that brings people together. Feminists have seized on this and added feminine images to describe God.

"Life force," "breath of life," "wellspring" are all meant to capture the pervasiveness and beauty of this aspect of God. The walk-in-the-woods God found in nature, usually engendered as Mother Nature, borders on this divine notion, but the Force is more than the sum total of the natural world. Obviously God as Force, or God as Guide, can be located within the library setting. God can be seen not only as the force that brought a person to the library but also that which sustains them to continue searching. God can also be seen as that which guides people in their quest, whether they are seeking help to lose weight, find a better job, or discover the ultimate meaning of life.

As Mark Edmundson notes in a book aptly titled *Why Read?* the world is full of "farmers, tradesmen and trades women, mechanics, lawyers, and, up to some crucial moment, layabouts, who've used books to turn their lives around." Of course, for those on outright religious journeys, the library can also be a natural setting for exploring the relational aspect of God. But no matter what subject brings someone to the library, the process of using a library can be seen as a secularized version of salvation. The person comes into the library because of some acknowledged lack or need, believing the answer will be found there. In the Bible people were invited: "Seek and ye shall find; knock and the door will be opened to you". A similar invitation could be made at the library. Here you will find what you need, with the help of an imagined or believed divine presence, possibly serving as a guide or force to help in your search.

HISTORY OF LIBRARY SALVATION

Well before the self-actualization, self-help era began in the 1960s, libraries had taken as their mission the lofty goal of improving individuals and society. For librarians deliverance to the promised land of enlightenment can be achieved through reading. The word "library" derives from the Latin *liber,* meaning free. American slaves were forbidden from learning to read because of the power that came with the act. Roman slaves were allowed to learn practical subjects such as math and engineering but were forbidden from reading literature, history, or philosophy for fear learning these "liberal" arts might inspire them to unite and rise up.

Librarians are obviously aware of reading's power. Literacy initiatives have been, and continue to form, a key aspect of library service. Going beyond simply encouraging reading, librarians have historically encouraged what they considered to be "right" reading. Bemoaning the public's demand for stories, librarians at one time strenuously tried to divert them to "worthier" forms of reading. Scorning popular demand, they waged what has been dubbed the "fiction wars." Librarians tried to shape patron tastes from the "cheap and tawdry reading of novels and newspapers towards a redeeming vision of high literary culture."

This uplifting-through-right-reading philosophy continued at least into the 1970s when I was in library school. Heated debates about the appropriateness of Nancy Drew mysteries in the children's section exemplified the continuing belief that "wrong reading" can bring dire consequences. The effort to uplift the masses with right reading actually predates the establishment of American public libraries. Library historian Matthew Battles dates the beginning of the saving mission of libraries to the nineteenth century, when librarians' role went from being "largely custodial to that of caregiver." As keeper of the books—their original mission—the librarian saw his primary duties as "counting the books, fetching them, and . . . returning them to the shelves."

By the turn of the century, though, librarians had become "the information social workers of modernity." Also called "intellectual physicians," librarians would diagnose and treat readers' aberrations. One of the first efforts to uplift the masses in America began in the 1900s and was a precursor to the public library movement in this country. Librarians would deliver a "home library"–consisting of a cupboard stuffed with as few as twenty books—to rural readers and settlement houses. A librarian or volunteer would deposit the chest of books and return in a week or so to collect them, discuss them, and offer another set of selections.

The acknowledged power and respect that emanated from this piece of furniture was at times palpable. This shrine to knowledge was often positioned proudly in people's living rooms or parlors. One writer even likened the bookcase to "an altar filling the room with the glow of books." The aim of these home libraries, which eventually became bookmobiles, was undeniably social uplift. As Battles put it, home libraries and the settlement-house outreach programme were designed "to bring untutored masses into the circle of readers, to set them on a path to right reading that would lead from adventure stories to travel to tales to geography, history and the trades."

In the early 1900s, libraries also played a key role in "Americanizing" newly arrived immigrants to this country. One 1920 Carnegie study of Americanization efforts at the time found that "amongst all the institutions in American life, libraries had achieved the best results." Librarians will be proud to know that libraries managed this task without "de-racializing, divesting, remodeling or otherwise 'Americanizing' immigrants; rather, libraries interested immigrants in American life by first interesting themselves in the life of the immigrant." Branch libraries were especially successful in serving as community centers for immigrant neighbourhoods.

Along with supplying books in foreign languages and providing easy-to-read books, libraries also conducted English classes and assisted users in obtaining citizenship. Beyond these services, some of which are still offered today, libraries also served their immigrant populations with innovative programmes. In his survey of historical library service to immigrants, Eric Novotny found reports of librarians writing condolence letters, naming babies, and loaning soap to "ragged and dirty school children."

Novotny grants that an undercurrent of paternalism can be found in some library efforts on behalf of immigrants, but he concluded that librarians generally provided services with "sympathy and understanding" and "an appreciation for the contributions immigrants made to American life." Along with intellectual and moral uplift, libraries promised their patrons other virtues as well. Melvil Dewey hoped an efficiently run library would promote "efficiency in readers' lives." John Stuart Mill believed libraries offered happiness, repose, and reflection.

Charles Dickens "was confident libraries would teach that capital and labour are not opposed, but mutually dependent and mutually supporting." More recently, Philadelphia Judge Matthew D. Carrafiello issued an injunction blocking that city from reducing library hours because such an action would pose irreparable harm to the city. "The local library is one of the strongest antidotes to the drug culture and violence affecting Philadelphia's children," claimed Judge Carrafiello.

LIBRARIES AND SOCIETAL REDEMPTION

But societal improvement was also central to the library saving mission, albeit usually one person at a time. Though most think of sin as an individual's actions against God, societal improvement depends on the actions of individuals, as a simple story can suggest: After living through the horrors of the holocaust and watching his best friend die of cancer, an old man angrily cries to God: "There is so much pain and anguish in the world, God. Why don't you send help?" "I did send help," God answers. "I sent you." Individuals organized and inspired through religions have been instrumental in bringing about societal justice.

Many credit Christianity with abolishing slavery in America. The Catholic social movement was instrumental in the establishment of a myriad of social programmes of the Progressive era. The Jewish prophetic tradition of social justice is credited with correcting countless injustices throughout history. In *The Gifts of the Jews,* Thomas Cahill credits Judaism for awakening civilization to the possibility that tomorrow can be different, and therefore better than today. Especially after the Enlightenment and scientific revolution, there existed a sense that everything–both personal and communal–was redeemable through knowledge.

By combining individual freedom and scientific progress, communal salvation seemed within reach. As Francis Bacon put it, even the fall of Adam and Eve was reversible through "thought and its products." Like religion, libraries have been active proponents of social change. Libraries have been intimately involved in freeing individuals, even if it was freeing only their minds through knowledge and books.

In compiling a book of essays on the library vision of the future, editor Gregg Sapp noted the library profession's "passionate commitment to democracy and societal improvement." The essays also revealed that the library's role in educating and improving society formed a common theme in futuristic writings. The possibility of societal improvement can be seen as a foundational belief of libraries. As Battles put it, "Librarians believed in the unlimited possibility of the library for the reformation of culture and society." It was assumed not only that right reading could enlighten an individual but that an educated, enlightened populace could bring about a better society.

For instance, John Stuart Mill said that library books "offered a greater good than reason." These books would "ultimately encourage the regard for one's fellow man" and form the foundation of altruism. Even now libraries continue their central role in maintaining democracy in this country. The National Issues Forum, which aims to improve the quality of civic discourse, is convening library-based public forums about thorny public policy issues. The library was chosen as the site for this programme to heal a societal ill: polarization and partisan gridlock. "Libraries can prove the antidote," explained the initiative founder, LBJ Presidential Library and Museum's Taylor Willingham.

LIBRARIES AS VIOLENT LIBERATORS

The Library as Liberator may seem an odd concept to those who picture libraries as refuges from the world at large. Libraries are thought of as safe sanctuaries far removed from the dangers and evils all around. Yet libraries are also powerful, potentially dangerous places. This library power exists both in the potentially destabilizing potential of its contents and the authority vested in those who control access to it. To understand the latter, consider how librarians have been portrayed historically.

Librarians were scary individuals. Scowling, mean, able to inspire fear with a mere eyebrow, these austere individuals were frightening. Not exactly thought of as witches, they were close to it. The awe-inspiring librarians were dangerous because the power they wielded was none other than the accumulated knowledge of civilization. When the right information was applied at the right time in the right amount in the right circumstances, library knowledge could be devastating. Kings could be toppled, revolutions begun, slaves set free. Knowledge is power may seem a cliché, but it is far from trivial.

Librarians and libraries have the power to change not only lives but the course of history. If that is not a liberator, what is? The saving mission of libraries through reading usually brings to mind a gentle, benign path to personal salvation, but at times library salvation has been imagined through violence. For instance, in 1935 German librarians adopted the slogan "The Book–A Sword of the Spirit" for their annual Book Week celebration, though they later retreated from this campaign when it was used malevolently by the Nazis. Realizing the potential for books to radically alter one's outlook on life, Kafka called books "the ice ax of the soul," an image far removed from one of a placid, gentle reader. Libraries and books have been credited with liberating enslaved people. Victor Hugo said that when Gutenberg invented movable type it "marked the transition of man-slave to the free-man."

Echoing the liberating power of libraries, Malcolm X said:

* I had never been so truly free in my life as when in the prison library. Ten guards and the warden couldn't have torn me out of those books. Months passed without even thinking about being imprisoned.... I don't think anybody ever got more out of going to prison than I did.

Perhaps one of the best descriptions of the library enabling personal triumph was offered by Henry Louis Gates Jr.:

* In tenth grade, when I was fourteen, I had a friend who played chess a lot. I thought, I'm better at games than all the rest of the kids, so I'm going to play this

> guy and beat him. He crushed me. It was ugly. Then one day when I was at the library, I came across a book on chess... it was love at first sight.... That's when I discovered that reading could open your mind to the wonders of everything you wanted to know. For the first time, I understood the power of books, because after I started reading them, I began crushing players I couldn't beat before.

LIBERATING GOD

Just as God the Force and God the Light can be imagined in a library setting, God as Liberator can be seen within a library context. The empowering righteousness experienced-allowing players to be beaten and crushed—approximates one of my favourite images of God. Depicted perfectly by Sally Field in the movie *Norma Rae*, the hero stands atop a table in an intolerable sweatshop, thrusting a poster overhead demanding one word: "UNION!" Here is the biblical prophetic voice of God, proclaiming justice and righting wrongs here on earth, the superhuman-conquering-evil version of the divine.

This prophetic voice of God combats institutional social injustice such as slavery, financial inequity, and racial and ethnic hatred. This aspect of God is perhaps the only matter most religious Americans seem to agree upon. Social critic Robert Bellah says the prophetic voice of American public life "to carry out God's will on earth" has been a characteristic of American thought since the days of Puritan New England. Liberation theology, founded to right injustices prevalent in Latin America, typifies this kind of God. God not only helps those in poverty but also questions the root causes of poverty. Closely allied to the liberating God is the frightening God. The meek, benevolent, peaceful God may inspire love but seems inadequate to confront factory owners or slaveholders.

Known in the Bible as the wrath of God, this dimension of the divine can be seen as Yahweh thundering from Mt. Sinai, drowning the Egyptian army, reigning "destruction upon those who oppress the helpless and grind down the poor." This second side of the holy, called *mysterium tremendum et fascinans* by theologian Rudolf Otto, has been depicted for thousands of years in different religious traditions. In Hinduism the god Kali is seen as the "malicious face of the divine, with a belt of dismembered arms and necklace of skulls."

Buddhist, especially Tibetan, iconography employs dreadful and grotesque images of deities. American religions scholar Cheryl Bridges Johns has noted the demise of such wrathful images of God. Studying grassroots religious movements in the United States, Johns uncovered a trend to "remold God into the most pleasant and obliging deity imaginable." God is now merciful, benevolent, or what Cox has dubbed the "oh-so-nice God."

No one shudders in its presence, for this reimagined divinity is now "a user-friendly God." Researchers have argued that, even though religions have toned down images of the powerful, awe-inspiring God, there remains a place for such an image within the human heart. A place for such an image can also be found within the library. It is true that libraries help people individually by helping each move from where they are to a better place. But combined social action can also deliver entire groups of people to a better place. Libraries have been key players in social justice movements. Believers may see God the Liberator as present in the library, providing not just knowledge to users but the inspiration to act on what they learn.

OTHER LIBRARY SINS

Because of their potential to deliver salvation and violence, librarians do not take their service lightly. Indeed, arguably one value librarians hold in common is the belief that withholding library service from any individual or group of potential users is a sin. Librarians today look back in horror at the Jim Crow period, when "some people were unsuited to be readers." Libraries delivered "unbearable pain" by withholding library service. Closely allied to the sin of withholding library service is another action librarians consider sinful: desecrating books.

Though appalling to librarians, this act is nothing new. In 1725 Thomas Hollis wrote, "Students take to their chambers, and tear out pictures and maps to adorn their Walls, such things are not good." Of course, the public is well aware of one other form of library sinning, requiring pennies rather than penance. The fine for overdue materials does provide financial support for libraries, though it may arrive at a rate of only five cents per day, per item, per sinner. Though it usually does not amount to much money for libraries, it does increase library guilt, which most suffer already by simply walking through the library doors.

12

Librarians and Libraries Promote Community

Recently discovered that a fellow librarian at work shares my passion for swimming. Since she swims almost daily, I asked if she had considered purchasing a home with a pool. "No, I don't want a private pool. I like the whole idea of a community pool instead of everyone having their own. I guess I'm just funny that way." Without realizing it, her being "funny" about community swimming pools may be another expression of the main reason she chose the library profession.

Librarians understand the benefits that derive from sharing resources rather than each one having his or her own. This preference for communal rather than individually owned resources is unusual in America's individualistic society. Whether liberal or conservative, capitalist or communist, librarians know the limits of personal property. You cannot be an effective librarian cloistered away in your own library. Especially with the accelerating rate of information creation, no library will ever be self-sufficient. In a library, no matter how much you amass, it will never be enough. You have to share to gain access to the riches of the world's intellectual property.

NEED FOR AND SOURCES OF COMMUNITY

Although libraries are inherently community institutions, they are rarely recognized as such. It was the communal aspect of libraries that she asked me to explain. "Everything about a library promotes community," I told her. "Its very existence is the result of a community coming together to share resources. Think about borrowing a cup of sugar from the next-door neighbour. Isn't that an act that promotes and sustains a community?

Libraries are the exemplary good neighbours. Their entire reason to exist is to enable neighbourly sharing." "I guess you're right," she said. "I never thought of it like that." It was understandable that my friend would miss the subtle communal aspect of libraries. Checking out a book from a library appears to be a solitary activity. The person comes to the library alone, usually finds the book on her own, then checks it out to read alone. But undergirding all of this apparent individual activity is the community at large.

Societies with libraries-be they municipalities, colleges, or corporations-recognize the universal benefit of individual intellectual pursuits but acknowledge that no one person could or should own enough books to serve this purpose. And so the community comes together to purchase, store, and share the resources freely among its members. Not only are the resources available to all, in our isolated society the library is also one of the few institutions that touch all. Whenever I would become upset by a student complaint about the library, a former boss would remind me: "On a college campus people complain about the cafeteria and library more than anything else. They are the only places *everyone* shares."

Despite the occasional complaint, people by and large like libraries and want them close at hand. Unlike the familiar "not-in-my-backyard" syndrome other institutions face, libraries are one of the top "desirable elements" people want in their residential areas. Only drugstores and food markets are more desired, and they nosed out libraries by just a fraction of a point. Libraries garner higher desirability ratings than schools, community centers, churches, hospitals, or playgrounds. What is more, the library is one of the few places *all* population groups want.

The elderly, households with children, without children, whites, blacks, Hispanics, upper income, lower income-everyone wants a library in their neighbourhood. Along with libraries, other features home buyers want are coffee shops, Kinko's, and clubhouses, all areas that promote interaction among residents. Sociability is so important that more people report wanting a friendly area than one safe or quiet. When all these features are put together, it appears that people long to create an atmosphere of community that has been lost.

Columnist David Brooks notes that until recently people lived around some definable place they all shared: a tribal ring, an oasis, a river junction, a port. These were the geographic entities around which the community survived. But now in exurbia, each individual has his or her own polycentric nodes: the church, the subdevelopment, the office park. Even schools, which used to be shared entities, often lose their universality when so many people opt for private alternatives to the neighbourhood public school. Not only do contemporary communities lack a shared geographic point, but residents are also growing farther apart. With the spread of gated communities and increasing home size, contact with one's neighbours grows ever rarer.

Especially as people gain in wealth, their isolation increases. They purchase bigger and bigger homes separated from each other, resulting in lifeless neighbourhoods that one critic said foster "segregation, isolation, compartmentalization, and sterilization." As one would expect, the isolation of residential housing has been accompanied by increasing feelings of loneliness and separation. Louis Harris polls, in 1966, 9 per cent of people said they felt left out of things going on around them. By 1986 that number had grown to 37 per cent. In 1966, 36 per cent said, "What I think does not matter." In 1986 it was 60 per cent. This increase in feelings of isolation has been attributed to a variety of causes. Andrew Solomon, an expert on depression, believes that spending a day watching television or a computer screen can contribute to feelings of isolation, noting that the rise in depression has accompanied increases in these activities. Others think basic changes in society are to blame.

Barry Schwartz, author of Paradox of Choice, observed:

* Our social fabric is no longer a birthright, but has

> become a series of deliberate and demanding choices. What was once given by neighbourhood and work now must be achieved; people have to make their own friends . . . and actively cultivate their own family connections.

Some blame the prevalence of today's celebrity culture for our estrangement. Sometimes we know more about the divorces, pregnancies, and intimate lives of Madonna or Britney Spears than we do about our neighbours. Whatever the causes, many warn that dire consequences can result from chronic isolation. Sociologist Ray Oldenburg posits that, in the absence of a communal outlet, people's expectations towards work and family escalate beyond anything reasonable or possible. When the home and workplace fail to deliver sufficient succor—and usually they do fail because the need is too great—the resulting stress and strain can be disastrous.

Oldenburg attributes the climbing divorce rate, absenteeism, and stress-related medical problems to lack of community. Something must be amiss, he notes, when the best-selling drugs in this country are tranquilizers and ulcer and hypertension medicine. On the other hand, connections with real people can evidently bring true happiness. Research has found that those who successfully weave social connections with others are rewarded with a sense of well-being that is lacking in loners. People who are married, have good friends, are close to their families, or participate in religious communities are happier than others.

Communities are also vital to maintain what one historian called "a healthy social order." The founders of the U.S. Constitution included the right to free assembly as an antidote to tyranny. Totalitarian rulers ban informal gatherings to solidify their power. Residents of the former Soviet Union were fearful of talking freely in public. And lest we forget, as part of his successful reign of terror, Hitler banned assemblies of more than three persons on the streets of Germany. Because contact with others is so vital to both human happiness and democracy, Americans turn to a variety of places where-as the *Cheers* television show put it-everyone knows your name.

THE THIRD PLACE

The First Place is home. The Second Place is work. But the Third Place, according to Oldenburg, the term's originator, is where you head for "regular, voluntary, informal and happily anticipated gatherings beyond the realms of either home or work." In France the Third Place is the café, in Germany the beer garden, in England the pub. But no matter what the locale or location, all of these Third Places alleviate loneliness and foster the public good. In his foundational work, *The Great Good Place,* Oldenburg laments the lack of a Third Place in America. Though we nostalgically remember life in Mayberry, USA, sidling up to strangers at Denny's would be bizarre for most Americans.

We don't even spend time talking to the people who live next door, let alone the person downing the Grand Slam Breakfast in the next booth. The teenager hamburger joints fondly remembered in *Happy Days* perhaps come as close to anything in America resembling a Third Place. But now these places, derogatorily referred to as "hangouts," evoke a more pejorative than desirable connotation. Arguably in America the neighbourhood bar once filled this function, but no more.

One telling statistic reveals the decline of these establishments: 90 per cent of drinking in this country used to be done in public; now it is barely 30 per cent. The national coffeehouse chain Starbucks was founded deliberately to create an Oldenburg-type Third Place. Major bookstore chains added eating and lounging areas for the same reason. Though these commercial entities have succeeded financially, none has been successful in creating the public discourse—or schmoozing, if you will—among patrons that is central to the idea of a communal Third Place.

WORK AS COMMUNITY

For many Americans, work is where they find their community. Because we no longer exist in tight geographic communities, the body of water around which we gather is more likely the water fountain than the well. Or, as one social commentator noted, community ties have moved from the front porch to the water cooler. One survey found that two-thirds of all conversations among working adults take place at work, and another revealed that people get about 90 per cent of their social connections from the workplace.

Many studies have shown that having social connections with coworkers is the strongest single predictor of one's job satisfaction. The trend of finding fellowship through employment is well known among librarians. Anecdotal evidence suggests that a high percentage of librarians befriend each other, socialize together outside work, and marry each other. Membership in professional associations such as the ALA has increased 50 per cent in the past two decades, perhaps as a result of the increasing attraction of socially gathering with colleagues. Often in America work is expected to yield much more than a paycheck.

Especially for those in professions such as librarianship, our "identity" is intertwined with what we do from nine to five. Indeed, some librarians approach retirement with trepidation, not only because they fear loosing their professionbased social community but because their identity is tied up with their work. Work also provides a more illusive, profound aspect to our lives. "Identification" is too weak and modern a term for what we expect from our jobs. We also want to be subsumed by Something beyond us. We want to be not only invested but enmeshed in what we do.

David Brooks noted that Americans have the unique ability "to slather endless amounts of missionary zeal on apparently trivial subjects and thereby transform them into harbingers of some larger transcendence." This imagined Something we long for came before us, will be here after us, and explains the essence of who we are and why we are here. Work becomes the avenue of this immersion. Fortunately for librarians, the universal, transcendent aspects of libraries as discussed in this book are more apparent-and I would argue more real-than those of many places of employment.

OTHER SECULAR COMMUNITIES

Beyond work, the secular venues to which people turn for community vary as widely as the people searching. Memberships in the local Democratic Party or the Flamingo Elementary School PTA provide an intimate sense of belonging, even bordering on the religious. "Sacred is the feeling that I belong here," explains community promoter Margaret J. Wheatley. Any shared hobby-whether it be birding, bingo, or scrapbooking-can provide some of the essential elements of a Third Place. By bringing together people on a regular basis for conversation and companionship, these shared interests create a warm and welcoming environment for all.

Sports is one venue that can create community among a diverse gathering of people. Indeed, one critic noted that generalized loneliness gets covered up with "a wealth of frantic activity. That's the reason tennis has gotten so big. They all go out and play tennis." Like the world of work, sports can lend meaning to people's lives far beyond what appears on the surface. In some respects sports can even fulfill religious functions. Like religious gatherings, sports provide opportunities to achieve intimacy with real and imagined others.

By wearing the colours of their team, sporting shirts emblazoned with logos and players' numbers, people can imagine themselves as part of the team. Baseball aficionados often bring gloves with them, hoping for the chance to participate in the game directly. With the emphasis on the character-building capacity of sportsmanship, sports can provide moral uplift. And the fervent loyalty fans express for their teams can be seen as nothing short of religious devotion. Sports is an excellent example of a secular community that resembles a religious congregation. So similar are these gatherings, scholars have difficulty defining the difference between them.

RELIGION AND COMMUNITY

When her child died, author Elaine Pagels sought and found comfort in the community of her church. As she put it,

"Here was a place to weep without imposing tears upon a child; and here was a heterogeneous community that had gathered to sing, to celebrate . . . and to deal with what we cannot control or imagine." Others seek this route for more mundane reasons. No matter what draws them, people seek out religious communities to fulfill their need for community-referred to in religious parlance as fellowship.

Though many people assume that a shared belief in a doctrine unites people of faith, it is the sense of community that serves as the attraction for many, if not most. As one Nazarene church member put it succinctly, "We agree with the doctrine, but the people are more important than doctrine." Especially among young people, the congregation rather than doctrine attracts. They, like many of their elders, believe that answers to philosophical questions such as the meaning of life and ultimate purpose-if they exist at all-will come through a community of the faithful.

The need for religious communion is especially pressing in a large, diverse, fragmented society such as America. When we can't agree on much, explain sociologists Michael Mazur and Kate McCarthy, religion provides shared acts of eating, dancing, and singing. "At least for a few moments, we can hold on to a slim thread of communal life." American Catholicism is famous for instilling communal loyalty among its members. Labour unions, political machines, government service-all communal organizations-have historically been encouraged and supported by Catholics.

Many Protestants convert to Catholicism because of its power to create community and overcome the isolation associated with American individualism. "People pull" is also an attraction in Judaism. One study of ultraorthodox Jewish women found that a sense of belonging to an all-inclusive group was as important as, if not more important than, the search for tradition. The study also revealed another important, though rarely acknowledged, religious attraction.

Since many of them were single, the possibility of finding a suitable mate led many women to become orthodox. Whether they were returning to their religious roots or joining from nonorthodox or secular upbringings, many women became orthodox because orthodox men, it was rumored, make good husbands and fathers.

LIBRARIES AS COMMUNAL SPACE

Religious institutions are far from the only places people go prospecting for potential mates. My husband remembers fondly using the public library for this purpose. "I used to go to the library to check out the babes, not the books," he says. My husband's choice of the library as the place to cruise chicks was no accident. Libraries are the central social gathering spot for many communities, colleges, and schools. Why else did the Internal Revenue Service select the library as its destination of choice for distributing tax forms? Libraries are the contemporary version of the communal well–the shared meeting spot for everyone in the community. Because of this social-gathering-spot function, many a married couple trace their start to the library.

Recently my own library was the site of a formal marriage proposal. The future groom got down on his knee in front of his beloved, who was studying in a carrel, and popped the question. If it were not for the shouts of approval by those studying in nearby carrels when she said "yes," no one ever would have known that the library had served as such a romantic location. Though libraries do not often host marriage proposals, they do provide a safe, central place where everyone in the supporting organization feels welcome. Though libraries provide refuge from society, they are also the center of it.

On most college campuses the library is positioned in the center of the campus and referred to as the "heart" of the institution, geographically symbolizing the pursuit of knowledge as the focus of the enterprise. Library architect Henry Myerberg reminds us that school libraries provide "the biggest bang for the buck." Though they consume the equivalent of only two large classrooms, or about 5 per cent of a school's real estate, libraries serve and inspire 100 per cent of the school's teachers and students.

Likewise, public libraries of old dominated their town squares, sitting proudly near other institutions representing permanence and trust: the courthouse, post office, bank. But more than any of these places, it was the library, along with the church, that was the physical and imagined center of a community. In libraries and houses of worship the group was recognized for being greater than its parts. Even the private acts of reading and praying were acknowledged to be more effective when done in the presence of others.

COMMUNITY THROUGH READING

Sharing books among people is obviously a communal activity. But so is reading. My editor and I vacillated over where a discussion on reading belonged in this book. Was it a solitary activity that should be discussed in the chapter on library as a place of solitude? Or was it communal? In truth, we decided, it is both. As psychologist Solomon noted, reading is neither a passive nor an isolating experience. "Reading is an entry into dialogue; a book can be a friend, talking not at you, but to you." A homeless man interviewed in a shelter reported that the library was his destination of choice because there he could read and lose his loneliness in conversation with a stranger.

"As long as I can read," claimed columnist Linda Weltner, "I am never alone." A community of readers may seem counterintuitive, but such a gathering fits perfectly into the contemporary definition of community. Perhaps because we lack a physical Third Place, in America communities are more imagined than real. As Brooks noted, "Our sense of belonging comes not so much from where the person believes they belong, but where they *want* to belong. The basis of community is what ideal state they aspire to." American communities come "from the person's head and heart rather than any place on earth."

The community of all people reading the same book could be imagined as such a congregation of the like-minded. But beyond just being a timespanning virtual community, the communal experience of reading also allows each individual to dissolve into Something larger, grander, greater, and longer lasting than herself. Indeed, when imagined thus, reading could be seen as a secular experience of the divine. Communion with that greater.

Something is one way religion scholars refer to experiencing God. For many of us, falling in love most closely expresses this feeling of total absorption of the self. In the Bible, Paul spoke of such a feeling as God "in whom we live and move and have our being". Harvey Cox describes this kind of divine feeling as being "not only around us but inside us, informing our senses and our feelings." According to Harold Bloom, romantic love, like reading, can be such an experience of the sublime.

Though he admits that he is "not exactly an erotics-of-reading purveyor," Bloom believes that both reading and falling in love can be secular moments of transcendence. While acknowledging that people read for a variety of reasons–to come to know other people profoundly, to know ourselves better, for knowledge of self and others–for Bloom "the most authentic motive for deep reading . . . is the search for a difficult pleasure." Bloom urges readers "not to believe, not to accept, not to contradict, but to learn to share in that one nature that writes and reads."

COMMUNAL MEMORY

Though experienced privately, reading is also an ongoing conversation between author and reader. Even death does not keep one from these communal conversations. Indeed, it could be argued that communicating from the grave is the main purpose of writing. Bloom noted that, though he turns to reading as a solitary praxis, he derives from it a sense of continuity with the past. In singing the praises of the institution, Alfred Kazin noted that the entire idea of the library is to connect seamlessly with those who came before. The communal memory one taps in a library differs from history. History is the record of what happened, but communal memory is the experience of the narrative story as it was and as it will continue.

For those from a strong ethnic or religious tradition, the group memory itself can become an object of reverence. It is not that the members of the group worship themselves; rather, it is the connection—the totality of the group's past, present, and future—that seems holy and immortal. Religions use ritual and prayer to evoke this remembered tradition among the faithful. An effective prayer, notes Cox, is one that provokes a sense of holiness by linking a person to a tradition that goes back thousands of years. The worshipper senses a kinship with others around the world, as well as with those in previous centuries. In my own experience, performing a ritual preparation of a body for burial gave me the feeling of a direct link with my historical tradition.

Washing the arm began my experience of time and space travel:

> * I began wondering if someone had washed my *bubbe*'s arm like that. From *bubbe* my thoughts moved to her *bubbe*, and to her *bubbe*, and then to all the *bubbes* who have washed and been washed by Jewish women just like me. Suddenly, I was part of the permanence of the Jewish people who have performed this ritual for centuries.

LIBRARY COMMUNAL MEMORY

For the secularly inclined, the religious milieu is not where an unending connection to previous generations is sought or found. Rather, the library embodies the union of past, present, and future. Libraries are imagined to include the history of anyone and everyone who ever managed to read or write a book. Beyond that, libraries also record the recording of history. Both the historical record of civilization and the history of the history can be found in the library. If God is imagined as Connection to History, library use becomes de facto worship. What else is library usage than the linking of a person with an ancient tradition?

An eighth-grader reading a commentary on *Macbeth* may not imagine herself communing with the divine. Nor does an amateur gourmet consulting a cookbook for a recipe for cheese soufflé think he is performing a religious act. But both are linking themselves to a tradition. The student may simply be praying for a good grade, and the cook praying for a puffy dish, but they are also unknowingly praying to a secular library god.

SILENT AND SPOKEN LIBRARY COMMUNICATION

Beyond an ethereal sense of community, libraries also enable and encourage communication among those physically present in the building. Sometimes this communication is deliberate, but sometimes it is spontaneous and nonverbal. Enormous amounts of information are transmitted over the carts of returned books. Without saying a word, members of a community exchange silent recommendations over the library version of the water cooler. What's good? What topics are hot these days?

The racks of returned books speak volumes, if you will. Before the days of automated circulation, the book pocket pasted to the back of the book would transmit the necessary secret information about good reads. Author Bel Kaufman remembers checking the card tucked inside as part of her selection process. "If the card was stamped with lots of dates, I knew I had a winner!" When talking is added to the process, the information exchanged can be better than any review in the *New York Times Review of Books*. "Was that any good?" asked of a patron returning a novel can provide a more direct and often accurate assessment than a hundred published book reviews.

READERS ADVISORY: A COMMUNITY EFFORT

The five words that head this section are not mine. They are the title of an article published recently in *Public Libraries*. The art of recommending titles to readers, known in the profession as readers advisory, remains a key element of librarianship. Learned through both formal classes and on-the-job training, librarians daily suggest books to their patrons. But when a reader finds a librarian who manages to suggest just the right book, that advisor becomes a friend for life. When

I was working at a public library, one day an elderly woman approached me, frantically asking, "Where's Mary? Where's Mary?"

* "She's on break," I explained. "Can I help you?"

* "No," she said emphatically. "I'll wait."

Responding to my quizzical look, she told me with combined desperation and affection, "I finished my book and I need Mary to tell me what to read now." To aid librarians missing the skills of Mary, various online sources have been created that enhance and expand title recommendation. As the *Public Libraries* article discusses, these services have become "a virtual meeting place for books and readers." Many allow readers to both select the titles to be included and record their own impressions.

BOOK DISCUSSION AS COMMUNITY

Some may argue that verbal and nonverbal exchanges about what to read next do not constitute a community, at least not in the classic sense of the word. Few, however, would take exception to characterizing a book discussion club as a community. There may be as many as 30 million members in 750,000 special interest groups devoted to discussing books or current events or to pursuing shared interests. Libraries have a long history of encouraging and facilitating discussions about books. In the early days of American libraries, home libraries regularly deposited a few shelves of books into people's homes. Along with the physical books, a librarian was also dispatched to the home to engage readers in discussion.

Book clubs with selected titles and discussion dates are now common features of many public libraries. Thanks to Nancy Pearl and her One Book/One Community Programme, communities grounded in books have expanded far beyond the confines of public libraries. The One Book concept began in 1998 when the Seattle Public Library and Washington Center for the Book introduced "If All Seattle Read the Same Book." Since then, similar book-based discussions have sprung up in cities, towns, communities, and organizations throughout the country.

Discussing books is a secular activity, but it forms the basis of many religious communities. Within Judaism not only are books sacred, but so is the discussion of their content. The weekly Jewish religious service features the ceremonial reading from the Torah. The Jewish tradition of discussing the Bible and its ancient commentary, the Talmud, is arguably the oldest continuous book club. By gathering to discuss these texts, many of which contain the varying points of view and opinions across generations, participants continue a seamless conversation over centuries.

Reading from holy texts also holds a central place in the worship service within Christianity and Islam. Bible study, which could be seen as the original One Book/One Community, is one of the fastest-growing programmes in many churches, most likely because people are turning to this ancient source to seek relevance for their lives today. Religion scholars have noted a hunger for serious, soul-searching discussions of sacred texts within many denominations.

Church leaders have been pleasantly surprised to find that participation in Bible study groups increases when the content becomes more rigorous. No longer satisfied to hear simply a recounting of the familiar Bible stories, congregants require discussions that plumb the meaning and history of the texts. Whether discussing sacred or secular topics, communities that revolve around books and shared information create powerful assemblies.

The University of Florida turned to communal reading when searching for a way to form esprit de corps and encourage racial dialogue among incoming freshmen. "Why Are All the Black Kids Sitting Together in the Cafeteria?" was the title chosen to encourage discussions of diversity and race. The programme organizers, requiring all the students from diverse backgrounds to read and discuss the same book promoted community interaction. By literally getting them all on the same page, reading successfully provided participants an avenue to talk about their shared experiences.

COMMUNITY-CREATING LIBRARY PROGRAMMES

Libraries also promote community through library

programmes such as current events discussions, lectures, and films. Most major public library systems employ adult services staffs to organize and operate such programmes. Even smaller public libraries manage to sponsor community events ranging from crafts demonstrations to spelling bees. Information and referral services, which identify major resources in a community and match individuals with them, have been a major activity of libraries for decades. The provision of such community-based information was deemed more important by library users than reference service or popular reading materials.

LIBRARY ARCHITECTURE REFLECTS COMMUNITY FUNCTION

In recognition of their community function, many libraries have been built with community rooms, lecture halls, and other spaces available for community groups. Even the activity of study, which was previously conducted by one person alone, has become a communal activity. "Study carrels are out; four-person tables are in," explains a building consultant. Likewise, students on college campuses are clamoring for group study space in their libraries because solitary reading assignments are often accompanied, or even replaced in some classes, by group projects. Since many libraries were not designed to support such activities, meeting this demand has been a challenge.

In many places, the library is the only facility with a publicly available community meeting room, so it becomes the de facto focal point for communitybased activities by virtue of this physical facility. Public access computers are another physical feature that brings people to libraries and enhances the library role as a central gathering spot. Librarians sometimes lament that these computers are used only to check e-mail or play games, activities not thought of as traditional library use. If, however, building community is seen as a central role of the library, use of this communal shared resource fits perfectly into this mission.

LIBRARY COMMUNITY-BUILDING PROGRAMMES

To find other ways to enhance their community building,

librarians might investigate a new national initiative that helps libraries fill this role. The Libraries for the Future programme, a division of Americans for Libraries Council helps libraries join foundations and community-based organizations to create and sustain community life.

This national programme currently operates three major programmes to assist libraries:

* Reading America, sponsored by the MetLife Foundation, provides training and technical support for libraries to use book and film discussions to foster intergenerational understanding and communication, especially in new immigrant families.
* The Equal Access Libraries programme, supported by the Bill and Melinda Gates Foundation, trains librarians to conduct needs assessment and create partnerships and public awareness programmes that will strengthen their role as the community's center for information and learning.
* The Family Place Libraries programme strives to build healthy families and enhance literacy by creating spaces where young children and their caregivers can play and learn together.

LIBRARY VALUES THAT PROMOTE COMMUNITY

It is not by chance that libraries have taken the lead in many of the communal activities. All libraries share the following values, which reinforce their role as community builders. Each of these values contributes to the library's central role as a communal institution that brings people together to share resources.

PUBLICLY AVAILABLE

From their beginning, libraries threw open their doors to everyone. The ancient library at Athens was *ad commenem delectationem*, "for the enjoyment of all." Even the practice of chaining books to the shelves was done "for the good of the community." Modern-day reserve collections in academic libraries continue this practice; though no longer chained to the desk, certain books are put away and handed out selectively, to make sure these books remain available "for the enjoyment of all." Libraries remaining open and making their riches accessible to all members of a community continues as a basic tenet of the library profession.

The ALA Library Bill of Rights demands that books and library resources be provided "for all people of the community" and that library use not be denied or abridged because of origin, age, background, or views. Because libraries are one of the few institutions that bring together individuals of all classes and castes, they have served as a great equalizer throughout history. Many have noted the diverse assemblage of human beings brought together in the public library.

Nearly one hundred years ago one library user noted seeing in the library "everything from frumpery to finery." In the 1700s the library was described as an institution to which "the curious and impatient Enquirer . . . and the bewildered Ignorant might freely repair." Alfred Kazin characterized the library as "an asylum and church of the unemployed." Another public library user counted among the patronage "the unprocessed, misfits, left-overs . . . hollow-cheeked, watery-eyed, shabby and furtively sad."

FREE

Rare in our consumer-based society, the library is open to all regardless of income. Everyone is invited to partake at no cost to the individual. Librarians sometimes forget just how remarkable this is. No other institution in American society exists for this purpose. Not even food-the very essential element for life-is provided in such a universal, free, all-you-want basis as books are in libraries. An immigrant from Venezuela, who later became a librarian himself, remembers his astonishment upon learning that the books in the library could be taken home for free.

"I absolutely could not believe it when they told me that I could take a book—or lots of books—home. And that it would not cost me anything. In my country we didn't have anything like that!" I remember my preschool daughter's confusion about this during one of our first trips to the library. Laden with an armload of picture books, she asked, "Where do we pay?"

* "We don't, honey. It's free."
* "Oh," she said and proceeded to the exit door.
* "No, come back," I told her. "We do need to check them out."
* "But I thought you said they were free."

Thus ensued a lengthy explanation on how checking out materials differed from purchase. An uncle of mine who spent his entire work life in the corporate world never grasped this concept. At family gatherings he would always ask me, "How's the library business?" Rather than engage him in a detailed discussion of how libraries are not commercial, I would just smile demurely and answer, "Just fine, thanks." To the credit of those of us in the "library business," we have consistently insisted that the storehouse of knowledge residing within library walls—and on library computers–remains available free of charge to all within the community of users.

User fees as a source of revenue for public libraries have been successfully opposed, even in those communities with residents who could easily afford them. Indeed, within American society, only the library and houses of worship are places one can go without expecting to pay anything. Museums and parks may have "Free Fridays" or such, but these are often the exception rather than the rule. So extraordinary is this cost-free feature of libraries, one author deemed the free library movement one of the most important developments in the history of libraries.

Even those with substantial financial means still use the public library. While conducting research on the history of the Charleston library, one historian found that many families owned extensive private libraries but still frequented the public library. A modern-day example of the same phenomenon was demonstrated through a library bond issue. One wealthy woman announced her support of the campaign: "I never use libraries myself," she admitted, "but I want them available anyway." One fund-raising consultant noted that more often than not major donations to libraries come from people who do not even own a library card. Though library resources are free, they can be priceless treasures.

Harvey Cox has observed that human beings, especially those with money, can own and dispose of anything they choose. However, there never seems to be enough, because an overwhelming desire to purchase more and more overtakes them. Unlike the emptiness created by tangible purchases, library usage can be deeply satisfying. Knowledge not only is free but can lead to priceless understanding. People may be infused with a desire to know more, which is rarely experienced as a hole to be filled.

VOLUNTARY

The use of libraries–like religious attendance in this country–is voluntary, an important aspect for community formation. Except for students brought by teachers, no one is forced to use the library. Actually, library usage is frequently overreported, especially by teens who have been known to claim to be using the library while partying at the beach. Self-selecting participation is an important feature of community formation. Tocqueville was especially taken with the vibrancy of the voluntary organizations he saw operating in this country, noting that these associations brought together diverse people in a way he did not witness in European countries.

David Brooks observed that Americans continue the tradition by creating their own social circles, each carrying its own status system, validation system, and role within society. People find their place in the world within these chosen groupings. Unlike families, which cannot be chosen, voluntary communities can be joined and left at will. Members must constantly affirm their affiliation to themselves and to others in order to justify their continued membership. Because no one is forcing anyone to remain, loyalty to the chosen community is high, which often translates into financial contributions.

Just as Americans join more groups than any other nationality, they donate more money per capita than any other people. On average, American adults donate $1,100 per year to their voluntary organizations, with $3,600 given per year on average from evangelical Christians. Libraries garner higher levels of community desirability than many other communal institutions. Therefore, the potential exists for libraries to capitalize on this loyalty through increased private donations.

ALL SIDES WELCOME

Not only are all people invited to use the library, they are also free to explore any and all opinions there. "Libraries should provide materials and information presenting all points of view," proclaims of the Library Bill of Rights. Nothing on the shelves of the library can be "proscribed or removed because of partisan or doctrinal disapproval."

Intrinsic to the philosophy of libraries is the belief that no one has a monopoly on the truth. Wrestling with ideas is not only possible but encouraged. Sir Francis Bacon said that one should read "not to contradict and confute, nor to believe and take for granted, nor to find talk and discourse, but to weigh and consider." The emphasis on the library's free exchange of ideas may seem pedestrian to Americans, but it is exceptional in much of the world.

A young woman from Latin America once told me that when she arrived in this country she found the teachers baffling:

* My teachers kept asking me, "What do *you* think?" "What do *you* think?" Whatever subject they were teaching, they all kept asking me what I thought. I would look at each one blankly. None of them understood. In my life before, in my country, no one had ever asked for my opinion on anything.

To guarantee that all opinions are exchanged freely, libraries value the protection of minority opinions and challenge attempts at censorship. Indeed, the academic world is based on and revolves around the free exchange of competing views. One author called academics' conferences and periodicals "outloud challenges of one another's work." Librarians steadfastly oppose efforts to suppress information and are loath to reveal the identity of those who have consulted their books and other materials.

Likewise, librarians have vociferously fought efforts to employ Internet filtering software lest they inadvertently restrict access to information. "Conflict among books is what the universal library is about," says library historian Matthew Battles. Librarians invite all members of their imagined community to come in and intellectually slug it out. Indeed, anyone who can read is invited into the intellectual free-for-all known as the library.

13

Creating a Positive Climate for Change

INTRODUCTION

One of the best recent articles on the subject of change was published in 1986 by Sara Fine. One of Fine's most relevant points is that resistance to change is inevitable, and management must be prepared to respond to it. Fine's research shows that "human beings tend to resist change, even when change represents growth and development... greater efficiency and productivity. [Since] changes in an organization affect the individuals within that organization, and individuals...have the power to facilitate or thwart the implementation of an innovation.

Why do employees resist change? Primarily because they fear the unknown. That is, they feel anxiety about how the change will affect them, their job performance, their relationship with other employees, and other job related factors. In fact, psychologists say that fear of the unknown is a rational, rather than an irrational, response to change. A small amount of uneasiness is to be expected from most people when the status quo shifts, simply because people need time to adjust their thinking, their job performance, and their social relationships to any changes made.

Thus, resistance to change is inevitable, and managers must allow for some resistance when they are planning to implement change. Indeed, some resistance to change may even be positive because it slows down the speed with which innovation might otherwise proceed and allows time for people to adjust to it.

Unfortunately, resistance to change sometimes goes beyond a healthy unease for the unknown, as some researchers have discovered. Nancy Feldman studied a series of changes in the Tulsa Public Library system and found the following types of employee resistance: task avoidance or postponement, hostility, resignation, and underproduction. A few years later, other library researchers found several more indicators of employee resistance to change: increased absentee-ism, increased employee impatience, frustration, and sabotage. To manage change effectively, administrators must understand why an employee's initial reaction to a new proposal, that is, uneasiness and fear of the unknown, sometimes accelerates into more negative behaviour like decreased job performance or sabotage.

WHAT CAUSES NEGATIVE BEHAVIOUR IN EMPLOYEES

Fine implies that a major cause of this acceleration is inept management. This object will, therefore, explore two questions: Can managers actually increase employee levels of resistance to change through poor planning, lack of support, or ignorance of employee needs? And, if so, how can managers avoid doing this in the future?

GENERAL UNCERTAINTY ABOUT THE EFFECTS OF CHANGE

Let us scrutinize the general uncertainty which people experience when a major change is announced by a hypothetical example. Upper managers in an academic library are concerned because employees do not have enough time to evaluate the library's collection. These managers are quite altruistic; they want to try to make their employees' jobs easier by bringing in a consultant to conduct the evaluation for them.

Sherry, the head of collection development, is asked to make this a top priority. Since she has not worked out all the details of who the consultant will be and what he will do, she makes a simple bald statement at the end of her next staff meeting. The statement is this: a consultant will be brought in to evaluate the library's collection, review collection development policies, and make suggestions for improving collection development efforts. Sherry does not encourage discussion about the matter because the meeting has already run over in time. When staff try to briefly question the need, she says upper management has asked her to implement this change and that she will try to answer people's questions later.

George is one of sixteen employees responsible for collection development at this library. He has a number of immediate reactions to the suggested change-that is, to the consultant's presence. He wants to know who the consultant will be and what is the consultant's level of expertise. He wants to know why management feels a consultant is necessary. He also wants to know whether the consultant will discuss matters fully with current staff before making decisions which will affect them and how any changes suggested will affect patron service in the long run.

George's boss, Sherry, is too busy with her normal work and with making arrangements for the consultant's visit to answer his questions. George's initial reaction to the announcement is uneasiness, but as Sherry continues to ignore his needs for more complete information on the topic, he begins to feel that she is hiding something from him. His anxiety about the consultant's presence grows. By the time the consultant arrives, George's stress about the situation has grown so much that he is unwilling to listen to any of the consultant's suggestions. Instead he tries to undermine the consultant's advice by disagreeing with everything.

In this case, Sherry has handled the introduction of the new change poorly. She has failed to see the extent of George's uneasiness about this change and to provide him and other employees with appropriate information to ease these fears. The literature of librarianship, of management, and of personnel psychology shows that employees respond better to change when management consciously tries to ease employee fears in a number of ways.

First, management should provide as much advance information about the actual change as possible. Sherry did not. She hadn't worked out all the details herself and may have been afraid of looking inept in front of her staff if she said this. But she should have provided as much information as possible and not worried about the details at this point.

Second, management should fully inform affected employees of the reasons behind the change. Management is trying to help employees by providing a person to perform a task which they have not had time to do. Since this rationale is not made clear, George assumes management is criticizing the ability of the staff to evaluate the collection and reacts accordingly.

Third, management should do everything possible to clarify employees' questions about the changes. Sherry did not realise how serious George's uneasiness about the change was. Thus she did not take the time to answer his questions, unwittingly making the situation worse.

Fourth, management should give employees time to reflect on how the proposed change will affect them, the organization as a whole, and their clientele. Sherry, told by upper management that bringing in the consultant is a top priority, rushes to do this rather than discussing matters fully with her staff and trying to give them time to adjust to the change.

In other words, workers who receive clear information about how a change will directly affect the organization and their role within it will accept change significantly better than those who do not receive this information.

A second example might make this even clearer. A 1985 article by two communications researchers described the results of a study of a government agency which was anticipating a move to a new office building. The employees had always worked in traditional offices, but management was asking them to move to a new building which used open landscaping. The move represented an environmental shift which could radically alter processes for accomplishing work. Six weeks before the move, management had provided little information to the employees about the change even though it had been planned for some time.

The researchers asked senior management at this agency if they could experiment with the levels of information employees got about the move. In effect, the researchers wanted to verify the fact that giving employees clear information in advance would help them adapt better to the change. But the researchers had a second purpose too. They wanted to see whether employees would respond differently if they were given positive information about the move than if they were given negative information.

They did this by emphasizing for one set of departments positive aspects of the move. For another set, they emphasized negative aspects. They gave no information to a third set. The researchers expected to find that employees would adapt to change better when they received positive information about the change and they did. However, employees who had received negative information about the move responded more positively than employees who had received no clarifying information at all. That is, workers who received clarifying information about a change accepted it significantly better than those who did not *euen when they viewed the change as a negative one.*

These findings clearly reinforce the idea that managers should share as much information about a proposed change as they can, even if there are negative aspects. That is, when the director of a small medical library is told his budget will be cut by 15 per cent next year, he should not try to keep the information under cover. Rather, he should share the news with the staff and then work to keep them informed of and involved about what changes will have to be made to stay within the budget and how these changes will affect them individually.

UNCERTAINTY ABOUT JOB PERFORMANCE

Another reason for employee fear of change is uncertainty about new work-related expectations associated with job performance. Specifically, the employee fears that he may not have enough skill to perform the changed task. A recent study supports this by showing that individuals with experience performing a specific task one way will resist change more than individuals with less experience. This was discovered in an experiment where two groups of high school students were asked to complete a series of simple manual tasks where they were rewarded for correct performance. One group was given more experience than the other, and developed more skill at the tasks.

They were then asked to adopt automated procedures for these tasks. The students with more experience resisted automation significantly more than those with less experience. This was because the experienced group of workers had a higher degree of confidence in their ability to do the job in the old way; when they were asked to automate, their initial anxiety was higher. The levels of uncertainty about performance for students with little experience in their jobs did not change when they were asked to automate. This was because they were still a bit unsure about their performance in the manual task and were thus more receptive to trying new work methods.

This research implies that managers need to follow two strategies when introducing new tasks. First, they need to provide employees with exact information about what the changed tasks will be because knowledge reduces fear. Second, managers need to reassure their employees that they will develop the skills to do these tasks. The latter can be accomplished if workers receive adequate and complete training and receive reassurance that they will not be punished if their performance levels drop initially while relearning the changed tasks.

EMPLOYEE PARTICIPATION IN CHANGE

Management can also lessen resistance to change by increasing employee involvement in the change process. Henry Lucas lists some of the strengths of encouraging employee participation in change. First, participation increases employee knowledge about the innovation thus lessening fear. Second, participation can be ego enhancing, intrinsically satisfying, and challenging, thus making workers feel needed and appreciated.

Finally, participation encourages employees to believe that they have some control over a system that will affect them. This last point is particularly important since psychologists have shown that even small amounts of individual control over adverse stimuli will reduce a person's opposition to these stimuli.

A recent article by Debra Shaw also supports the idea that participation can reduce resistance to change. In 1983 the Indiana State Library surveyed employees to determine their initial feelings about installing an automated catalog and circulation system. Management then attempted to involve as many staff as possible in planning for the automated system.

Participation was encouraged through a library automation planning committee and through a committee which concentrated on staff development for automation. Each committee was comprised of senior management and volunteers. Both committees shared information about their tasks with various library departments and invited suggestions from the departments for consideration. Several other techniques were also used to keep staff involved and informed, ranging from a regular news memo to programmes which acquainted staff with automation terminology and with various automated systems. One year after the study began, staff attitudes were significantly more positive about the proposed new system.

Two cautions need to be offered about participative management. Token participation for employees is not enough. Participative management will only ease resistance to innovation when employees truly believe they can influence the change. In fact, Wilson Luquire found that attitudes relating to innovation were directly related to the real level of participative management in the libraries. Real level refers to the level to which employees were actually allowed to influence decisions rather than the level to which managers said employees were allowed to influence decisions.

A second caution is also in order. Not all staff members are interested in participatory management. The Indiana State Library appropriately encouraged involvement by volunteers. This approach may be the wisest if a number of people are not interested in participating in the decision-making process.

FEAR OF CHANGE DUE TO SOCIAL CONSEQUENCE

One other major type of employee fear is caused when the potential social consequences of the change are not anticipated and allowed for. Perhaps this is best illustrated when looking at the effects of hiring a new director in a fairly small public library. Let's say that the old director had been at the library for twenty years and is retiring. The ten employees have been trained by, and have worked well with, the old director. In this situation each of the employees is not only nervous about whether the new director will be satisfied with their individual performance, but also they are nervous about how the new director will relate to them both as a person and as an employee. In other words, they are nervous that the change might have unanticipated social consequences.

In fact, the levels of employee stress just after the hiring of a new director tend to be very high. One main way the new director can reduce stress levels is to be very careful during his first few months on the job to treat employees as if he likes each and every one of them and as if he recognizes the unique contributions that each is offering the library.

RESISTANCE BECAUSE OF FAILURE TO PROVE CHANGE IS NEEDED

Resistance to change also occurs when managers fail to convince employees that the change is needed. In one public library in Ohio, library staff resisted efforts to reintegrate the genre fiction collection into the general fiction collection. Management wanted to do this because they felt one interfiled system would make it easier for the technical services staff to inventory the collection since they wouldn't have to look in three or four possible places for a particular book. However, the staff noted that patrons liked having mysteries and other genre areas separated out from the regular collection and that inventories were conducted only once every ten years. In this case, the employees perceived that the proposed change was not a valid one. Ultimately management agreed to let the collection remain separate by genre.

Change should only be implemented when a performance gap exists-that is, when people become highly dissatisfied with some aspect of a task or process. Remember the study of high school students performing the simple manual tasks. The experienced group was finally persuaded to change by an astute manager who made them consider the performance gap, showing them that automation would enable them to complete the work in a fraction of the time. The implication here is that management must do a good job identifying and publicizing areas where true performance gaps exist if they expect employees to feel that they have valid reasons for changing. It also implies that if a performance gap does not really exist, management should reconsider the change.

FAILURE TO COMMIT SUFFICIENT RESOURCES TO THE CHANGE

Increased resistance to change can also result when managers do not follow through by committing sufficient resources to the change. In one public library, initial employee reactions to the introduction of an automated circulation system and online catalog were generally positive. However, upper management failed to hire an expert to introduce automation, skimped on system specifications, purchased an inferior automated system, and overworked existing personnel to get the system started. Several years later, the automated circulation system was down as much as it was up, required an average twenty second response time when it was up, and had increased both employee and patron dissatisfaction with the library.

In addition, machine-readable information on the library's collection had to be input twice since system failures caused much of the data to be erroneously erased from the computer's memory banks. The staff who were initially supportive of the system developed higher and higher levels of frustration and eventually turned against the system. This is clearly a case where administrators failed to commit sufficient resources to planning and implementing a large change and directly increased employee resistance.

Actually, Fine suggests that it is not uncommon for resources to be overextended or with-drawn just when staff is experiencing the greatest stress of change. Moreover, she adds that administrators often skimp on really necessary items, *e.g.*, complete training by experts may be viewed as an extravagance rather than as a necessary expenditure associated with change. Thus, it is important for managers to be particularly sensitive to this issue, and to critically examine if they have supported the innovation by providing all necessary resources-be it money, time, increased attention to detail by management, added personnel, or whatever.

RESISTANCE DUE TO FAILURE TO TIE LIBRARY VALUES TO THE CHANGE

Another reason that employees resist change is that management often forgets to emphasize the positive aspects of the change on professional and library values-e. g., improved service to patrons. Unfortunately, some managers fail both to keep employees informed of the library's values, and then to tie the positive effects of the change to these values. Remember George, the worker who resisted efforts to hire a consultant to evaluate the collection. He might have responded more appropriately if management had tied the positive effects of the change to a goal which he supported, *i.e.*, matching collections to patron needs. In other words, if managers insist on hiring a collection evaluation consultant, they need to explain that they are doing this to make sure that collection development efforts are really meeting user needs.

RESISTANCE DUE TO FAILURE TO CREATE A CLIMATE CONDUCIVE TO CHANGE

General resistance to change may also result when managers fail to create a positive climate where change can flourish. The best illustration of this might be a library where management allows employees little participation and in fact does not encourage new ideas in any way. Research has shown that employees resist change less when they are given opportunities to participate in continuing education activities, in professional organization activities, and in professional training, *e.g.*, the MLS degree. Each of these activities encourages employees to think and to act for themselves. The activities both expose workers to new ideas and give them confidence in their abilities to respond to new situations. Therefore, workers become more receptive to changes which are proposed and shown to be valid. This implies that managers need to both encourage and reward employee efforts to learn and grow as this will reinforce receptivity to change.

CONCLUSION

Fine originally implied that inept management strategies can cause resistance to change to accelerate. Both logic and research support this statement and show us the need for corrective management action. Corrective action can include providing adequate information about change and being generally sensitive to employee fears about change. Other positive steps include convincing employees that a real reason exists for the change and committing sufficient resources to the change to ease the transition process and alleviate employee frustration. Managers should also tie the change to improved patron service and should constantly work to create a climate where employees are encouraged to explore new ideas and try them out.

Bibliography

AAL Newsletter: *The Newsletter of the Association of Architectural Librarians*, Washington, D.C.: Washington Association, 1987.

Abbott, Ethelred: *Art Museum Libraries*, London: Bowker-Saur, 1996.

Abid, Ann B.: *Loss Liability: Risk, Responsibility, Reco very*, North America: Art Documentation, 2002.

Allan, B.: *Standards for Art Libraries and Fine Arts Slide Collections*, New Jersey: Facet Publishing, 2007.

Allan, M.: *Cataloging Art, Architecture, and their Visual Images*, New Jersey: Facet Publishing, 2002.

Allen, Nancy S.: *The Art and Architecture Program of the Research Libraries Group*, North America: Art Libraries Journal 1988.

Allen, Susan M.: *Towards an International Art Library*, UK: Getty Research Institute, 2002.

Anderson, T.: *Introduction to Art Image Access, Issues, Tools, Standards, Strategies*, India: Cambridge University Press, 2008.

Depuis, E.A.: *Procedural Guide to Automating an Art Library*, India: Neal Schuman Publishers, 2003.

Hodges, C. B.: *International Bibliography of Art Librarianship*, Scotland: University of Glasgow, 2004.

Johnston, P.: *Museum Librarianship: A Guide to the Provision and Management of Information Services*, UK: Clarkson University, 2001.

Jolliffe, A: *Library Instruction for Students in Design Disciplines: Scenarios, Exercises, & Techniques*, UK: Taylor and Francis, 2005.

Kapoor, Bupesh.: *The Library and the Accreditation Process in Design Disciplines: Best Practices*, India: Cambridge University Press, 2003.

Khan, B.H.: *Selection and Acquisition in an Art School Library*, India: Educational Technology Publications, 2001.

Lee, S.: *Library Acquisitions: Practice and Theory*, Minnesota: Univesity of Minnesota, 2003.

Lewis, D.: *Cataloging Architectural Drawings*, India: Open University Press, 2006.

Moshinskie, J.: *How Libraries Collect and Handle Artists' Books*, UK: Univesity of Minnesota, 2000.

Newton, R.: *Staff Attitudes to the Development in Library*, India: Cambridge University Press, 2005.

Rowlands, J.: *Collection Development Policies for Libraries*, California: Sandia National Laboratories, 2002.

Salmon, A.: *Encyclopedia of Library & Information Science*, UK: Taylor and Francis, 2006.

Salmon, G.: *Digital Images and Art Libraries in the Twenty-First Century*, UK: Taylor and Francis, 2002.

Schank, R.: *Indivisibility of Art Librarianship*, Scotland: University of Glasgow, 2000.

Scholten, E.J.: *Introduction to Librarianship*, Switzerland: Elmepress International, 2004.

Tucson, Ariz: *Handbook and List of Members*, USA; Art Libraries Society, 1982.

Tucson: Staffing *Standards for Art Libraries and Visual Resources Collections*, N.C.: Art Libraries Society of North America, 1996.

Index